Propositions has two main goals. The first is to show that there are propositions. The second is to defend an account of their nature. While pursuing these goals, Trenton Merricks draws a variety of controversial conclusions about related issues, including, among others, supervaluationism, the nature of possible worlds, truths about non-existent entities, and whether and how logical consequence depends on modal facts.

An argument is modally valid just in case, necessarily, if its premises are true, then its conclusion is true. *Propositions* begins with the assumption that some arguments are modally valid. Merricks then argues that the premises and conclusions of modally valid arguments are not sentences. Instead, he argues, they are propositions. So, because there are modally valid arguments, there are propositions.

Merricks defends the claim that propositions are not structured and are not sets of possible worlds. He thereby presents arguments against the two leading accounts of the nature of propositions. Those arguments are intended not only to oppose those accounts, but also to deliver conclusions about what a satisfactory account of the nature of propositions should say. Of particular importance in this regard are arguments concerning the alleged explanations of how a set of possible worlds or a structured proposition would manage to represent thing as being a certain way. Merricks then defends his own account of the nature of propositions, which says only that each proposition is a necessary existent that essentially represents things as being a certain way.

Trenton Merricks is Commonwealth Professor of Philosophy at the University of Virginia.

Propositions

TRENTON MERRICKS

CLARENDON PRESS · OXFORD

OXFORD
UNIVERSITY PRESS

Great Clarendon Street, Oxford, OX2 6DP,
United Kingdom

Oxford University Press is a department of the University of Oxford.
It furthers the University's objective of excellence in research, scholarship,
and education by publishing worldwide. Oxford is a registered trade mark of
Oxford University Press in the UK and in certain other countries

First published 2015
First published in paperback 2018

Published in the United States of America by Oxford University Press
198 Madison Avenue, New York, NY 10016, United States of America

British Library Cataloguing in Publication Data
Data available

Library of Congress Cataloging in Publication Data
Data available

ISBN 978–0–19–873256–3 (Hbk.)
ISBN 978–0–19–881209–8 (Pbk.)

For Al Plantinga

ACKNOWLEDGMENTS

I presented parts of this book as talks at Georgetown University, the College of William and Mary, the University of Virginia, Colgate University, Virginia Commonwealth University, the University of Vermont, and at conferences at the University of Southern California, the University of South Florida, and the University of Notre Dame. Thanks to those who attended those talks, and especially to those who asked questions and pointed out problems. Thanks also to Elizabeth Barnes, Mike Bergmann, Tal Brewer, Paddy Blanchette, Jim Cargile, Lorraine Juliano Keller, Steve Kuhn, Joungbin Lim, Jonathan Rutledge, Charlie Tanksley, David Vander Laan, Brian Weatherson, and Nick Wolterstorff for comments on parts of the manuscript.

I am grateful to Ross Cameron, Chad Carmichael, Dan Korman, Antonia Lolordo, Brannon McDaniel, Mark Murphy, Jeff Speaks, and three anonymous referees for Oxford University Press, all of whom provided detailed feedback on the entire manuscript. So too did those who participated in a workshop on a draft of this book at the University of Notre Dame; I thank all those participants, especially Andrew Brenner, Jack Himelright, Michael Longenecker, Mike Rea, Bradley Rettler, Amy Seymour, and Meghan Sullivan. I cannot overstate how much I owe to everyone mentioned above for their tremendously generous and instructive advice and objections. I am also grateful to my friend, Greg Breeding, who designed this book's cover, and did so just for the fun of it.

My biggest debt is to the following graduate students at the University of Virginia who worked with me, page by page, through a draft of the whole manuscript in a series of meetings stretching over a semester, and most of whom then went and did it all over again with another draft the following year: Jonathan Barker, Matt Duncan, Corin Fox, Dave Ingram, Derek Lam, Joe Lenow, John Mahlan, Andrei Marasoiu, Andrew Morgan, Paul Nedelisky, Nick Rimell, Peter Tan, Craig Thompson, and Adam Tiller.

T. M.
Charlottesville, VA

CONTENTS

INTRODUCTION

Let an argument be modally valid just in case, necessarily, if its premises are true, then its conclusion is true. This book begins with the assumption that some arguments are modally valid. Chapter 1—'Propositions and Modal Validity'—argues that the premises and conclusions of modally valid arguments exist necessarily, have their truth conditions essentially, and are the fundamental bearers of truth and falsity. Again, some arguments are modally valid. So there are the premises and conclusions of modally valid arguments. So there are necessarily existing fundamental bearers of truth and falsity that have their truth conditions essentially. I shall call these entities 'propositions'. So there are propositions.

Chapter 1 argues that the premises and conclusions of modally valid arguments are propositions (not sentences). Chapter 2—'Logical Validity and Modal Validity'—argues that the premises and conclusions of logically valid arguments are sentences (not propositions). Chapter 2 also argues that modally valid arguments cannot be supplanted by logically valid arguments, thus buttressing Chapter 1's argument for the existence of propositions. In fact, Chapter 2 defends the claim that an argument is logically valid only if the sentences that are its premises and conclusion express propositions that are themselves the premises and conclusion of a modally valid argument. And Chapter 2 delivers both a way to block a major objection to supervaluationism and also a solution to Kripke's 'puzzle of belief'.

Chapter 3—'Propositions Are Not Sets of Possible Worlds'—opposes the arguments in support of the thesis that propositions are sets of possible worlds. Moreover, this chapter defends a number of objections to that thesis. If propositions really are sets of possible worlds, then possible worlds really do exist. And if possible worlds really do exist, then they have a nature. This chapter's most sustained objection to the thesis that propositions are sets of possible worlds maintains that that thesis cannot be combined, without incurring new and serious problems, with any standard account of the nature of possible worlds. In fact, this chapter argues that the best account of the nature of possible worlds rules out the thesis that propositions are sets of possible worlds.

The thesis that propositions are sets of possible worlds is one of the two leading accounts of the nature of propositions. The other leading account endorses structured propositions. The central line of argument in Chapter 4—'Against Structured Propositions'—turns on the idea of a proposition's representing things as being a certain way. (For example, the proposition *that dogs bark* represents dogs as barking, and for this reason is true if and only if dogs bark.) Chapter 4 assumes that if there are structured propositions, then there is an explanation of how each proposition manages to represent things as being a certain way. This chapter then argues that if there are structured propositions, that explanation must be in terms of a proposition's constituents and structure. But this chapter also argues that a structured proposition's constituents and structure would not explain how that proposition manages to represent things as being a certain way. So this chapter concludes that there are no structured propositions.

Let a singular proposition be a proposition that is 'directly about' an entity. Chapter 5—'Singular Propositions'—argues that while there are singular propositions, a singular proposition does not have the entity that it is directly about as a constituent. Chapter 5 thereby objects to the most widely defended versions of structured propositions, versions that claim that a singular proposition does have the relevant entity as a constituent.

Along the way, this chapter argues that there are singular propositions about entities that no longer exist, and indeed about entities that never have existed and never will exist. By arguing that we ought to reject the most widely defended versions of structured propositions, this chapter supports Chapter 4's conclusion that we ought to reject structured propositions.

Chapters 3 through 5 consider the leading accounts of the nature of propositions, and therefore consider the principal rivals to any other account, including the account I defend. But I do not pretend to consider, much less refute, every possible rival to my own account. Nor need I. For—as far as supporting my own account of the nature of propositions goes—the point of Chapters 3 through 5 is not to refute all rivals in order to leave a void that only my account can then rush in to fill. Rather, the point of those chapters—at least as far as supporting my own account goes—is to defend claims about what a satisfactory account of the nature of propositions should, and should not, say. Of particular importance in this regard are objections raised in those chapters to alleged explanations of how a set of possible worlds or a structured proposition would manage to represent things as being a certain way.

Chapter 6—'The Nature of Propositions'—presents and defends my account of the nature of propositions. My account says that each proposition is a necessary existent that essentially represents things as being a certain way. That is it. This simple account is supported by arguments earlier in this book for the conclusion that propositions really do exist necessarily and really do essentially represent things as being a certain way. And this account is supported by its explaining why propositions have the further features and play the roles that—so I argue in various places throughout this book—propositions really do have and really do play. As we shall see, one of the implications of my account of the nature of propositions is that there is no explanation of how a proposition manages to represent things as being a certain way. Much of Chapter 6 focuses on this implication. I find this implication plausible partly because of arguments in Chapters 3 and 4 for the claim that our cognitive activity cannot play a role in explaining how a proposition manages to represent things as being a certain way. And I find this implication plausible partly because of arguments in those same chapters for the claim that how a proposition represents things as being would not—not even if that proposition had constituents—be explained by its constituents and structure.

I

PROPOSITIONS AND MODAL VALIDITY

AN ARGUMENT is *modally valid* just in case, necessarily, if its premises are true, then its conclusion is true. This book's starting point is that there are some modally valid arguments. As we shall see, this starting point has an impressive pedigree. Moreover, it is obvious that certain arguments are modally valid. Or so it seems to me.

There are modally valid arguments. So there are the premises and conclusions of modally valid arguments. This chapter argues that those premises and conclusions have certain features. For example, they exist necessarily, have their truth conditions essentially, and are the fundamental bearers of truth and falsity. I shall, with good reason, call them 'propositions'. So there are propositions.

I. Modal Validity

Aristotle says:

> A deduction is a discourse in which, certain things being stated, something other than what is stated follows of necessity from their being so. I mean by the last phrase that it follows because of them, and by this, that no further term is required from without in order to make the consequence necessary. (*Prior Analytics* 24b 19–22 [1984, 40])

So, according to Aristotle, necessarily, if a deduction's premises are true, then its conclusion is true. Similarly, Stoic logicians took the truth of a valid argument's premises to necessitate the truth of its conclusion (Bobzien, 2006).

Aristotle's logic, with deduction as its centerpiece, was taught in the West 'by and large without rival' from the fourth century AD up to the nineteenth century (Bobzien, 2006). And even after Aristotle's logic was superseded in the nineteenth century, the view that the truth of the premises of certain arguments necessitates the truth of their respective conclusions remained common. For example, Gottlob Frege (1879 [1997, 57]) says that we can state the claim that A follows from B and Γ as: 'A is the necessary consequence of B and Γ.'

Plenty of twentieth-century philosophers also agree that the truth of the premises of certain arguments necessitates the truth of their respective conclusions. Alfred Tarski supports his account of logical consequence by saying:

> It seems that everyone who understands the content of the above definition [of logical consequence] must admit that it agrees quite well with common usage. This becomes still clearer from its various consequences. In particular, it can be proved, on the basis of this definition, that every [logical] consequence of true sentences *must* be true... (1936 [1956, 417], emphasis added)

Irving Copi (1978, 32) says: 'A deductive argument is *valid* when... premisses and conclusion are so related that it is absolutely impossible for the premisses to be true unless the conclusion is true also.' Graham Priest (1999, 184–5) says: 'A valid deductive argument is one where, in some sense, the conclusion cannot but be true, given the premises.' And, finally—although many more examples could be given—John Etchemendy says:

> The premises of a logically valid argument cannot be true if the conclusion is false; such conclusions are said to 'follow necessarily' from their premises. (1990, 81)

And:

> For an argument to be genuinely valid, it does not suffice for it to have a true conclusion or a false premise, for it simply to 'preserve truth.' The truth of the premises must somehow *guarantee* the truth of the conclusion. (1990, 82)

The above passages illustrate that the following view is venerable and widespread: Some arguments are such that, necessarily, if their premises are true, then their conclusions are true. In other words, some arguments are *modally valid*.

I endorse the venerable and widespread view that some arguments are modally valid. This is partly because of my deference to the wisdom of the past and of the crowd. And it is also because certain arguments seem to me to be obviously modally valid. For example:

(1) All men are mortal.
(2) Socrates is a man.
Therefore,
(3) Socrates is mortal.

Some philosophers reject metaphysical necessity and possibility. They will deny that there are modally valid arguments. They might even attempt to undermine my support for modally valid arguments. They might, first, claim that the venerable idea of the truth of an argument's conclusion being necessitated by the truth of its premises was but an inchoate attempt to describe that argument's conclusion being a logical consequence of its premises (cf., e.g., Quine, 1982, 102–8). Second, they might add that my example of an 'obviously modally valid' argument is, instead, an example of an obviously logically valid argument.

Modal validity is defined in terms of necessity. *Logical validity* is defined in terms of form (see Ch. 2, §I). So they are different concepts. But, in Chapter 2, I shall argue that there are logically valid arguments only if there are modally valid arguments. In that same chapter, I shall respond to the above attempt to undermine my support for modally valid arguments (Ch. 2, §VI).

But all that is in Chapter 2. For now I shall simply ignore the above attempt to undermine my support for modally valid arguments. And I shall continue to claim both that the view that there are modally valid arguments is venerable and widespread and also that certain arguments are obviously modally valid. And the rest of this chapter will build on the claim that there are modally valid arguments.[1]

II. The Premises and Conclusions of Modally Valid Arguments Are Not Sentences

Consider again this modally valid argument:

(1) All men are mortal.
(2) Socrates is a man.
Therefore,
(3) Socrates is mortal.

(1) is true just in case all men are mortal. (2) is true just in case Socrates is a man. And (3) is true just in case Socrates is mortal.

(1), (2), and (3) have the truth conditions just noted. But suppose that it is possible for them to have had different truth conditions. Even more, suppose, for reductio, that the following are all jointly possible: (1) is true if and only if dogs bark and (2) is true if and only if the sky is blue and (3) is true if and only if pigs fly; and dogs bark and the sky is blue and pigs do not fly.

[1] That is, this chapter will build on the claim that there are premises whose truth necessitates the truth of certain conclusions. I do not make the added assumption that those premises and conclusion compose some further entity, which further entity is a modally valid argument.

Our supposition for reductio implies that it is possible for (1) and (2) to be true and (3) false. So it implies that the above argument is not modally valid. But that argument is modally valid. So what we supposed for reductio is false. So there are certain truth conditions that the above argument's premises and conclusion—that is, (1), (2), and (3)—could not possibly have.

I think that the most plausible moral to draw here is that (1), (2), and (3) have their truth conditions essentially. I conclude, in other words, that it is not possible for (1), (2), and (3) to exist and to have truth conditions other than those that they actually have. The above reasoning in support of this moral could be adapted to the premises and conclusions of other modally valid arguments. So I conclude that, in general, the premises and conclusions of modally valid arguments have their truth conditions essentially (cf. Cargile, 1969 and 1979, 104–5).

Semantic drift occurs when a word gradually changes in meaning. And when a word changes in meaning, so too do the sentences of which that word is a part. Because sentences can change in meaning, sentences can also change with respect to their truth conditions. Since an entity cannot change with respect to its essential features, sentences do not have their truth conditions essentially. So I conclude that the premises and conclusions of modally valid arguments are not sentences. In other words, I conclude that modally valid arguments are not 'constituted by' sentences.

Here is a related point. The word 'guy' once meant *effigy* (Algeo, 2001, 512). So the sentence 'A guy is on the street' once meant that an effigy is on the street. At that same time, presumably, 'A human being is on the street' meant that a human being is on the street. So, possibly, 'A guy is on the street' means that an effigy is on the street and 'A human being is on the street' means that a human being is on the street. So, possibly, 'A guy is on the street' is true and 'A human being is on the street' is false. So the argument whose premise is the sentence

'A guy is on the street' and whose conclusion is the sentence 'A human being is on the street' is not modally valid.

But we can surely exhibit a modally valid argument thus:

(i) A guy is on the street.
Therefore,
(ii) A human being is on the street.

The argument just exhibited—being modally valid—does not have the aforementioned sentences as its premise and conclusion. So it does not have sentences as its premise and conclusion. More generally, and once again, modally valid arguments are not constituted by sentences.

A sentence has truth conditions only in a context of use. And the truth conditions of many sentences can differ from one context of use to another. For example, the sentence 'I am a philosopher', when uttered by me, is true if and only if I am a philosopher. When uttered by you, that same sentence is true if and only if you are a philosopher. An entity's essential properties cannot differ from context to context. So the sentence 'I am a philosopher' does not have its truth conditions essentially.

This same point can be made with sentences that do not use indexicals. 'Jones is tall' has certain truth conditions when uttered by sports commentators discussing what Jones brings to her professional basketball team. But it has different truth conditions when uttered by her colleague from the philosophy department. (Jones has an unusual array of skills.) Because that sentence's truth conditions vary with its context of use, that sentence does not have its truth conditions essentially.

The fact that sentences have truth conditions only in a context of use shows that sentences do not—at least not in general—have their truth conditions essentially.[2] But the premises and

[2] A single sentence type can occur in multiple contexts of use, and so the above reasoning shows that sentence types have their truth conditions contingently. But the same goes for sentence tokens. First, imagine a sentence token printed on a

conclusions of modally valid arguments do have their truth conditions essentially. This is the first way in which a sentence's having its truth conditions only in a context of use implies that the premises and conclusions of modally valid arguments are not sentences.

There is a second way. Let S be the sentence 'It is raining'. Suppose we both utter S and that one of us (standing in a downpour) thereby says something true, and the other (in sunnier climes) thereby says something false. I do not think that this forces us to conclude that S is both true and false. That is, I do not think this forces us to conclude that S is both true simpliciter and false simpliciter. For sentences have truth conditions only in a context of use. So a sentence is true only in a context of use. And a sentence is false only in a context of use. So we can say that sentence S is both true in one context of use and false in another context of use. We can then deny that S is true (or false) simpliciter. And we can deny that any sentence is true (or false) simpliciter.

All of this not only blocks a quick and easy road to dialetheism, it also shows that sentences do not constitute modally valid arguments. For suppose that no sentence is true simpliciter. Then no argument with sentences as its premises and conclusion is such that, necessarily, if its premises are true simpliciter, then its conclusion is true simpliciter.[3] An argument is modally valid just in case, necessarily, if its premises are true (simpliciter), then its conclusion is true (simpliciter). So no argument constituted by sentences is modally valid.

card, a token that finds itself put to use on a variety of occasions. Second, the mere possibility that a sentence token can occur in a context of use other than its actual context implies that some such tokens have their truth conditions contingently.

[3] That is, no argument with sentences as its premises and conclusion satisfies this description except vacuously, in virtue of the necessary falsehood of the claim that its premises are true simpliciter. But vacuously satisfying this description cannot suffice for modal validity, lest every argument constituted by sentences be modally valid.

I think that all of this is right. But this might seem to threaten some of my above arguments. To see why, suppose, for example, that the sentence 'dogs bark' is not true simpliciter, but is instead true in context C. Then you might object that it is not the case that 'dogs bark' is true just in case dogs bark. Instead, you might say, 'dogs bark' is true-in-context-C just in case dogs bark. And then you might add that this example shows that sentences do not have truth conditions at all (but instead only truth-in-context-C conditions, truth-in-context-C* conditions, etc.). And if sentences do not have truth conditions, then some of my above arguments go astray. For some of those arguments conclude that sentences do have truth conditions, but have them contingently.

Here is my reply. To say that a sentence is true in a context of use is shorthand for saying that, in that context of use, that sentence expresses a true proposition. To say that a sentence has certain truth conditions in a context of use is shorthand for saying that, in that context of use, that sentence expresses a proposition that has those truth conditions. And to say that a sentence has certain truth conditions contingently is shorthand for saying that that sentence contingently (and, of course, in a context of use) expresses a proposition with those truth conditions.

That is my reply. My reply allows me to make sense of the claim that sentences do have truth conditions, and have them contingently, even though sentences are true (or false) only in a context of use. My reply also allows me to avoid dialetheism. But despite these benefits, I do not want to rely on my reply here. For I want this section to play a role in this chapter's overall argument for the conclusion that there are propositions. So I do not want this section to presuppose that there are propositions, lest my argument for the conclusion that there are propositions beg the question. And, obviously, my reply presupposes that there are propositions. So set my reply aside.

Having set my reply aside, consider afresh the following charge. Some of my arguments above conclude that sentences have truth conditions, albeit contingently. But there is some reason to worry that sentences might not have truth conditions at all (instead having only truth-in-context-C conditions, truth-in-context-C* conditions, etc.). So there is some reason to worry that some of my arguments above go astray.

Having set my reply aside, I now respond that my main point in this section is that the premises and conclusions of modally valid arguments are not sentences. And I have argued above that this main point follows from the claim that sentences do not have their truth conditions essentially. That claim—and so my main point—is true if sentences do not have truth conditions at all. For if sentences do not have truth conditions at all, then they do not have truth conditions essentially. So the claim that sentences do not have truth conditions at all is not a threat to my main point in this section, even though it does suggest that some of my above arguments in support of that main point go astray, namely, those that claim that sentences do not have truth conditions essentially because they do have truth conditions, but only contingently.

Besides, the most serious challenge to my main point—the point that the premises and conclusions of modally valid arguments are not sentences—turns on an alternative definition of 'modally valid' in terms of truth *at* a possible world. I take this challenge seriously. And I shall respond to this challenge in the following section. But that challenge is cut off at the knees if sentences do not have truth conditions at all, not even contingently. For that alternative definition of 'modally valid' supports the idea that modally valid arguments are constituted by sentences only if sentences have truth conditions. So I assume that those who want to defend this most serious challenge to my main point will agree with me—and so will allow my arguments above to conclude—that sentences do have truth conditions, even if only contingently (and only in a context of use).

And there is another reason—a reason that does not involve truth conditions—to conclude that modally valid arguments are not constituted by sentences. That reason starts with this modally valid argument:

(a) There are no philosophers.
Therefore,
(b) It is not the case that Socrates is a philosopher.

This argument is modally valid. So, necessarily, if (a) is true, then (b) is true. A conclusion cannot be true unless it exists.[4] So, necessarily, if (a) is true, then (b) exists.

Again, necessarily, if (a) is true, then (b) exists. But it is false that, necessarily, if the sentence 'There are no philosophers' is true, then the sentence 'It is not the case that Socrates is a philosopher' exists. So it is not the case that (a) is identical with the sentence 'There are no philosophers' and (b) identical with the sentence 'It is not the case that Socrates is a philosopher'. So the premise and conclusion of the above modally valid argument are not sentences. More generally, the premises and conclusions of modally valid arguments are not sentences.

Modally valid arguments are not constituted by sentences. This does not imply, of course, that sentences do not constitute other sorts of arguments. In fact, I shall argue in Chapter 2 that the premises and conclusions of logically valid (as opposed to modally valid) arguments are sentences. But this chapter's focus is modally valid arguments. And this section's conclusion is that the premises and conclusions of modally valid arguments are not sentences.

[4] In this chapter and elsewhere, I rely on the claim that, necessarily, if an entity is true (or has truth conditions), then that entity exists. I defend this claim in Ch. 5 (§VII).

III. Two Alternative Definitions of 'Modally Valid'

Recall Etchemendy's remark that in a valid argument 'the truth of the premises must somehow *guarantee* the truth of the conclusion'. This coheres with my definition of 'modally valid', which says that an argument is modally valid just in case, necessarily, if its premises are true, then its conclusion is true.

But Etchemendy then adds:

> The exact source of the guarantee, whether it be the meanings of the expressions contained in the argument, brute logical intuition, or something else entirely, need not concern us at the moment. (1990, 82–3)

Etchemendy entertains the idea that 'the meanings of the expressions' are the source of the relevant guarantee. That idea inspires an alternative definition of 'modally valid': An argument is modally valid just in case, necessarily, if its premises are true *and have their actual truth conditions and its conclusion has its actual truth conditions*, then its conclusion is true.

Let S1 be the sentence 'All men are mortal', S2 be the sentence 'Socrates is a man', and S3 be the sentence 'Socrates is mortal'. Necessarily, if S1 and S2 are true *and have their actual truth conditions* and S3 *has its actual truth conditions*, then S3 is true. Thus this alternative definition counts the argument with S1, S2, and S3 as its premises and conclusion as modally valid, even though S1, S2, and S3 do not have their truth conditions essentially. Moreover, since, necessarily, S3 has truth conditions only if S3 exists, this alternative definition can count the aforementioned argument as modally valid despite the truth of S1 and S2 failing to necessitate the existence of S3. All of this illustrates how this alternative definition threatens Section II's defense of the claim that modally valid arguments are not constituted by sentences.[5]

[5] As Section II emphasized, sentences have truth conditions only in a context of use. So defenders of this first alternative definition should restate that definition in

But consider this argument with—let us stipulate—a sentence as its premise and a sentence as its conclusion:

(I) Electrons exist.
Therefore,
(II) A sentence exists.

A sentence must exist to have truth conditions; so if (II) has its actual truth conditions, then (II) exists; (II) itself is a sentence; so, necessarily, if (II) exists and has its actual truth conditions, then (II) is true. Moreover, necessarily, if (I) is true, then (I) exists; (I) itself is a sentence; so, necessarily, if (I) is true and (II) exists and has its actual truth conditions, then (II) is true. For these two reasons, the argument from (I) to (II) is such that, necessarily, if its premise is true *and has its actual truth conditions and its conclusion has its actual truth conditions*, then its conclusion is true. Thus the above alternative definition counts the argument from (I) to (II) as modally valid.

So that alternative definition is wrong. That is, that alternative definition of 'modally valid' does not capture the venerable and widespread idea of the truth of an argument's premises necessitating the truth of that argument's conclusion. For all devotees of that idea should agree—since the existence of electrons is no guarantee of there being sentences—that the truth of (I) does not appropriately necessitate the truth of (II).

Here is another argument with—let us stipulate—a sentence as its premise and a sentence as its conclusion:

(A) Dogs bark.
Therefore,
(B) The sentence 'dogs bark' is true if and only if dogs bark.

terms of truth conditions in an actual context of use (as opposed to actual truth conditions). Similarly, defenders of the second alternative definition below should say that a sentence is true *at* a particular possible world only in a context of use. But making all of this explicit, all the way through this section, would be cumbersome. So, in this section, I shall leave the role of context of use implicit.

Necessarily, if sentence (A) has its actual truth conditions, then the sentence 'dogs bark' is true if and only if dogs bark. Thus, necessarily, if (A) is true and has its actual truth conditions and (B) has its actual truth conditions, then (B) is true. So the above alternative definition of 'modally valid' counts the argument from (A) to (B) as modally valid.

So, again, that alternative definition is wrong. That is, that alternative definition of 'modally valid' does not capture the venerable and widespread idea of the truth of an argument's premises necessitating the truth of its conclusion. For all devotees of that idea should agree—since barking dogs guarantee neither the existence of English sentences nor such sentences having specific truth conditions—that the truth of (A) does not appropriately necessitate the truth of (B).

Here is a final problem with the above alternative definition.[6] Again, let S1 be the sentence 'All men are mortal', S2 be the sentence 'Socrates is a man', and S3 be the sentence 'Socrates is mortal'. Consider a possible world in which S1 is true just in case dogs bark, S2 is true just in case the sky is blue, and S3 is true just in case pigs fly. And suppose S1 and S2 are true in that possible world, but S3 is false. Now imagine that someone in that possible world presents an argument from S1 and S2 to S3. The argument she has presented has true premises and a false conclusion. So her argument is not modally valid. But the above alternative definition of 'modally valid' counts her argument as modally valid. For, necessarily, if S1 and S2 are true *and have their actual truth conditions and S3 has its actual truth conditions*, then S3 is true. So, again, that alternative definition must be rejected.

[6] Thanks here to Dan Korman.

Let a premise or conclusion be true *in* a possible world just in case, necessarily, if that possible world were actual, then that premise or conclusion would be true. And let a premise or conclusion be true *at* a possible world (as opposed to *in* a possible world) just in case the actual truth conditions of that premise or conclusion are satisfied *in* that possible world. That is, a premise or conclusion is true *at* a possible world just in case that premise or conclusion actually has truth conditions and, necessarily, if that possible world were actual, then those truth conditions would be satisfied.

We can illustrate the notion of truth *at* a possible world—and how it differs from truth *in* a possible world—with sentence S*, the sentence 'No sentences exist'. There are possible worlds such that, necessarily, if they were actual, then there would be no sentences. That is, there are possible worlds *in* which there are no sentences, not even S*. So S* is not true *in* those possible worlds. But S*'s actual truth conditions are satisfied *in* those possible worlds. So S* is true *at* those possible worlds.

The notion of truth *at* a possible world can be used to articulate a second alternative definition of 'modally valid'. That second alternative definition says that an argument is modally valid just in case its conclusion is true *at* all possible worlds (as opposed to *in* all possible worlds) *at* which (as opposed to *in* which) its premises are true.

Sentence S1 ('All men are mortal') is true if and only if all men are mortal. So S1 is true *at* all possible worlds in which all men are mortal. By the same token, S2 ('Socrates is a man') is true *at* all possible worlds in which Socrates is a man, and S3 ('Socrates is mortal') is true *at* all possible worlds in which Socrates is mortal. In fact, because all possible worlds in which all men are mortal and Socrates is a man are also possible worlds in which Socrates is mortal, S3 is true *at* all possible worlds *at* which S1 and S2 are true.

Thus the second alternative definition counts the argument from S1 and S2 to S3 as modally valid.[7] More generally, the second alternative definition will count a variety of arguments constituted by sentences as modally valid, and will do so even though the premises and conclusions of those arguments have their truth conditions contingently, and even if the truth of such an argument's premises does not necessitate the existence of its conclusion. All of this illustrates how this second alternative definition threatens Section II's defense of the claim that modally valid arguments are not constituted by sentences.

But this second alternative definition must be rejected. To begin to see why I say this, consider that S3 (the sentence 'Socrates is mortal') is true *at* a possible world if and only if Socrates is mortal in that possible world. Again, for every possible world W, S3 is true *at* W if and only if Socrates is mortal in W. So S3 has the same truth conditions *at* all possible worlds. It would be natural to conclude from this that S3 thereby has its truth conditions essentially. But that conclusion is wrong. For sentences, including S3, do not have their truth conditions essentially (§II).

So S3's having the same truth conditions *at* all possible worlds does not imply that S3 has its truth conditions essentially. Nor, for that matter, does S3's having the same truth conditions *at* all possible worlds imply that S3 has its truth conditions contingently. Indeed, S3 has the same truth conditions *at* all possible worlds regardless of the modal status of S3's having those truth conditions. This is why we can all agree that S3 has the same truth conditions *at* all possible worlds even if we disagree about

[7] Truth *at* a possible world, as opposed to truth *in* a possible world, makes all the difference here. For suppose that there is a possible world W, which is such that if it were actual, the following would be the case: S1 ('all men are mortal') is true if and only if dogs bark; dogs bark; S2 ('Socrates is a man') is true if and only the sky is blue; the sky is blue; S3 ('Socrates is mortal') is true if and only pigs fly; but pigs do not fly. If W were actual, S1 and S2 would be true, but S3 would not. So S3 is not true *in* all possible worlds *in* which S1 and S2 are true.

the modal status of S3's having those truth conditions. And all of this shows—perhaps surprisingly—that the claim that S3 has the same truth conditions *at* all possible worlds is not a claim about the modal status of the truth conditions of S3.

A parallel result holds for the claim that S3 is true *at* all possible worlds *at* which S1 and S2 are true. For that claim does not imply that the sentence S3 is essentially such that it is true if those other sentences are true. Nor does it imply that S3 is contingently such that it is true if those other sentences are true. More generally, S3 is true *at* all possible worlds *at* which S1 and S2 are true regardless of what—if any—modal connection there is between, on the one hand, S3's being true and, on the other, S1's being true and S2's being true. All of this shows—perhaps surprisingly—that the claim that S3 is true *at* all possible worlds *at* which S1 and S2 are true is not a claim about any modal connection between the truth of S3 and the truth of S1 and S2.

Defenders of the venerable and widespread idea that some arguments are modally valid should all agree that an argument is modally valid only if there is some modal connection between the truth of a modally valid argument's conclusion and the truth of its premises. But the claim that an argument's conclusion is true *at* all possible worlds *at* which its premises are true does not imply that there is any modal connection between the truth of its conclusion and the truth of its premises. So we should deny that an argument is modally valid just in case its conclusion is true *at* all possible worlds *at* which its premises are true. So we should reject the second alternative definition of 'modally valid', the alternative put in terms of truth *at* a possible world.[8]

[8] As was just shown with an argument constituted by sentences, the mere claim that an argument's conclusion is true *at* all possible worlds *at* which its premises are true does not imply that there is any modal connection between the truth of its conclusion and the truth of its premises. But—whatever constitutes a modally valid argument—the mere claim that an argument is modally valid does imply that there is some modal connection between the truth of its conclusion and the truth of its

None of this is to deny that the claim that S3 is true *at* all possible worlds *at* which S1 and S2 are true implies some modal connections. On the contrary—as its invocation of 'possible worlds' should make clear—that claim is a modal claim and, unsurprisingly, it does imply certain modal connections. For example, a claim's truth depends on how things are (see Merricks, 2007). So consider not S1 itself, but the way things have to be in order for S1 (given its actual truth conditions) to be true. And consider also not S2 or S3, but the way things would have to be in order for S2 and S3 (given their actual truth conditions) to be true. It is impossible for things to be as they must be in order for S1 and S2 to be true (given their actual truth conditions) and also for things to fail to be as they must be in order for S3 to be true (given its actual truth conditions). Thus we have a modal connection among ways that things are or could be, a modal connection implied by the claim that S3 is true *at* all worlds *at* which S1 and S2 are true.

And I think that S3's being true *at* all possible worlds *at* which S1 and S2 are true implies another modal connection. For I think that S1 and S2 each express a proposition, as does S3 (in a context of use) (see §V). And I think that, necessarily, if the propositions (actually) expressed by S1 and S2 are true, then so is the proposition (actually) expressed by S3. And that too is a modal connection. Moreover, I think that this modal connection delivers a modally valid argument. For, as we shall see, I think that the premises and conclusion of a modally valid argument are propositions (see §IV and Ch. 2, §IV).[9]

premises. So an argument is not modally valid in virtue of its conclusion's being true *at* all possible worlds *at* which its premises are true even if that conclusion and those premises are not sentences, but are instead propositions.

[9] The modal connection between 'ways things are or could be' does not deliver a modally valid argument. For one thing, it is false that those 'ways' are the premises and conclusions of modally valid arguments. This is in part because premises and conclusions have truth-values, but those ways do not. Instead, those ways are that on which the truth of this or that premise, or this or that conclusion, depends.

We have considered two alternative definitions of 'modally valid'. Those two alternative definitions were considered because—as noted above—they threaten Section II's defense of the claim that modally valid arguments are not constituted by sentences. But those threats have been neutralized and the arguments of Section II reaffirmed. This is because there are good reasons to reject those two alternative definitions of 'modally valid'.

IV. The Premises and Conclusions of Modally Valid Arguments Are Propositions

Some of the premises and conclusions of modally valid arguments are necessarily true, and some are necessarily false. Necessarily, if a premise (conclusion) is true, then it exists. So if a premise (conclusion) is necessarily true, then that premise (conclusion) exists necessarily. For parallel reasons, I think that if a premise (conclusion) is necessarily false, then it too must exist necessarily. So I conclude that some of the premises and conclusions of modally valid arguments exist necessarily.

You might object that necessary truth (falsity) should be understood as truth (falsity) *at* all possible worlds. If your objection were right, this would undermine the argument just given. For a premise or conclusion can be true (false) *at* all possible worlds even if that premise or conclusion does not exist necessarily.

But necessary truth is not truth *at* all possible worlds. To see why, let S be a sentence whose truth conditions are satisfied in all possible worlds. Then S is true *at* all possible worlds. S could have had different truth conditions. So S could have been false. So the claim that necessary truth is truth *at* all possible worlds yields the result that some necessary truths could have been false. I think that result is mistaken. So I deny that necessary truth is truth *at* all possible worlds. And so I stay with my claim that a premise's (conclusion's) being necessarily true implies that that premise (conclusion) exists necessarily.

As we saw above (§II), the truth of the premises of a modally valid argument necessitates the existence of that argument's conclusion. I think that this should have an explanation. Suppose that all the premises and conclusions of modally valid arguments exist necessarily. Then the conclusion of each modally valid argument exists necessarily. Then, necessarily, if a modally valid argument's premises are true, its conclusion exists. In this way, the necessary existence of all the premises and conclusions of modally valid arguments directly and elegantly explains why the truth of a modally valid argument's premises necessitates the existence of its conclusion.

I accept this explanation. I accept this explanation because it is direct and elegant. But I would not have accepted this explanation if it were not believable. And it is believable. It is believable because we have already seen that at least some of the premises and conclusions of modally valid arguments—those that are necessarily true and those that are necessarily false—exist necessarily. So being the premise or conclusion of a modally valid argument does not rule out existing necessarily. So it is believable—absent a compelling argument to the contrary—that the premises and conclusions of modally valid arguments exist necessarily.

The premises and conclusions of modally valid arguments exist necessarily. Sentences exist contingently. Thus we have another reason—in addition to those of Section II—to conclude that sentences do not constitute modally valid arguments.

Consider two premises, one to the effect that 2 plus 1 equals 3 and another to the effect that all dogs are dogs. The first premise is true just in case 2 plus 1 does equal 3. The second premise is true just in case all dogs are dogs. But 2 plus 1 equals 3 just in case all dogs are dogs. So the first premise is true just in case the second premise is true. So those two premises have the same truth conditions.

Those two premises have the same truth conditions. But they differ in some ways. For example, and obviously, they differ in what they are *about*. One of those premises is about integers (and not about dogs) and the other is about dogs (and not about integers). Relatedly, those premises differ in how they *represent things as being*. One of them represents the sum of 2 and 1 as being 3. The other represents every dog as being a dog.

Those two premises have the same truth conditions but differ in how they represent things as being. So a premise's (or conclusion's) having certain truth conditions is not one and the same thing as that premise's (or conclusion's) representing things as being a certain way. Rather, I think that how a premise (or conclusion) represents things as being explains its truth conditions. For example, the premise to the effect that all dogs are dogs is true just in case all dogs are dogs because that premise represents all dogs as being dogs. And the conclusion to the effect that Socrates is mortal is true just in case Socrates is mortal because that conclusion represents Socrates as being mortal. And so on.

Relatedly, how a truth-bearer represents things as being is part of the explanation of its being true. In general, an entity is true because, first, it represents things as being a certain way and, second, things are that way (Merricks, 2008, 343). Similarly, an entity is false because, first, it represents things as being a certain way, and, second, things are not that way.[10]

[10] This allows us to explain why a claim's truth depends on how things are, which is assumed not only above (§III), but also throughout my book *Truth and Ontology*. A claim's truth depends on how things are because (a) each entity that is capable of being true or false represents things as being a certain way and (b) that entity is true (false) because things are (are not) as that entity represents them as being.

This suggests a new sort of deflationism about truth. That sort of deflationism says, first, that there is no property *being true*. And, second, that the predicate 'is true' applies to a proposition just in case that proposition represents things as being a certain way, and things are as that proposition represents them as being. This sort of deflationism is consistent with everything defended in *Truth and*

Each premise and conclusion of a modally valid argument has its truth conditions because of how that premise or conclusion represents things as being. Recall that each such premise and conclusion has its truth conditions essentially (§II). Therefore, each premise and conclusion of a modally valid argument not only represents things as being a certain way, but essentially represents things as being that way.

This section and Section II have defended a number of claims about the premises and conclusions of modally valid arguments: They are not sentences. They exist necessarily (see also Ch. 3, §VII and Ch. 5, §II). They have their truth conditions essentially. They essentially represent things as being a certain way. And they are bearers of truth and falsity. Moreover, I shall argue in the next section that the premises and conclusions of modally valid arguments are the fundamental bearers of truth and falsity.

In light of these claims about the premises and conclusions of modally valid arguments, I conclude that we should apply the label 'propositions' to these premises and conclusions. For consider the following familiar claims: Propositions are not sentences. But propositions are bearers of truth and falsity. (All believers in propositions accept these first two claims.) Indeed, propositions are the fundamental bearers of truth and falsity (see, e.g., Bealer, 1998; McGrath, 2012). Propositions have their truth conditions essentially (see, e.g., Stalnaker, 2011, 511; cf. Lewis, 1986a, 179–80), which implies that they essentially represent things as being a certain way (see, e.g., Jubien, 2001, 47). And propositions exist necessarily (see, e.g., Plantinga 1993, 118–19).

There are modally valid arguments. Those arguments have premises and conclusions. Those premises and conclusions are rightly called 'propositions'. So those premises and conclusions are propositions. So there are propositions. This is not the only argument one could give for the existence of propositions (see,

Ontology other than its claim—in its concluding sections—that there is the property *being true*.

e.g., §VI). But it is the argument I have focused on. I have focused on this particular argument for two reasons. First, I find it compelling. Second, this particular argument shows not only that propositions exist, but also reveals some of their features. For example, as we have seen, it reveals that propositions essentially represent things as being a certain way.

V. Fundamental Bearers of Truth and Falsity

Let us say that an entity is a *fundamental* bearer of truth just in case that entity meets two conditions. First, that entity is true. Second, its being true is not (even partly) analyzed in terms of its being related to some other entity that is true. Similarly, a *fundamental* bearer of falsity is false, and its being false is not (even partly) analyzed in terms of its being related to some other entity that is false. This section will argue that what I am calling 'propositions'—that is, those entities that exist necessarily and each of which essentially represents things as being a certain way—are the fundamental bearers of truth and falsity.[11]

A thousand years ago, no sentence had ever expressed, and no one had ever believed, the true proposition *that a water molecule is constituted by two hydrogen atoms and an oxygen atom.* Indeed, there are surely true propositions that have never been, and never will be, expressed or believed. (See Appendix for examples.) So the truth of those propositions cannot be analyzed in terms of the truth of the sentences that express them, or the truth of beliefs that have them as their contents or, it seems,

[11] The claim that an entity is a fundamental bearer of truth (or falsity) does not imply that there is no explanation of that entity's being true (or false). My own view, as we have seen, is that a proposition's being true is explained by a combination of that proposition's representing things as being a certain way and things being that way.

the truth of any other truth-bearers. So those propositions are fundamental truth-bearers. So some propositions are fundamental truth-bearers. I think that if some true propositions are fundamental truth-bearers, then each proposition is a fundamental bearer of truth or falsity.[12] So propositions are fundamental bearers of truth and falsity.

Here is another argument for this same conclusion. Propositions exist necessarily. But all other bearers of truth—such as, for example, sentences—exist contingently. It is possible that no contingent truth-bearers exist at all. So, possibly, proposition *p* (exists and) is true and no non-propositional truth-bearer exists. Therefore, possibly, proposition *p* is true and stands in no relation to a true non-proposition. Therefore, possibly, proposition *p* is true and its being true is not analyzed in terms of its standing in a relation to a true non-proposition. In light of this, I conclude that, possibly, proposition *p* is a fundamental bearer of truth. Presumably, necessarily, a fundamental truth-bearer is essentially a fundamental bearer of truth or falsity. Therefore, proposition *p* is a fundamental bearer of truth or falsity.

Proposition *p* is an almost arbitrarily chosen possibly true proposition. But the argument just given turns on the premise that, possibly, proposition *p* is true and no non-propositional truth-bearer exists. So *p* cannot be, for example, the proposition *that some true sentences exist*. For it is not the case that, possibly, *that some true sentences exist* is true and no non-propositional truth-bearer exists.

But consider the following: Possibly, the proposition *that some true sentences exist* is false and no non-propositional falsity-bearer exists. Therefore, possibly, that proposition is false

[12] You might object that, for example, the truth of the 'complex' proposition *p and q* is analyzed in terms of how it is related to the truth of *p* and the truth of *q*. Then you might say that only 'atomic' propositions are the fundamental bearers of truth. I disagree (see Ch. 6, §II). But no matter. Even if you are right, propositions—albeit only atomic ones—are still the fundamental bearers of truth and falsity.

and stands in no relation to a false non-proposition. Therefore, possibly, that proposition is false and its being false is not analyzed in terms of its standing in a relation to a false non-proposition. In light of this, I conclude that, possibly, that proposition is a fundamental bearer of falsity. Presumably, necessarily, a fundamental falsity-bearer is essentially a fundamental bearer of truth or falsity. Therefore, that proposition is a fundamental bearer of truth or falsity.

We have just seen that each proposition whose falsity does not necessitate that there is a contingently existing falsity-bearer is itself a fundamental bearer of truth or falsity. And before that we saw that each proposition whose truth does not necessitate that there is a contingently existing truth-bearer is itself a fundamental bearer of truth or falsity. Any proposition whose truth necessitates that there is a contingently existing truth-bearer is a proposition whose falsity does not necessitate that there is a contingently existing falsity-bearer. So we should conclude that all propositions are fundamental bearers of truth and falsity.

I think that there is only one kind of entity whose members are fundamental bearers of truth and falsity. So I think that since propositions are fundamental bearers of truth and falsity, sentences are not also fundamental bearers of truth and falsity. But sentences are bearers of truth and falsity. So I conclude that a sentence has a truth-value in virtue of how it is related to a proposition that has that truth-value. So let us say that sentences are *derivative* bearers of truth and falsity.

A sentence has a truth-value in virtue of how it is related to a proposition that has that truth-value. So let us say that a sentence is true (false) in virtue of *expressing* a true (false) proposition.[13] Recall that a sentence has a truth-value only in a context of use (§II). So a sentence expresses a proposition only in a context of use. But I shall often leave contexts of use implicit.

[13] Supervaluationists will want to tweak this claim. See Chapter 2 (§VII).

For example, I shall often say things along the lines of: The sentence 'dogs bark' expresses the proposition *that dogs bark*.

There is another reason to conclude that sentences are derivative bearers of truth and falsity. Consider the sentence '2 plus 1 equals 3'. Because that sentence has its truth conditions contingently, it could have been false. Moreover, that sentence could have failed to exist, and so could have failed to have any features, and so could have failed to have a truth-value, and so could have failed to be true. So the sentence '2 plus 1 equals 3' is not necessarily true.

Even so, the claim that the sentence '2 plus 1 equals 3' is necessarily true is not bizarre or unmotivated. Something in the neighborhood of that claim is surely right. These observations can easily be accommodated if sentences are derivative truth-bearers. For then the sentence '2 plus 1 equals 3' is true in virtue of (contingently) expressing a proposition that itself really is necessarily true. Indeed, we may even say 'The sentence "2 plus 1 equals 3" is necessarily true' after all, just so long as we thereby mean that the sentence '2 plus 1 equals 3' is thus *derivatively* necessarily true.[14]

[14] For much of the twentieth century, it was standard to hold—indeed, it was even a Dogma of Empiricism—that the fundamental bearers of necessary truth were analytic sentences (Quine, 1951). But only sentences—not propositions—are analytic. And, as I have here argued, only propositions—not sentences—are the fundamental bearers of truth, necessary or otherwise. So it is false that if a sentence is analytic, then it is a fundamental bearer of necessary truth.

Moreover, it is false that if a sentence is analytic, then it expresses a necessarily true proposition. I say this because I think that the instances of the T-schema are analytic, but express contingently true propositions. For example, it is contingently true that 'snow is white' expresses the proposition *that snow is white*. As a result, the following sentence expresses a contingently true proposition: '"Snow is white" is true if and only if snow is white'. But I also think that that sentence is analytic. For I think that a sufficient condition for a sentence's being analytic is that one can be justified in accepting that sentence solely by understanding the words (and expressions) that constitute it (along with understanding its syntax) (cf. Boghossian, 1997). And one can be thus justified in believing the sentence '"Snow is white" is true if and only if snow is white'.

I have argued that propositions are the fundamental bearers of truth and falsity. We can square this with the idea that we often have true (and false) beliefs. One way to do this is to identify a belief with a proposition, that is, to take a belief to be the proposition that is believed. Then what it is for an agent to have a true (false) belief is for that agent to stand in the *believing* relation to that true (false) proposition. (There may be further *relata*, such as a 'guise' (see Ch. 2, §§II–III).) Then propositions are the objects of belief.

Similarly, some might claim that a belief is not the proposition that is believed, but is instead a certain sort of mental event, a mental event constituted by an agent's standing in the *believing* relation to (perhaps among other things) a proposition. Then propositions are the objects of belief.[15]

There are at least the above two ways to square the truth or falsity of this or that belief with propositions' being the fundamental bearers of truth and falsity. For all I know, there may be others. Even so, I think it is clear that if propositions are the fundamental bearers of truth and falsity, then propositions are, in one way or another, the objects of belief. (Cf. Merricks, 2009a.)

Recall that an entity is true because it represents things as being a certain way and things are that way; and an entity is false because it represents things as being a certain way and things are not that way. Assume, for reductio, that a sentence represents things as being a certain way, but not (even partly) in virtue of standing in any relation to a proposition. Then that

[15] It is a substantive and controversial metaphysical thesis that if an object exemplifies a property, then there is the event or, in other words, the state of affairs of that object's exemplifying that property. More generally, it is a substantive and controversial metaphysical thesis that there are events or, in other words, states of affairs (see, e.g., Lewis, 1986b). I do not endorse this thesis (see my discussion of Koslicki, 2008 in Merricks, 2009b). But, just for the sake of argument, I shall assume, when discussing both alleged mental events (Ch. 6, §V) and alleged propositions-as-states-of-affairs (Ch. 4), that there are events, that is, states of affairs.

sentence has a truth-value, but not in virtue of standing in any relation to a proposition. Thus our assumption for reductio leads to a false conclusion.

The only way to avoid this false conclusion is to say that sentences derivatively represent things as being a certain way. More carefully, the only way to avoid this conclusion is to say that a sentence represents things as being a certain way in virtue of expressing a proposition that represents things as being that way. Something similar goes for all other non-fundamental bearers of truth and falsity. Likewise, because propositions are the fundamental bearers of truth or falsity, propositions fundamentally represent things as being a certain way. That is, a proposition represents things as being a certain way, but not (even partly) in virtue of how it is related to something else that represents things as being that way.[16]

Propositions fundamentally represent things as being a certain way. An entity has the truth conditions that it does because of how it represents things as being (§IV). So propositions have their truth conditions fundamentally. Sentences and other contingently existing bearers of truth and falsity derivatively represent things as being a certain way. So sentences and any other contingently existing bearers of truth and falsity have their truth conditions derivatively. For example, for a sentence to have certain truth conditions (in a context of use) is for that sentence (in that context of use) to express a proposition that has those truth conditions.

Recall from Section II that the claim that a sentence has its truth conditions thus derivatively allows us to reconcile two

[16] The claim that an entity fundamentally represents things as being a certain way does not automatically imply that there is no explanation of that entity's representing things as being that way. In fact, the search for an explanation of how a proposition manages to fundamentally represent things as being a certain way will play a central role in much of what follows, especially in Chapter 4. But, as we shall see, my own view is that there is no such explanation (Ch. 6, §II).

positions that seem to be correct, but that also might have seemed to be incompatible. The first is that a sentence has a truth-value only in a context of a use. The second is that a sentence can have truth conditions (and not just truth-in-context-C conditions, etc.). This reconciliation lends further support to the claim that propositions have their truth conditions fundamentally and that sentences have their truth conditions derivatively.

I am a parent. Suppose I utter the sentence 'I am a parent'. Then that sentence—in this context of use—is true. So that sentence—in this context of use—expresses a true proposition. Similarly, when I truly believe that I am a parent I stand in the *believing* relation to a true proposition. Given the reasoning in this section, these remarks are unremarkable. But these unremarkable remarks give us a reason to reject the influential view defended by David Lewis in 'Attitudes *De Dicto* and *De Se*'.

According to Lewis's view, when I believe that I am a parent, I ascribe the property *being a parent* to myself, but I do not stand in the *believing* relation to a proposition. For Lewis (1979, 521) says of cases just like this: 'Some belief and some knowledge *cannot be understood as propositional*, but can be understood as self-ascription of properties' (emphasis added; see also Lewis, 1979, 525–6). Likewise, Lewis would say that when I utter 'I am a parent', I do not express a proposition.

Again, given the reasoning of this section, we must reject Lewis's view. For my belief that I am a parent is true. And the sentence 'I am a parent' is—in this context of use—true. So, given the views defended in this section, that belief and that sentence are each true in virtue of being appropriately related to a true proposition. So that belief is 'propositional' and that sentence expresses a proposition.

Of course, Lewis gives reasons for his view. Lewis's first main reason stems from the account of the nature of propositions endorsed in 'Attitudes *De Dicto* and *De Se*', according to which propositions are sets of possible worlds (see esp. Lewis, 1979, 515). I shall argue that that account is false (Ch. 3).[17]

Lewis's second main reason is that his view allows him to solve certain puzzles involving indexicals. I shall say a bit more about these sorts of puzzles in the next section. And in Chapter 2 (§§II–III) it will be clear that the solution to these puzzles that I endorse, which turns on believing a proposition 'under a guise', does not require us to say that some belief and some knowledge cannot be understood as propositional.

VI. Two Sentences Can Express the Same Proposition

Here is a familiar argument:

> You say: 'Smith is a doctor.' I say: 'Smith es un médico.' We have asserted the same thing. But we have not uttered the same sentence. So what we have asserted is not a sentence. It is, instead, a proposition. So there are propositions.

This sort of argument is defended widely in conversation, and endorsed in print by—among many others—James Cargile (1979, 105), Richard Cartwright (1962), Jeffrey King (2011), and Scott Soames (1999, 15–16). I think this is the single most common argument for the existence of propositions.

I am sympathetic with the following objection to this common argument. There are cases of two numerically distinct sentences 'meaning the same thing' even when there is no proposition that is their meaning. I say: 'Good morning' and

[17] It would be misleading to say, without qualification, that Lewis's own considered account of the nature of propositions is that propositions are sets of possible worlds. Rather, Lewis replaces the question 'What are propositions?' with 'Which entities play the propositional roles?' He then answers that sets of possible worlds play most of the propositional roles. (See Lewis, 1973, 46n.; Lewis, 1986a, 54–5.) As a result, we shall consider Lewis's views and arguments not only when exploring propositions-as-sets-of-possible-worlds (Ch. 3), but also when exploring structured propositions (Chs 4–5).

you say: 'Buenos días'. Or I ask: 'How many doctors are in town?' and you ask: 'How many physicians are in town?' Or I say: 'Shut the door now' and you say: 'Shut the door immediately'. Two numerically distinct sentences—such as greetings and questions and commands—can mean the same thing without there being a proposition that is their meaning. So—this objection concludes—it does not automatically follow from two numerically distinct declarative sentences asserting the same thing that there is a proposition that is what they assert.

Maybe this is a fantastic objection to the most common argument for propositions. Or maybe it is terrible.[18] Or maybe something in between. But all that matters here is that what I am about to say is not vulnerable to this objection, fantastic or otherwise. For—despite points of similarity with the most common argument for the existence of propositions—what I am about to say is not an argument for the existence of propositions at all. Rather, it is an argument that starts with the claim that there are propositions, and concludes that two (or more) sentences can express the same proposition.

There are propositions (§IV). Propositions are the fundamental bearers of truth (§V). For a sentence to be true (in a context of use) is for it to express a true proposition (in that

[18] The ancient Stoics believed in *lekta*, which are expressed by greetings, questions, commands, and so on. *Lekta* are incorporeal. *Lekta* are not sentences in a language. The Stoics believed in a species of *lekta* called '*axiomata*'. *Axiomata*, unlike other *lekta*, have truth-values; indeed, *axiomata* are propositions. (See Bobzien, 2003 and 2006.) I presume the Stoics would not be sympathetic to the above objection to the familiar argument; they would say that whenever two distinct sentences 'mean the same thing', there really is a *lekton* that is their meaning, and when those sentences have truth-values, that *lekton* is a proposition.

Robert Stalnaker says: 'Propositions are things people express when they make predictions or promises, give orders or advice' (1976, 79). And John Searle (1970, 22–9) claims that the same proposition is 'expressed' by all of the following sentences: 'Sam smokes habitually', 'Does Sam smoke habitually?', 'Sam, smoke habitually!', and 'Would that Sam smoked habitually'. Stalnaker and Searle, no less than the Stoics, would not be sympathetic to the above objection to the most common argument for propositions.

context of use) (§V). So if two sentences assert the same truth, they express the same proposition. Sometimes two sentences do assert the same truth, such as, for example, 'Smith is a doctor' and 'Smith es un médico'. So I conclude that different sentences can express the same proposition.

Or look at it this way. There are propositions (§IV). A sentence represents things as being a certain way only in virtue of expressing a proposition that represents things as being that way (§V). Sometimes two distinct sentences are exactly alike in how they represent things as being. For example, 'Smith is a doctor' and 'Smith es un médico' each represent Smith as being a doctor. So the proposition expressed by 'Smith is a doctor' represents things as being a certain way and the proposition expressed by 'Smith es un médico' represents things as being exactly that same way. So those two sentences express the same proposition. So I conclude that different sentences can express the same proposition.

Perhaps it was unnecessary for me to argue for the conclusion that, if there are propositions, then different sentences can express the same proposition. For believers in propositions all agree that different sentences can express the same proposition. But this conclusion is crucial to Chapter 2's arguments. So it is worth being sure about.

In fact, let me give one final argument for that same conclusion. This argument involves the idea of a *just-for-me proposition*. A just-for-me proposition is a proposition that exactly one person—and no one else—can use a sentence to express. My final argument's key premise is that there are no just-for-me propositions.[19]

[19] That is, a just-for-me proposition is a proposition that, necessarily, exactly one person can express. If only one person existed, or only one person was clever enough to use a sentence to express a particularly hard-to-grasp proposition, then there would be a proposition that only that person—and so only one person—was able to express. But that would not imply that that proposition was a just-for-me proposition.

The premise that there are no just-for-me propositions is plausible. And it has defenders (see, e.g., Kaplan, 1989). But it is not uncontroversial. For some have

I can use the sentence 'I am a parent' to express a true proposition (§V). Let us name this proposition *p*. There are no just-for-me propositions. So *p* is not a just-for-me proposition. So it is false that I alone can use a sentence to express *p*. So at least one other person can use a sentence to express *p*. Let A be one of those other persons.

A cannot use the sentence 'I am a parent' to express *p*. This is because when A uses the sentence 'I am a parent', A expresses a proposition that is true if and only if A is a parent. But *p* is true if and only if I myself am a parent and irrespective of whether A is a parent. So—given the preceding paragraph—A can use some other sentence to express *p*. So at least two different sentences can express *p*. So different sentences can express the same proposition.

Imagine that—as in John Perry (1979)—I see someone in a store mirror who is spilling sugar. So I accept the sentence 'That person is spilling sugar'. But I reject the sentence 'I am spilling sugar', even though I am 'that person'. I say (and Perry agrees) that those sentences, in the context here imagined, express the same proposition. But given that I accept one sentence and reject the other, a puzzle looms. As Chapter 2 will make clear, such puzzles loom whenever (or almost whenever) two distinct sentences express the same proposition—and not just when the sentences involve indexicals (or demonstratives, or proper names).

argued that there are propositions that only one person can grasp. And if there is a proposition that only one person can grasp, then presumably that one person is the only person who can use a sentence to express that proposition. Similarly, others have made claims about the nature of a proposition expressed by a sentence using the word 'I' that seem to imply that such propositions can be expressed only by a single person. (See, e.g., Frege, 1918–19; Chisholm, 1976, 36–7; Chalmers, 2011; Stanley, 2011, 98–110; and Hanks, 2013.)

VII. Conclusion

This chapter has argued that there are entities that have truth conditions, and have those truth conditions essentially. Those same entities, this chapter has argued, exist necessarily. This chapter also argued that those entities are, among other things, the fundamental bearers of truth and falsity, expressed by sentences that have truth-values, and the objects of belief. We should call those entities 'propositions'. So there are propositions.

2

LOGICAL VALIDITY AND MODAL VALIDITY

LOGICAL *validity* is defined in terms of an argument's form. But *modal validity* is not (Ch. 1, §I). So the concept of logical validity is not identical with the concept of modal validity. Even so, logical validity is related in important ways to modal validity. This chapter defends, among other things, an account of that relationship.

I. Logical Validity and 'Cicero' and 'Tully'

In his classic textbook *Introduction to Mathematical Logic*, Alonzo Church articulates the uncontroversial idea that logical validity is a matter of an argument's form:

> Our subject is *logic*... logic is concerned with the analysis of sentences or of propositions and of proof with attention to the *form* in abstraction from the *matter*... To take a relatively simple argument for illustrative purposes, consider the following:
>
> Brothers have the same surname; Richard and Stanley are brothers; Stanley has surname Thompson; therefore Richard has surname Thompson.
>
> ...The argument, it may be held, is valid from its form alone. (1956, 1–2)

Today's textbooks, written more than fifty years after Church's, still describe logical validity in this way. For example:

> ... logical consequence is *truth-preservation by virtue of form*. To say that an argument preserves truth is to say that *if* its premises are all true, *then* its conclusion is true. 'By virtue of form' requires that the truth-preservation be due solely to the form, not to the content, of the argument. (Sider, 2010, 2)

Logical validity is truth preservation in virtue of an argument's form.

Let us assemble the sentences 'Cicero is an orator' and 'Tully is an orator' into an argument, Argument A. And—because the nature of Argument A's premise and conclusion is central to what follows—let us present that argument in a way that makes it evident that it is constituted by sentences (as opposed to propositions):

'Cicero is an orator.'
Therefore,
'Tully is an orator.'

Argument A has a sentence as its premise and a sentence as its conclusion. No argument constituted by sentences is modally valid (Ch. 1, §§II and IV). So Argument A is not modally valid. We shall see that some arguments constituted by sentences are logically valid. But Argument A is not logically valid. That is, it is false that Argument A, simply in virtue of its form, preserves the truth of its premise.

I think it is fairly obvious that Argument A is not logically valid, even though—let me now add explicitly—'Cicero' and 'Tully' co-refer. Nevertheless, I shall defend, in three ways, this fairly obvious claim. Three defenses of the fairly obvious might seem to be overkill. But each defense will cast light on logical validity in ways that will be relied on at various points throughout the chapter. So each of those three defenses will eventually earn its keep.

My first defense begins by noting that Argument A's logical form seems to be: a is F; therefore, b is F. It is easy to see that arguments of the form *a is F; therefore, b is F* are not logically valid. For an argument is logically valid if and only if that argument's conclusion is true in all models in which its premises are true. Now consider a model that assigns 'a' to me, 'b' to my daughter, and 'F' to the set of males. In that model, 'a is F' is true but 'b is F' is false. So Argument A's conclusion is not true in every model in which its premise is true. So Argument A is not logically valid.

I have just focused on *predicate logic*. But there is also *sentential logic*.[1] The logical form of Argument A by the lights of sentential logic is: P; therefore, Q. There is a model that assigns the value *true* to 'P' and *false* to 'Q'. So arguments of the form *P; therefore, Q* are not valid in sentential logic. Thus, by the lights of sentential logic, Argument A is not logically valid.

Argument A does not have a logically valid form by the lights of predicate logic. Nor does Argument A have a logically valid form by the lights of sentential logic. Nor does Argument A have a logically valid form by the lights of any reasonable extensions of those logics (e.g., modal logic) or any reasonable revisions of those logics (e.g., free logic). So I conclude, without qualification, that Argument A does not have a logically valid form. This completes my first defense of the claim that Argument A is not logically valid.

None of us reasons perfectly. So perhaps we cannot recognize a priori all the logical consequences of everything we accept. Even so, there is good reason to conclude that an *ideal reasoner* can do this. For suppose that an ideal reasoner

[1] This section and the next will make it clear why I prefer the label 'sentential logic' (as in, e.g., Burgess, 2009, 3–7; see also Tarski, 1938 [1956]) to its perhaps more common synonym 'propositional logic'.

understands the premises and the conclusion of an argument. Then it seems that no further empirical evidence is required for that ideal reasoner to discover that argument's logical form—assuming it has one—or to discover whether arguments of that form are logically valid. So, at least as far as ideal reasoners go, there is good reason to endorse the standard claim that a 'consequence that could not be recognized as such a priori would never qualify as a logical consequence' (Etchemendy, 1990, 89). So I conclude that, necessarily, sentence T is a logical consequence of sentence S only if an ideal reasoner who understands both S and T can know a priori that T is a consequence of S.

Possibly, there is an ideal reasoner who understands both the sentence 'Cicero is an orator' and also the sentence 'Tully is an orator', but who does not know that 'Cicero' and 'Tully' co-refer. That ideal reasoner cannot know a priori that 'Tully is an orator' is a consequence of 'Cicero is an orator'. So 'Tully is an orator' is not a logical consequence of 'Cicero is an orator'. So Argument A's conclusion—that is, 'Tully is an orator'—is not a logical consequence of that argument's premise—that is, 'Cicero is an orator'. This completes my second defense of the claim that Argument A is not logically valid.

My third defense of the claim that Argument A is not logically valid begins with Greg Restall's remark:

> Logical consequence must have some . . . grip on agents like us. But what could this grip be? Consider again the case of the [logically] valid argument from A to C, and suppose . . . that an agent accepts A. What can we say about the agent's attitude to C? The one thing we can say about the agent's current attitude is that if she rejects C, she has made a mistake. (2005, 193; see also Beall and Restall, 2006, 16)

Similarly, Quine says:

> Now of these relations of statements to statements, one of conspicuous importance is the relation of logical implication: the relation of any statement to any that follows logically from it. If one statement is

to be held as true, each statement implied by it must also be held as true. (1982, 3–4)

Etchemendy (1990, 89) quotes this passage from Quine, and follows it up with: 'If you accept the premises of a valid argument, you must also accept the conclusion (to which we sometimes add "on pain of irrationality").'

I cannot see every logical consequence of everything that I accept. Neither can you. Perhaps those logical consequences that we cannot see make no epistemic demands on us. Or perhaps they do and we are all guilty, to some degree, of making a mistake, of failing to believe what we must, or of being somewhat irrational. But however we sort this out, we should all agree that an *ideal reasoner* who accepts the premises of a logically valid argument will—on pain of irrationality—not reject that argument's conclusion, at least not if that ideal reasoner understands that conclusion. After all—and as noted above—an ideal reasoner who understands an argument's premises and conclusion can see a priori what that argument's form is, and can also see a priori that all arguments of that form that have true premises also have true conclusions.[2]

Possibly, there is an ideal reasoner who understands both 'Cicero is an orator' and 'Tully is an orator', but who does not know that 'Cicero' and 'Tully' co-refer. That ideal reasoner could rationally both believe that the sentence 'Cicero is an orator' is true and also believe that the sentence 'Tully is an orator' is false. This shows that the conclusion of Argument A—'Tully is an orator'—can lack a certain sort of epistemic purchase on an

[2] Caveat: One moral of the 'paradox of the preface' is that even an ideal reasoner might accept the many premises of a logically valid argument whose conclusion is the conjunction of those premises, but rationally reject that conclusion, since she figures that she is probably mistaken about the truth of at least one of the many premises (Beall and Restall, 2006, 16–17). In what follows, I shall consider only very short arguments. Moreover, it should be uncontroversial that, for each of those arguments, an ideal reasoner who accepts its premises, could not—if that argument were logically valid—rationally reject its conclusion.

ideal reasoner who accepts the premise of Argument A—'Cicero is an orator'. But if Argument A were logically valid, its conclusion would have that sort of epistemic purchase on every ideal reasoner who accepts its premise. Thus my third and final defense of the claim that Argument A is not logically valid.

Argument A is not logically valid. But some arguments constituted by sentences are. An obvious example is Argument B, whose premise is the sentence 'Cicero is an orator' and whose conclusion is that same sentence:

'Cicero is an orator.'
Therefore,
'Cicero is an orator.'

Argument B's predicate logic logical form is: a is F; therefore, a is F. And Argument B's sentential logic logical form is: P; therefore, P. Moreover, it is a priori knowable that Argument B's conclusion is a consequence of its premise. Finally, anyone who accepts Argument B's premise must, on pain of irrationality, not reject its conclusion. In light of all these facts about Argument B, I conclude that Argument B is logically valid.

Argument B is constituted by sentences, as opposed to propositions. But propositions are not irrelevant to Argument B's being logically valid. This is because logical validity involves truth preservation, and a sentence is true in virtue of expressing a true proposition (Ch. 1, §V). So Argument B is logically valid just in case its form guarantees that the sentence that is its premise expresses a true proposition only if the sentence that is its conclusion expresses a true proposition.

A sentence expresses a proposition only in a context of use (Ch. 1, §V). So sentences constitute a logically valid argument (or, for that matter, a logically invalid argument) only in a context of use. In arguing above that Argument B is logically valid, I was presupposing a context of use in which its premise and conclusion express the same proposition.[3]

Indeed, throughout this section I have presupposed—rather than explicitly described—contexts of use in which this or that sentence expresses the relevant proposition, and so contexts of use in which this or that sentence (derivatively) has a truth-value and (derivatively) represents things as being a certain way. In what follows I shall continue to presuppose, as opposed to explicitly note, the relevant contexts of use.

II. Logical Validity and Propositions

Sometimes two sentences are exactly alike in how they represent things as being. For example, 'Cicero is an orator' represents Marcus Tullius Cicero as being an orator, and so does 'Tully is an orator'. A sentence represents things as being a certain way in virtue of expressing a proposition that represents things as being that way (Ch. 1, §V). So the proposition expressed by

[3] In fact, I am presupposing not only a context of use in which Argument B's premise expresses the same proposition as its conclusion, but also a context of use in which the occurrences of 'Cicero' in Argument B are appropriately *linked*. To see why I say this, suppose that Peter believes that there are two men named 'Paderewski', one a politician, the other a pianist. But suppose further that there is just one such man—a musical prime minister (Kripke, 1979, 265–6). Now suppose that, thinking of—as Peter would say—'the pianist', Peter accepts the sentence 'Paderewski is a musician', but, thinking of—again, as Peter would say—'the prime minister', he rejects the sentence 'Paderewski is a musician'. Add that Peter then takes the accepted sentence as a premise in an argument and the rejected sentence as that argument's conclusion. Is that argument, in the context just described, logically valid? I am inclined to say 'no'. I am inclined to say this because, with regard to epistemic purchase and what is knowable a priori, that argument is more like Argument A than Argument B. So I am inclined to conclude that that argument has the logical form *a is F; therefore, b is F*. Its having this logical form is not explained, in this context of use, by the premise expressing a different proposition than that expressed by the conclusion. Rather, it is explained by the fact that, in this context of use, the occurrences of 'Paderewski' are not appropriately linked (cf. Fine, 2007; Pinillos, 2011).

'Cicero is an orator' represents things as being exactly the same way as does the proposition expressed by 'Tully is an orator'. So I conclude that those two sentences express the same proposition (cf. Ch. 1, §VI).

Fregeans about names deny that the sentence 'Cicero is an orator' and the sentence 'Tully is an orator' express the same proposition. I think I have just given a good reason to conclude that they are wrong. And in the next section I shall raise further problems for Fregeanism about names. Moreover, the next section will defend this section's main point in a way that sidesteps Fregeanism about names. But for now—if just for the sake of argument—assume that 'Cicero is an orator' and 'Tully is an orator' do express the same proposition. And let us give that proposition the following name: *that Cicero/Tully is an orator*.

Modally valid arguments have propositions (as opposed to sentences) as their premises and conclusions (Ch. 1, §IV). So an argument can have a proposition as a premise and a proposition as a conclusion. Argument C is just such an argument. And—because the nature of that argument's premise and conclusion is central to what follows—let us present Argument C in a way that makes it evident that its premise is a proposition and its conclusion is a proposition:

That Cicero/Tully is an orator
Therefore,
That Cicero/Tully is an orator

I shall argue that Argument C is not logically valid.

My first reason for concluding that Argument C is not logically valid begins with an ideal reasoner who does not know that 'Cicero' and 'Tully' co-refer. She then asserts what she rationally believes: 'Cicero is an orator, and it is not the case that Tully is an orator.' So she rationally both believes the proposition expressed by 'Cicero is an orator' and also believes to be false the proposition expressed by 'Tully is an orator'. That is, she rationally believes and also believes to be false the proposition *that Cicero/Tully is an orator*.

That Cicero/Tully is an orator is the premise and also the conclusion of Argument C. An ideal reasoner can believe the premise of Argument C while also rationally believing that the conclusion of Argument C is false. So Argument C's conclusion lacks a sort of epistemic purchase on ideal reasoners who believe its premise. But if Argument C were logically valid, then its conclusion would have that sort of epistemic purchase on ideal reasoners who believe its premise (§I).[4] So Argument C is not logically valid.

A second reason to conclude that Argument C is not logically valid begins with an ideal reasoner who understands both 'Cicero is an orator' and 'Tully is an orator', and so who thereby understands the proposition that each expresses. But that ideal reasoner does not know that 'Cicero' and 'Tully' co-refer. That ideal reasoner then expresses Argument C by saying: 'Cicero is an orator; therefore, Tully is an orator.' When expressing Argument C in this way, that ideal reasoner cannot know a priori that its conclusion is a consequence of its premise. But an ideal reasoner who understands the premises and conclusion of a logically valid argument can always know a priori that that conclusion is a consequence of those premises (§I). So Argument C is not logically valid.

You might object to both of my above reasons for concluding that Argument C is not logically valid. For you might object that just so long as Argument C's premise and conclusion *are*

[4] I take Restall's formulation of the relevant epistemic purchase to be better than Quine's and Etchemendy's. Restall says that one who accepts the premises of a logically valid argument must not reject its conclusion. Quine and Etchemendy say that one who accepts the premises of a logically valid argument must accept its conclusion. Argument C's conclusion is identical with its premise; any agent who accepts C's premise thereby—simply because of the indiscernibility of identicals, as opposed to because of that agent's rationality—accepts its conclusion.

expressed by the right sentences, then that conclusion does have epistemic purchase on ideal reasoners who believe that premise and, moreover, ideal reasoners who understand those sentences can know a priori that that conclusion is a consequence of that premise. For example, you might continue, this is the way things are when both Argument C's premise and Argument C's conclusion are expressed by the sentence 'Cicero is an orator'.

Recall Argument B from the previous section:

'Cicero is an orator.'
Therefore,
'Cicero is an orator.'

Argument B just is the expression of both Argument C's premise and Argument C's conclusion by the sentence 'Cicero is an orator'. So the idea that both the relevant epistemic purchase holds and also the relevant consequence relation can be known a priori when Argument C's premise and conclusion are each expressed by the sentence 'Cicero is an orator' simply repeats two points from the previous section. First, an ideal reasoner who accepts Argument B's premise cannot, on pain of irrationality, reject its conclusion. Second, an ideal reasoner who understands both argument B's premise and conclusion can know a priori that its conclusion is a consequence of its premise.

With all of this in mind, I say that the idea that Argument C's conclusion has the relevant epistemic purchase on ideal reasoners who believe Argument C's premise only when that premise and that conclusion *are expressed by the right sentences* supports—rather than undermines—my conclusion that Argument C itself is not logically valid. For it supports the claim that the relevant epistemic purchase concerns accepting and not rejecting sentences that express propositions, as opposed to believing and believing to be false propositions in and of themselves (and so regardless of which sentences express them).

Likewise, the idea that an ideal reasoner can know a priori that Argument C's conclusion is a consequence of its premise only when that premise and conclusion *are expressed by the right sentences* supports—rather than undermines—my conclusion that Argument C itself is not logically valid. For it supports the claim that what is known a priori is that a proposition-expressing sentence is a consequence of a proposition-expressing sentence, as opposed to that a proposition, in and of itself (and so regardless of which sentence expresses it), is a consequence of a proposition, in and of itself (and so regardless of which sentence expresses it).

Again, Argument C is not logically valid. For what it is worth, I think that the above reasons to conclude that Argument C is not logically valid suggest that propositions are typically believed 'under a guise'. Here is how Nathan Salmon explains this idea:

> ... whatever mode of acquaintance of an object is involved in a particular case of someone's entertaining a singular proposition about that object, that mode of acquaintance is part of the means by which one apprehends the singular proposition, for it is the means by which one is familiar with one of the main ingredients of the proposition. This generates something analogous to an 'appearance' or a 'guise' for singular propositions. (1986, 109)

I am inclined to say that those who reject the sentence 'Tully is an orator' do not believe the proposition *that Cicero/Tully is an orator* under the 'guise' associated with the sentence 'Tully is an orator'. And this is so even if they believe that proposition under the guise associated with 'Cicero is an orator', and so believe that proposition.[5]

[5] Perhaps *believing* is a three-part relation between an agent, a proposition, and a guise. Or perhaps *believing* is a two-part relation between an agent and a proposition, and a guise gets in on the action in some other way. All of this is consistent with a variety of views on just what the semantic content, and pragmatic implications, of a 'belief report' are. And all of this is consistent with a variety of

There is one more reason to conclude that Argument C is not logically valid. As noted above (§I), an argument is logically valid if and only if its conclusion is true in all models in which its premises are true. The models for sentential logic map sentences to truth-values. The models for predicate logic map parts of sentences to objects and sets. As a result, the only arguments that can be logically valid are arguments constituted by sentences. So Argument C, which is not constituted by sentences, is not logically valid.

You might want to introduce new sorts of models as a way to try to resist this final reason for concluding that Argument C is not logically valid. Thus Jason Turner (2005, 200) says: 'What does it *mean*, though, for one proposition to "follow logically" from another? Logical implication is supposed to be a sentential relation.' (So far I agree!) But then he goes on:

> In predicate logic, a sentence 'p' is said to follow from another sentence 'q' if and only if every interpretation (i.e., function from terms to objects, properties, and relations) that renders 'q' true renders 'p' true also. Since our propositions have syntactic structure, we can provide interpretations for them as well; these would be functions from propositional elements to objects, properties and relations... I will say that one proposition is 'semantically implied' by another if the former is true on every interpretation that renders the latter true. (2005, 200)

Turner's idea is to expand what counts as a model in predicate logic so that such models do not merely map parts of sentences to objects and sets, but also *constituents of structured propositions* to objects and sets (or properties and relations).

Turner's idea works only if there are structured propositions. But Chapters 4 and 5 will argue that there are no structured propositions. Finding those arguments compelling, I conclude that Turner's idea does not work. More generally—and because

views on what guises *are*. (In particular, I do not say that guises are themselves sentences, but instead only that there are guises 'associated with' sentences.)

of Chapters 4 and 5—I conclude that the models in predicate logic cannot be expanded to accommodate arguments constituted by propositions. So arguments constituted by propositions cannot be logically valid by the lights of predicate logic. So Argument C is not thus logically valid.

Suppose you agree with me about predicate logic. Even so, you still might want to expand what counts as a model in sentential logic to accommodate logically valid arguments constituted by propositions. The standard models map sentences to truth-values. And, you might say, we can easily introduce new models that map propositions to truth-values. And so you might conclude that Argument C is itself logically valid by the lights of sentential logic. And so you might conclude that Argument C is logically valid.

This illustrates that simply denying that propositions are structured—and so concluding that propositions cannot constitute arguments that are logically valid by the lights of predicate logic—does not all by itself deliver the conclusion that propositions do not constitute logically valid arguments. Besides, in Chapter 4 (§III), I shall use that conclusion to undermine a standard motivation for structured propositions. So, even setting sentential logic aside, I need to defend that conclusion without presupposing that propositions are not structured. This is what I shall do for the rest of this section.

It would be a mistake to expand the models in sentential logic to include functions from propositions to truth-values. To begin to see why, consider a confused 'argument' whose sole premise is the sentence 'Is Turkey in Asia?' and whose conclusion is the sentence 'Is Turkey in Asia?' This confused 'argument' is not logically valid. For no 'argument' constituted by questions is logically valid. Therefore, it would be a mistake to expand the models in sentential logic to include functions from questions to truth-values.

Here is a related point. Any argument of the logical form *P; therefore, P* is logically valid. The 'argument' *'Is Turkey in Asia?';*

therefore, 'Is Turkey in Asia?' is not logically valid. So that 'argument' does not have the logical form *P; therefore, P*. So the identity of an 'argument's' sole premise with its conclusion is not sufficient for that 'argument' to have the logical form *P; therefore, P*.

Questions are not the right kind of entity to constitute logically valid arguments at least in part because questions do not have truth-values. But there are some other entities that (unlike questions) do have truth-values, yet nevertheless (like questions) are not the right kind of entity to constitute logically valid arguments.

To see why I say this, return to Argument C: *that Cicero/Tully is an orator*; therefore, *that Cicero/Tully is an orator*. Recall that Argument C's conclusion does not have the relevant epistemic purchase on ideal reasoners who believe Argument C's premise. Recall further that, possibly, an ideal reasoner who understands Argument C's premise and conclusion cannot know a priori that that conclusion is a consequence of that premise. Both of these points show that Argument C is not logically valid.

Argument C is not logically valid. But Argument C is as good a candidate for being logically valid as any argument constituted by propositions could be. That is, if any argument constituted by propositions were logically valid, Argument C would be logically valid. So I conclude that no argument constituted by propositions is logically valid.

Because no argument constituted by propositions is logically valid, it is a mistake to expand models in sentential logic to include functions from propositions to truth-values. Moreover, because no argument constituted by propositions is logically valid, it is a mistake—and would still be a mistake even if propositions were structured—to expand models in predicate logic to map constituents of propositions to objects and sets.

Here is a related point. Any argument of the logical form *P; therefore, P* is logically valid. Thus no argument constituted by propositions has the logical form *P; therefore, P*, not even if that argument's sole premise is identical with its conclusion. Similarly, if the premises and conclusion of an argument are propositions, then that argument does not have the logical form *a is F; therefore, a is F*, not even if, for example, its premise and conclusion are each the proposition *that Cicero/Tully is an orator*.

III. Logical Validity and 'Doctor' and 'Physician'

The main conclusion of the previous section is that no argument constituted by propositions is logically valid. I shall now defend that main conclusion in a way that sidesteps Fregeanism about names. My defense begins with the following argument—Argument A*—which is constituted by sentences:

'Smith is a doctor.'
Therefore,
'Smith is a physician.'

Argument A*'s predicate logic logical form is: a is F; therefore, a is G. Argument A*'s sentential logic logical form is: P; therefore, Q. So Argument A* does not have a logically valid form by the lights of either predicate logic or sentential logic. Nor does it seem to have a logically valid form by the lights of any reasonable extensions or revisions of those logics. So Argument A* is not logically valid.

Some will object. For some will endorse a recursive account of logical validity according to which an argument is logically valid if replacing a word in that argument with a synonym of that word delivers a logically valid argument (cf. Mates, 1972, 14–15). If we replace 'physician' in Argument A* with the synonymous 'doctor', we get an argument whose predicate logic logical form is *a is F; therefore, a is F* and whose sentential logic logical form is *P; therefore, P*. Thus defenders of this recursive account of logical validity will insist that Argument A* is logically valid.

This recursive account of logical validity is mistaken. To begin to see why, consider a second recursive account of logical validity, an account that (to my knowledge) no one defends. The second recursive account of logical validity says that an argument is logically valid if replacing a name in that argument with a co-referring name delivers a logically valid argument.

We can show that the second recursive account is mistaken by returning to Argument A:

'Cicero is an orator.'
Therefore,
'Tully is an orator.'

The second recursive account counts Argument A as logically valid. But Argument A does not preserve truth in virtue of form (§I). This shows that the second recursive account runs afoul of the fact that logical validity is truth preservation in virtue of form. The second recursive account runs afoul of this fact because it counts an argument as logically valid not only if that argument preserves truth in virtue of form, but also if that argument would preserve truth in virtue of form were it changed in a particular way (by replacing a name in that argument with a co-referring name).

The first recursive account, just like the second recursive account, runs afoul of the fact that logical validity is truth preservation in virtue of form. For the first recursive account counts as logically valid some arguments that do not preserve truth in virtue of form. In particular, it counts an argument as logically valid not only if that argument preserves truth in virtue of form, but also if that argument would preserve truth in virtue of form were it changed in a particular way (by replacing a word in that argument with a synonymous word). So I conclude that the first recursive account of logical validity is mistaken. And I stick with the claim that Argument A* is not logically valid.

Argument A* is not logically valid because—as noted above—it does not have a logically valid form. Or so I say. But maybe you are not yet fully convinced that Argument A* does not have a logically valid form. And so maybe you are not yet fully convinced that Argument A* is not logically valid. So I shall now offer further motivation for the claim that Argument A* is not logically valid (and, as a result, further reason to reject the first recursive account of logical validity).

Peter is an ideal reasoner. But Peter made it to adulthood without learning the words 'doctor' or 'physician'. Then Peter became seriously ill and was admitted to a hospital for a lengthy stay. The hospital personnel spoke American English and knew that 'doctor' and 'physician' are synonyms. But as a matter of hospital policy, the doctors at that hospital were always called 'doctors', never 'physicians'. Peter came to understand the word 'doctor' as well as do many other competent users of the term, and certainly well enough to assert that Smith is a doctor by saying: 'Smith is a doctor.'

Years later, Peter was struck with another serious illness. He was admitted to a new hospital for a lengthy stay, where he saw many doctors, including Jones. In the new hospital everyone spoke American English, but as a matter of policy the doctors were always called 'physicians', never 'doctors'. At a certain point, Peter came to understand the word 'physician' as well as do many other competent users of the term, and certainly well enough to assert that Jones is a physician by saying: 'Jones is a physician.'

As far as Peter could tell, the physicians at his new hospital did the same things as the doctors did at his old hospital. So to this day Peter is a little puzzled by—let me put it in his words—'the fact that the doctors at the old hospital are not physicians'. But Peter is a humble man, and assumes that he is missing some subtle difference between—as he would put it—'doctors and physicians'. While musing on this, his thoughts occasionally return to his first doctor, and he thinks to himself—let me put it in his words—'Smith is a doctor, but not a physician'.

Peter understands and accepts Argument A*'s premise, which is the sentence 'Smith is a doctor'. Peter understands and rationally rejects Argument A*'s conclusion, which is the sentence 'Smith is a physician'.[6] So Argument A*'s conclusion lacks a certain sort of epistemic purchase on an ideal reasoner—namely, Peter—who accepts Argument A*'s premise. But if Argument A* were logically valid, its conclusion would have that sort of epistemic purchase on every ideal reasoner who accepts its premise (§I). So Argument A* is not logically valid.

Because Peter does not know that 'doctor' and 'physician' are synonyms, he cannot—even though he is an ideal reasoner—know a priori that the sentence 'Smith is a physician' is a consequence of the sentence 'Smith is a doctor'. But, necessarily, if sentence T is a logical consequence of sentence S, an ideal reasoner who understands both S and T can know a priori that T is a consequence of S (§I). So 'Smith is a physician' is not a logical consequence of 'Smith is a doctor'. So, again, Argument A* is not logically valid.

I have just given two arguments involving Peter's case for the conclusion that Argument A* is not logically valid. Those arguments succeed only if Peter understands the words 'doctor' and 'physician'. And I say that he does. Indeed, the whole point of the story involving Peter is to show that even an ideal reasoner

[6] Now suppose that Peter—applying some logic to what he already accepts and rejects—comes to understand and reject the sentence 'All doctors are physicians'. 'All doctors are physicians' is surely analytic. So I conclude that even an ideal reasoner can understand and rationally reject an analytic sentence (cf. Williamson, 2006; Sorensen, 2001, 57–60). But an ideal reasoner cannot understand and rationally reject a sentence that is itself logically valid (cf. §I). So there are two closely related morals here. The first is that 'All doctors are physicians' is not itself logically valid, which gives us another reason to reject the first recursive account of logical validity introduced at the start of this section. The second is that not all analytic sentences are logically valid.

who understands both 'doctor' and 'physician' can fail to recognize that they are synonyms, and so can fail to recognize that 'Smith is a doctor' is true just in case 'Smith is a physician' is true.

And there is more—besides Peter's story—to support the claim that even an ideal reasoner can understand 'doctor' and 'physician' yet fail to recognize their synonymy. For one can understand a word even if unacquainted with some of its synonyms. So one can understand the word 'doctor' even if unacquainted with the word 'physician'. Such a person would not know that 'doctor' is synonymous with 'physician'. So understanding 'doctor' is not even partially constituted by knowing that it is synonymous with 'physician'. By parity of reasoning, understanding 'physician' is not even partially constituted by knowing that it is synonymous with 'doctor'. This too—in addition to Peter's story—supports the claim that one can understand 'doctor' and 'physician' yet fail to recognize their synonymy.

But some will object that this claim must be wrong. For example, Michael Dummett says:

> It is an undeniable feature of the notion of meaning—obscure as that notion is—that meaning is *transparent* in the sense that, if someone attaches a meaning to each of two words, he must know whether these meanings are the same. (1978, 131)

And here is Saul Kripke:

> What if a speaker assents to a sentence, but fails to assent to a synonymous assertion? Say, he assents to 'Smith is a doctor' but not to 'Smith is a physician.' Such a speaker either does not understand one of the sentences normally, or he should be able to correct himself 'on reflection.' (1979, 276 n. 23)

Dummett and Kripke both seem to be suggesting something along the following lines: Suppose one understands 'doctor'. Then one knows what 'doctor' means. Suppose one also understands 'physician'. Then one also knows what 'physician' means. One then recognizes—perhaps only 'on reflection'—that their meanings are the same. One then concludes that 'doctor' and 'physician' are synonyms.

But I object that it is possible—even for an ideal reasoner—to understand two expressions with the same meaning while failing to recognize that those expressions have the same meaning. For suppose that you understand two synonyms—for example, 'F' and 'G'—unusually well. Then you will recognize a lot of overlap in what you know about their meanings. But the overlap is not total, in part because—let us now add—you do not know every single thing about their meanings. Because the overlap is not total, you do not recognize that 'F' and 'G' are synonyms. In fact, this is just the phenomenon illustrated by the above case involving Peter.

And it is not only in contrived cases—such as the one involving Peter—that one understands a word but fails to know everything about its meaning. On the contrary, I doubt that any of us knows everything about the meaning of most of the workaday words that we clearly do understand, including 'doctor' and 'physician'. So I deny that those of us who understand 'doctor' and 'physician' are thereby—that is, simply in virtue of our understanding those words—able to deduce that they have exactly the same meaning.[7] So I conclude that one can understand two synonymous words and not recognize that they have exactly the same meaning (cf. Salmon, 1989a; Williamson, 2006).[8]

[7] Of course, you and I do know that 'doctor' and 'physician' have exactly the same meaning; I suspect that we know this because we have been told that they are synonyms.

[8] Exceptions include stipulatively defined technical words (and expressions). For example, suppose 'iff' is an operator whose meaning is exhausted by the fact that it joins two sentences S and S* into a resulting sentence that is true just in case the truth-value of S is the same as that of S*, and otherwise false. Then you know everything there is to know about the meaning of 'iff'. Make parallel assumptions about the technical expression 'just in case'. Then you can, in virtue

Some might grant me this conclusion, but still resist my reasons for concluding that Argument A* is not logically valid that turn on the case involving Peter. For some might charge that in judging whether 'Smith is a physician' is a logical consequence of 'Smith is a doctor', we should not focus on an ideal reasoner who merely understands those sentences. Rather, they charge, we should focus on an ideal reasoner who has *absolutely complete* understanding of those sentences, and so of the words 'doctor' and 'physician'.

Those who charge this will correctly point out both of the following: Such a reasoner who knows that the sentence 'Smith is a doctor' is true needs no further empirical evidence in order to conclude that the sentence 'Smith is a physician' is true. And if such a reasoner accepts the sentence 'Smith is a doctor', she may not—on pain of irrationality—reject the sentence 'Smith is a physician'.

These points are correct. But they are also irrelevant to the claim that 'Smith is a physician' is a logical consequence of 'Smith is a doctor'. To begin to see why I say this, recall why it is that an ideal reasoner who understands the premises and conclusion of a logically valid argument can know a priori that that conclusion is a consequence of those premises. This is because once such a reasoner understands those premises and conclusion, she can then—without any further empirical evidence—recognize both the form of that argument and also that that argument preserves the truth of its premises in virtue of having that form (§I).

Recall also why an ideal reasoner who understands the premises and conclusion of a logically valid argument and who also accepts those premises cannot—on pain of irrationality—reject that conclusion. This is because, as just noted, that reasoner thereby knows enough to recognize both the form of that

of understanding 'iff' and 'just in case', come to see that they have exactly the same meaning.

argument and also that that argument preserves the truth of its premises in virtue of having that form. And so that ideal reasoner can see that by accepting those premises—that is, by taking them to be true—she is thereby committed to the truth of that conclusion (§I).

With all of this in mind, suppose that an ideal reasoner who grasps the form of Argument A* cannot see that Argument A*'s conclusion follows from its premise. Then that conclusion does not follow from that premise in virtue of that argument's form alone. Then Argument A* is not logically valid. Thus the case above involving Peter, who is an ideal reasoner, shows that Argument A* is not logically valid. For although Peter does not have absolutely complete understanding of 'Smith is a doctor' and 'Smith is a physician', Peter's ordinary understanding of 'Smith is a doctor' and 'Smith is a physician' is good enough. His ordinary understanding of those sentences is good enough because it is sufficient for him to grasp the form of Argument A*.

Here is an instructive comparison. Imagine an ideal reasoner who not only understands the sentences 'Cicero is an orator' and 'Tully is an orator', but also knows that 'Cicero' and 'Tully' co-refer. That ideal reasoner does not need any additional empirical evidence to conclude that 'Tully is an orator' is a consequence of 'Cicero is an orator'. And if that ideal reasoner accepts the sentence 'Cicero is an orator', she may not—on pain of irrationality—reject the sentence 'Tully is an orator'. All of this is correct. And all of this is irrelevant to the claim that 'Tully is an orator' is a logical consequence of 'Cicero is an orator'. And so all of this is irrelevant to the claim that Argument A—'Cicero is an orator'; therefore, 'Tully is an orator'—is logically valid.

All of this is irrelevant because none of this shows that Argument A preserves truth in virtue of form. And Argument A does not preserve truth in virtue of form. We already showed this by considering an ideal reasoner who does grasp its form—in virtue of understanding its premise and conclusion—but who does not know that 'Cicero' and 'Tully' co-refer (§I). That reasoner cannot see that Argument A's conclusion is a consequence of its premise and that reasoner can rationally accept Argument A's premise while rejecting its conclusion. So Argument A is not logically valid.[9]

Here again is Argument A*:

'Smith is a doctor.'
Therefore,
'Smith is a physician.'

I have been arguing throughout this section that Argument A* is not logically valid. So I shall now build on the conclusion that Argument A* is not logically valid.

Two sentences sometimes express the same proposition (Ch. 1, §VI). And, surely, if any two sentences express the same proposition, then the premise and conclusion of Argument A*—that is, 'Smith is a doctor' and 'Smith is a physician'—express the same proposition. Let *that Smith is a doctor/physician* be that proposition.

Recall that Argument A from Section I—'Cicero is an orator'; therefore, 'Tully is an orator'—is not logically valid. Building on the fact that Argument A is not logically valid, Section II showed that Argument C—that is, *that Cicero/Tully is an orator*;

[9] Consider this argument: If two names used in an argument co-refer, then they ought to be symbolized with the same term; therefore, an ideal reasoner who does not know that 'Cicero' and 'Tully' co-refer does not know enough to grasp the form of Argument A, which is the logically valid *a is F; therefore, a is F*. I think that this argument is unsound, and in particular that its premise is false. This is because I think—for all the reasons given in this chapter—that Argument A is not logically valid. I also think—for all the reasons given in this chapter—that Argument A* is not logically valid. So I conclude that the following is false, and that the argument for Argument A*'s logical validity that it leads to is unsound: If two predicates used in an argument are synonymous, then they ought to be symbolized with the same letter.

therefore, *that Cicero/Tully is an orator*—is not logically valid. Argument A* is not logically valid. So the reasoning in Section II that shows that Argument C is not logically valid can easily be adapted to show that the following argument is not logically valid: *that Smith is a doctor/physician*; therefore, *that Smith is a doctor/physician*. But if any argument constituted by propositions were logically valid, then that argument would be. So I conclude—as I did in Section II—that no argument constituted by propositions is logically valid.

The main point here—the only point that matters for the rest of this book—is that no argument constituted by propositions is logically valid. I have just established that point by way of the case involving Peter. And there are other ways to establish that same point. Here is one. Let 'Henrietta' name a particular bit of gorse; in other words, let 'Henrietta' name a particular bit of furze. Then consider an argument whose sole premise is 'Henrietta is gorse' and whose conclusion is 'Henrietta is furze'. Then imagine a case involving an ideal reasoner who (understands and) accepts that argument's premise but (understands and) rationally rejects its conclusion.

Because 'gorse' and 'furze' (unlike 'doctor' and 'physician') are natural kind terms, some will find the sort of case I have just asked you to imagine acceptable even if they find Peter's case, as I described it, unacceptable (see, e.g., Kripke, 1979, 268 and 277 n. 23). So replace Argument A* with the argument that has the sentence 'Henrietta is gorse' as its sole premise and the sentence 'Henrietta is furze' as its conclusion. Then add that the sentence 'Henrietta is gorse' expresses the same proposition as the sentence 'Henrietta is furze'. Then reason as above to establish the point that propositions never constitute logically valid arguments.

Here is another way to establish that point. Suppose that Fregeanism about names is false. Suppose then that 'Cicero is an orator' and 'Tully is an orator' express the same proposition. If 'Cicero is an orator' and 'Tully is an orator' express the same proposition, Section II has already shown that no argument constituted by propositions is logically valid. At the very outset of that section, I raised a problem for Fregeanism about names. And we are now equipped to raise more problems for Fregeanism about names, thereby strengthening Section II's defense of the claim that no argument constituted by propositions is logically valid.

Fregeans about names make speeches like the following:

> ...other than using bribery, threats, hypnosis, or the like, there is simply nothing you can do to get most people to say that Smith believes that Tully was an orator, once they know that Smith sincerely denies 'Tully was an orator', understands it, and acts on his denial in ways appropriate thereto. In particular, pointing out that Smith can express something he believes with 'Cicero was an orator' seems simply irrelevant to most people. (Richard, 1990, 125)

Fregeanism about names allows us to avoid the result that someone might understand and sincerely reject the sentence 'Tully is an orator' but also believe that Tully is an orator. I take avoiding such results to be the central motivation for Fregeanism about names. But I say—in light of the arguments of this section—that Peter's case shows that someone who understands and rejects 'Smith is a physician' might also believe that Smith is a physician. Once we have accepted that result, there is no good reason to resist the parallel result involving believing that Tully is an orator.[10]

[10] Many invoke belief under a guise to make sense of how someone could believe the proposition *that Cicero/Tully is an orator*—and so believe that Tully is an orator—while rejecting the sentence 'Tully is an orator'. I think that they should also invoke belief under a guise to make sense of how Peter could believe that Smith is a physician while rejecting the sentence 'Smith is a physician'. Thus one moral of the case involving Peter is that there is a guise associated with sentences containing 'physician' no less than with sentences containing 'Tully'. But most of the literature on believing propositions under a guise—as in the passage from Salmon quoted in Section II—is focused on guises associated with sentences containing proper names (such as 'Tully'), indexicals (such as 'I'), or demonstratives (such as 'that person in the mirror'). See, among others, Richard

Or look at it this way. Fregeans about names insist that 'Cicero is an orator' and 'Tully is an orator' express different propositions. They insist on this because of their central motivation. But then, in light of the case involving Peter, Fregeans ought also to insist that 'Smith is a physician' and 'Smith is a doctor' express different propositions. And this is a reductio of their central motivation. For different sentences can express the same proposition. And if any two sentences express the same proposition, then 'Smith is a physician' and 'Smith is a doctor' do (cf. Ch. 1, §VI).[11]

Along similar lines, recall the case in which I would accept the sentence 'That person is spilling sugar' and reject the sentence 'I am spilling sugar', even though I am 'that person' (Ch. 1, §VI). I think that, in that case, I express the same proposition with 'I am spilling sugar' as I do with 'That person is spilling sugar'. So I conclude that, in that case, I believe that I am spilling sugar even though I understand and sincerely reject the sentence 'I am spilling sugar'. Fregeans about names

(1983), Perry (1979), Salmon (1986, 109), Crimmins and Perry (1989), Kaplan (1989), and Soames (1989).

[11] Frege says:

> In an article ('Über Sinn und Bedeutung') I distinguished between sense and *Bedeutung* [reference] in the first instance only for the case of proper names... The same distinction can also be drawn for concept words. (before 1895 [1997, 172])

I think this indicates a tension in Frege's overall view. For he also says: 'The same sense has different expressions in different languages and even in the same language' (1892a [1997, 153]); this implies that two distinct sentences can express a single proposition. More importantly—as Patricia Blanchette (1996, 323–4) shows—Frege's understanding of logic requires some distinct sentences in the same language to express the same proposition. And I suspect that among the cases in which Frege thinks two sentences can express the same proposition, there will be some in which one could rationally accept one of those sentences and reject the other. But if so, there will be cases analogous to the case of someone's rejecting 'Tully is an orator' but believing Tully is an orator. (Among contemporary followers of Frege, most follow Frege only with regard to names. But Chalmers (2011, esp. 613–15) endorses a Fregean approach to indexicals and terms like 'attorney' and 'lawyer'.)

should find this no more acceptable than the claim that you believe that Tully is an orator even though you understand and sincerely reject the sentence 'Tully is an orator'.

So Fregeans about names should say that I express one proposition *p* with 'I am spilling sugar' and a distinct proposition *q* with 'That person is spilling sugar'. More generally, and in light of their central motivation, I think that Fregeans about names are committed to there being a different sense for each denoting expression. Of course, no one besides me can express proposition *p* with the sentence 'I am spilling sugar'. And those who try to express *p* by referring to me with some denoting expression other than 'I' will—given the Fregean commitment just noted—end up expressing a proposition other than *p*. In this way, Fregeans about names are committed, unacceptably, to 'just-for-me' propositions (see Ch. 1, §VI).

Here is one final reason for concluding that propositions never constitute logically valid arguments, a reason that illustrates just how familiar and unsurprising this conclusion should be. Much of the literature explicitly takes logic to deal with sentences, as opposed to propositions (see, e.g., Tarski, 1936 [1956]; Mates, 1972, 10; and Burgess, 2009, 3–7). Indeed, logically valid arguments have been taken to be constituted by sentences at least as far back as the Middle Ages.[12] Most importantly, the typical models used to establish logical validity involve sentences or parts of sentences, as opposed to propositions or parts of propositions. So it is natural to assume that logically valid arguments are always constituted by sentences. This assumption implies that logically valid arguments are never constituted by propositions.

[12] Certain medievals used the word 'propositio' simply to mean *premise*—and a *propositio* was taken by all to be a sentence (Kretzmann, 1970; Gracia, 1975).

IV. The Current Orthodoxy and its Epistemic Corollary Are False

Among those who believe that there are modally valid arguments, it seems to be uncontroversial that if an argument is logically valid, then that argument is modally valid. Let me illustrate this with a few passages, starting with one from Tarski that was also quoted in Chapter 1:

> It seems that everyone who understands the content of the above definition [of logical consequence] must admit that it agrees quite well with common usage. This becomes still clearer from its various consequences. In particular, it can be proved, on the basis of this definition, that every [logical] consequence of true sentences *must* be true ... (1936 [1956, 417], emphasis added)

Theodore Sider says:

> ... logical consequence is *truth-preservation by virtue of form* ... 'By virtue of form' is also usually thought to require that the argument preserve truth of necessity. (2010, 2)

J. C. Beall and Greg Restall say:

> One of the oldest features determining properly *logical* consequence is its *necessity*. The truth of the premises of a [logically] valid argument *necessitates* the truth of the conclusion of that argument. (2006, 14)

William H. Hanson says:

> The importance of necessity for logical consequence has been recognized by numerous philosophers for more than two millennia. Aristotle, Leibniz, and Tarski are among the many who have taught that a proper account of logical consequence will contain necessity as a component. The rationale for this is not difficult to see. We want logic to guarantee that when the premises of a [logically] valid argument are true, the conclusion will also be true. And we want this guarantee to hold no matter how things are or might have been. (1997, 373)

And here is John Etchemendy:

> The most important feature of logical consequence, as we ordinarily understand it, is a modal relation that holds between implying sentences and the sentence implied. The premises of a logically valid argument cannot be true if the conclusion is false; such conclusions are said to 'follow necessarily' from their premises... That this is the single most prominent feature of the consequence relation, or at any rate of our ordinary understanding of that relation, is clear from even the most cursory survey of texts on the subject... (1990, 81)

Etchemendy then cites Copi (1972, 23), Mates (1965, 3), and Bell and Machover (1977, 5) as affirming that all logically valid arguments are modally valid.

Moreover, consider the common view that logical necessity is a species of *de dicto* metaphysical necessity. Defenders of this view include those with otherwise very different approaches to modality, such as, for example, Alvin Plantinga (1974, 1–2) and Theodore Sider (2011, 266–74). This common view implies that all logically valid arguments are modally valid.

Again, among those who believe that there are modally valid arguments, it seems to be uncontroversial that if an argument is logically valid, then that argument is modally valid. Thus I give you:

The Current Orthodoxy: Every logically valid argument is modally valid.

The Current Orthodoxy says that every logically valid argument is modally valid. Suppose we know that an argument is logically valid. Then—given the Current Orthodoxy—we can conclude that that argument is modally valid. And this may seem to be the best way to come to know that an argument is modally valid, since it seems to skirt all the controversies that bedevil modal epistemology.[13] Thus we get:

[13] To know that an argument is modally valid—to know that it is not possible for its premises to be true and its conclusion false—is to have a bit of modal

The Epistemic Corollary of the Current Orthodoxy: The best way to come to know that an argument is modally valid is to conclude this from its being logically valid.

No logically valid argument is constituted by propositions (§§II–III). But every modally valid argument is constituted by propositions (Ch. 1, §IV). So no logically valid argument is modally valid. So the Current Orthodoxy is false. (So the common view that logical necessity is a species of *de dicto* metaphysical necessity is false.) Again, no logically valid argument is modally valid. So it is false that if we know that an argument is logically valid, then we should conclude that it is modally valid. So the Epistemic Corollary of the Current Orthodoxy is false.

The Current Orthodoxy and its Epistemic Corollary are false. But there are true claims in the neighborhood of each. Here is the first true claim: The propositions expressed by (the sentences that are) a logically valid argument's premises and conclusion are themselves the premises and conclusion of a modally valid argument. Let us summarize this first true claim by saying that if an argument is logically valid, then that argument *expresses* a modally valid argument. And the second true claim is that if we know that an argument is expressed by a logically valid argument, then we know that that argument is modally valid.

Perhaps some of those quoted at the start of this section would be happy to reject the Current Orthodoxy and say instead that every logically valid argument expresses a modally valid argument. So perhaps the Current Orthodoxy is not as uncontroversial as I have suggested. That would be fine. For what matters here is that the Current Orthodoxy is false, not that the Current Orthodoxy is the current orthodoxy.

If an argument is logically valid, then it preserves the truth of its premises in virtue of its form. Indeed, truth preservation in

knowledge. See Gendler and Hawthorne (2002) for some of the controversies in modal epistemology.

virtue of form is what makes an argument logically valid (§I). But such truth preservation is not the only characteristic of logically valid arguments. For example, if an argument is logically valid, then an ideal reasoner who understands that argument's premises and conclusion can always know a priori that its conclusion is a consequence of its premises (§I). And if an argument is logically valid, then an ideal reasoner who accepts the premises of that argument must not—on pain of irrationality—reject that argument's conclusion (§I). In light of this section's discussion, we should add that there is yet another characteristic of logically valid arguments. We should add that if an argument is logically valid, then the truth of its premises guarantees the truth of its conclusion.

The Current Orthodoxy is one way to make this guarantee more precise. My claim that every logically valid argument expresses a modally valid argument is another way. And there are others.[14] But the Current Orthodoxy is false. Moreover, every logically valid argument really does express a modally valid argument. So I shall take the truth of a logically valid argument's premises guaranteeing the truth of its conclusion to just be that argument's expressing a modally valid argument.

V. Another Comment on the Relationship Between Logical Validity and Modal Validity

Consider *X-logic*. (I am making it up right now.) By the lights of X-logic, the sentence 'coyotes howl' is a logical consequence of the sentence 'dogs bark'. But the truth of 'dogs bark' does not

[14] Here is another way: Every logically valid argument's conclusion is true *at* all worlds *at* which its premises are true. This way of making the guarantee more precise is—like my way and like the Current Orthodoxy—modal, turning on a modal connection between how things have to be in order for a logically valid argument's premises (in that context of use) to be true and how things have to be in order for its conclusion (in that same context of use) to be true (see Ch. 1, §III).

guarantee the truth of 'coyotes howl'. And logical consequence guarantees preservation of truth (§IV). So 'coyotes howl' is *not* a logical consequence of 'dogs bark'. So X-logic gets logical consequence wrong.

Of course, X-Logic is not a respectable logic. I made it up simply to illustrate the point that a first sentence's being a logical consequence of a second sentence *according to some logic* does not imply that the first sentence is a logical consequence of the second. In other words, I made it up to illustrate that a logic can get logical consequence wrong. In yet other words, I made it up to illustrate that a logic can be mistaken.

We can also illustrate this same point with a respectable logic. Consider the respectable Simple Quantified Modal Logic (SQML). The following is a theorem of SQML:

The Converse Barcan Formula: $\Box\forall x\mathrm{F}x \rightarrow \forall x\Box\mathrm{F}x$

As is well known, the Converse Barcan Formula has a startling result. SQML, via the Converse Barcan Formula, implies that 'everything exists necessarily' is a logical consequence of 'necessarily, everything exists'.[15]

Logical consequence guarantees preservation of truth (§IV). The truth of 'necessarily, everything exists' does not guarantee the truth of 'everything exists necessarily'. This is easy to see. For 'necessarily, everything exists' is true. But 'everything exists necessarily' is false. (You and I, among other things, are contingent.) So 'everything exists necessarily' is not a logical consequence of 'necessarily, everything exists'. So SQML gets logical consequence wrong. So SQML is mistaken.

[15] The Converse Barcan Formula is of course named after Ruth Barcan Marcus (1946). 'Simple Quantified Modal Logic' is the name used by Linsky and Zalta (1994) and Sider (2010, 230), among others, for the logic I am here discussing. Williamson (1998, 257) calls it 'the simplest and strongest sensible quantified modal logic'.

Of course, some will disagree with me about the merits of SQML.[16] Philosophy being what it is, some might even disagree with me about the merits of X-Logic. But for my purposes here, it does not matter whether SQML, X-Logic, or any other particular logic is mistaken. Here is what does matter: First, an argument can be 'logically valid' by the lights of a given logic, but not really be logically valid. Second, sometimes we know that that argument is not really logically valid—and so know that the given logic is mistaken—because we know that the truth of that argument's premises does not appropriately guarantee the truth of its conclusion.[17]

The truth of a logically valid argument's premises guaranteeing the truth of its conclusion just is that argument's expressing a modally valid argument (§IV). So knowing whether the appropriate guarantee is present is to have a bit of modal knowledge. And it is just this sort of modal knowledge—in particular, seeing that that guarantee is not present—that makes me (and you) reject X-Logic. Moreover, seeing that the appropriate guarantee is present—and so, again, having some modal knowledge—is part of why we accept a system of logic.

While discussing the Epistemic Corollary of the Current Orthodoxy, I said that some take knowledge of logical validity to be the best way to know that an argument is modally valid, since (they hold) knowledge of logical validity is less controversial than modal knowledge (§IV). But we have seen that some

[16] For example, Linsky and Zalta (1994) and Williamson (1998; 2013) accept SQML along with its unsavory metaphysical consequences. They would all replace the claim that a given concrete object might not have existed (and so is contingent) with the claim that it might not have been concrete (but is necessary).

[17] In Chapter 5, I shall argue that there are singular propositions about entities that do not exist. For example, I shall argue that there is a true singular proposition expressed by the sentence 'Lincoln does not exist'. I deny that the truth of this sentence implies that there is some *x* such that *x* does not exist. Thus it may be that I must reject existential generalization, and so classical logic, in favor of some sort of free logic. If so, then this is another example of how the metaphysical facts ought to inform our logic.

modal knowledge is prior to accepting a system of logic, and so prior to knowledge of logical validity. Thus knowledge of logical validity stands on a foundation of modal knowledge.[18]

VI. The Replacement View is False

The *Replacement View* says that there is no metaphysical necessity or possibility, and so there are no modally valid arguments. And the Replacement View adds that logically valid arguments 'replace' modally valid arguments in the following two ways. First, the venerable idea that some arguments are modally valid was but an inchoate attempt to articulate the idea that some arguments are logically valid. And, second, what might seem to be obvious examples of modally valid arguments are instead examples of logically valid arguments.[19]

The ways in which the Replacement View 'replaces' modal validity with logical validity constitute an objection to how I motivated the claim that there are modally valid arguments back in Chapter 1 (§I). In fact, I even presented this objection when I was motivating that claim. But I did not then respond to this objection. In this section, I shall respond to this objection by opposing the Replacement View. This section thereby defends Chapter 1's (§I) contention that there are modally valid arguments, thus reinforcing that chapter's overall argument for the claim that there are propositions.

[18] On the other hand, once we have (in part owing to some modal knowledge) settled on a logical system, we can then use that system to give us further modal knowledge, in particular, further knowledge of cases of modal validity. As I said in Section IV, if we know that an argument is expressed by a logically valid argument, then we know that that argument is modally valid.

[19] Those who deny that there is metaphysical necessity and possibility include—to offer just two particularly illustrious examples—Bertrand Russell (1905 [1994]; 1918–19 [1985, 96–7]) and W. v. O. Quine (1951). Quine (1982, 102–8) seems to endorse the Replacement View, and I think other foes of modality would as well.

The Replacement View says that there are logically valid arguments. I have argued for the conclusion that logically valid arguments express modally valid arguments (§IV). If I could rely on that conclusion here, refuting the Replacement View would be short work. Unfortunately, my argument for that conclusion has roots that go back to this book's starting point, which is that there are modally valid arguments. And that starting point is what is now at issue. So, in this section, I shall not rely on my conclusion that logically valid arguments express modally valid arguments.

Everyone—including defenders of the Replacement View—must acknowledge that the truth of the premises of a logically valid argument somehow guarantees the truth of its conclusion (§IV). Obviously, defenders of the Replacement View cannot understand that guarantee in my way, in terms of logically valid arguments' expressing modally valid arguments. Nor can they understand that guarantee in any other way that invokes modality, such as, for example, the Current Orthodoxy. I think that this alone threatens the Replacement View, since the very notion of a guarantee strikes me as inherently modal.

Of course, defenders of the Replacement View will not agree that the very notion of a guarantee is modal. On the contrary, just as they replace modal validity with logical validity, I assume that they will replace a modal guarantee with a logical guarantee. That is, I think that defenders of the Replacement View will say that the truth of a logically valid argument's premises guaranteeing the truth of its conclusion just is the truth of those premises *logically* guaranteeing the truth of that conclusion.[20]

[20] Some defenders of the Replacement View might instead take the guarantee to be epistemic. For example, they might say that what it is for the truth of a logically valid argument's premises to guarantee the truth of its conclusion is for an ideal reasoner to be able to see a priori that the truth of the premises is preserved, in virtue of form, in the conclusion. But I object that this gets things backwards. In particular, I say that an ideal reasoner would recognize that truth is thus preserved because such preservation is guaranteed, and not the other way around. More

Recall X-Logic. I rejected X-logic on the grounds that the truth of 'dogs bark' does not guarantee the truth of 'coyotes howl' (§V). But now assume—for reductio—that the relevant guarantee is a logical guarantee. Then my objection to X-Logic turns out to be the claim that 'dogs bark' does not logically guarantee the truth of 'coyotes howl'. And that objection obviously begs the question against X-logic, which says that the sentence 'coyotes howl' is a logical consequence of 'dogs bark'. But my objection to X-logic does not thus beg the question. So what we assumed for reductio is false. So the relevant guarantee is not a logical guarantee.

Look at it this way. When I denied that 'dogs bark' guarantees the truth of 'coyotes howl', I was not simply asserting that 'coyotes howl' is not a logical consequence of 'dogs bark'. Instead, I was giving a reason for concluding that 'coyotes howl' is not a logical consequence of 'dogs bark'. The claim that the relevant guarantee is a logical guarantee precludes recognizing this reason for what it is—a genuine reason to reject X-logic. But this is a reason that everyone should recognize, including those who do not understand the relevant guarantee in my way, in terms of expressing a modally valid argument. So I conclude that it is false that the relevant guarantee is a logical guarantee.

Those who wish to take the relevant guarantee to be a logical guarantee cannot sidestep this verdict simply by spelling out the logical details. For example, suppose that those who say that the relevant guarantee is a logical guarantee elaborate as follows: What it is for a logically valid argument's premises to guarantee the truth of its conclusion is for every model in which that argument's premises are true to be a model in which its conclusion is true.

generally, I think that any way of taking the relevant guarantee to be epistemic would get things backwards in more or less this way.

I say that SQML is a mistaken logic (§V). 'Everything exists necessarily' is true in every model for SQML in which 'Necessarily, everything exists' is true. So I say those models are defective.[21] I say that they are defective because the truth of 'Necessarily, everything exists' does not guarantee the truth of 'Everything exists necessarily'.[22]

You might think my objection to those models is mistaken. Even so, my objection is still a reason—even if a mistaken one—for deeming the models of SQML defective. But if the relevant guarantee is understood in the above model-theoretic terms, then my objection is not a mistaken reason for deeming those models defective, but is instead simply the bald assertion that they are defective. But, again, my objection *is* a reason for deeming those models defective, a reason that is correct if some things exist contingently. And since the claim that the relevant guarantee is logical precludes recognizing this reason as a reason, I conclude, again, that it is false that the relevant guarantee is a logical guarantee.

The truth of a logically valid argument's premises guarantees the truth of its conclusion. That guarantee is not a logical guarantee. And I do not think that the Replacement View can accommodate an appropriate non-logical guarantee. So the Replacement View cannot accommodate logically valid

[21] In Section I, I said that an argument is logically valid if and only if that argument's conclusion is true in all models in which its premises are true. Let me now add explicitly that when I made that remark, I was taking the models to be non-defective.

[22] Those models do not vary with respect to domains, which I think is the source of the trouble. Here is another reason to think that models that do not vary with respect to domains are defective. At least *n* entities exist. So, given such models, 'At least *n* entities exists' turns out to be a logical truth, logically equivalent to: '$\exists x$, $\exists y\ldots$ ($x \neq y$ & . . .)' (see Etchemendy, 1990, 73–4 and 111ff.). And so those models tell us that any argument—no matter what its premises are—with the sentence 'At least *n* entities exist' as a conclusion comes out as logically valid. But, I object, it is false that just any arbitrarily selected premises guarantee that there are at least *n* entities.

arguments. But—as the Replacement View itself implies—there are logically valid arguments. So the Replacement View is false.

VII. A Comment on Supervaluationism

I say that a sentence is true (false) in virtue of expressing a single true (false) proposition (Ch. 1, §V). Supervaluationists will not agree. But they can still agree that sentences have truth-values derivatively, in virtue of how they are related to propositions. For supervaluationists can say that a sentence is true (false) just in case all the propositions that are its precisifications are themselves true (false). In other words, supervaluationists can take *supertruth* (*superfalsity*) to be the derivative sort of truth (falsity) had by sentences. And they can identify the precisifications of a sentence with propositions.

I think that this is the best version of supervaluationism. This is partly because I think that Chapter 1's arguments for the conclusion that propositions are the fundamental bearers of truth (and falsity) are compelling. And it is partly because this version—when combined with other moves made in this chapter and the previous—is immune to a major objection to supervaluationism. (I shall call it 'the Major Objection'.)

An argument is *globally valid* just in case, necessarily, if its premises are supertrue, then its conclusion is supertrue. It is standardly assumed that supervaluationists should take the following argument—Argument D—to be globally valid:

Harry is bald.
Therefore,
'Harry is bald' is true.

Harry is borderline bald. So supervaluationists must deny that the following conditional sentence is true:

If Harry is bald, then 'Harry is bald' is true.

They must deny this because—given supervaluationism—Harry's being borderline bald implies two things. First, there are some precisifications of the above conditional on which its antecedent is true. Second, there are no precisifications on which its consequent is true. So there are some precisifications on which that whole conditional is not true. So that conditional is not supertrue. So it is not true.

Suppose that supervaluationists must take Argument D to be globally valid and must deny that the corresponding conditional sentence is true. Then, given supervaluationism, there are cases in which the argument from sentence S to sentence T is globally valid, but 'If S then T' is not true. Supposedly, supervaluationists are thereby forced to reject conditional proof. And this would lead to supervaluationists having to reject other classical forms of proof, including reductio ad absurdum and proof by cases. That supervaluationists must reject classical forms of proof is the Major Objection. (See, e.g., Fine, 1975, 90 and Williamson, 1994, 151–2.)

We can put the Major Objection in terms of the DEF operator. The DEF operator is standardly introduced in this way: DEF S if and only if S is supertrue. The right-hand side of the bi-conditional attributes supertruth to S; sentences (not propositions) are supertrue; so the right-hand side attributes supertruth to sentence S. So a more explicit account of the DEF operator is: DEF S if and only if sentence 'S' is supertrue.

Now consider Argument D*:

Harry is bald.
Therefore,
DEF (Harry is bald)

Argument D* is standardly assumed to be globally valid. But, since Harry is borderline bald, 'If Harry is bald, then DEF

(Harry is bald)' is not true. So—according to the Major Objection—supervaluationists must reject conditional proof (etc.).

I think that the Major Objection fails. I think this for two reasons.

To begin to understand the first reason, recall that an argument is modally valid just in case, necessarily, if its premises are true, then its conclusion is true (Ch. 1, §I). Now consider an argument with sentences as its premises and conclusion. Add that sentence truth is supertruth. Then it follows that that argument is modally valid just in case, necessarily, if its premises are supertrue, then its conclusion is supertrue; that is, it follows that that argument is modally valid just in case it is globally valid.

With this in mind, we can see that global validity is most naturally understood as modal validity for arguments constituted by sentences, with sentence truth taken to be supertruth.[23] But, as was argued in Chapter 1 (§§II–IV), no argument constituted by sentences is modally valid. The arguments of Chapter 1 (§§II–IV) are not adversely affected by the claim that sentence truth is supertruth. So, in light of those arguments, we should conclude that even if sentence truth is supertruth, no argument constituted by sentences is modally valid. So no argument is globally valid. So neither Argument D nor Argument D* is globally valid. This is the first reason that the Major Objection fails.

Here is the second reason. Conditional proof is part of classical logic. Conditional proof is a kind of logical proof. So supervaluationism violates conditional proof only if supervaluationism has the result that, for some sentence S and some sentence T, S *logically* implies T and the sentence 'If S then T'

[23] This is how Williamson understands global validity. He says: '[Supervaluationists] identify truth with supertruth; since validity is necessary preservation of truth, they should identify it with necessary preservation of supertruth ... an argument is valid just in case ... necessarily if its premises are supertrue then its conclusion is supertrue. The latter property may be called *global validity*' (1994, 148).

is not true. No modally valid argument is logically valid.[24] So conditional proof is not violated even if both the argument from S to T is modally valid and 'If S then T' fails to be true. Similarly, conditional proof would not be violated even if Arguments D and D* were globally valid and the corresponding conditionals failed to be true.

We might try to rehabilitate the Major Objection. For starters, we might give 'global validity' a new definition. (Or, if you prefer, we might clarify how the original definition should be understood, once we add that propositions are the fundamental bearers of truth and falsity.) Let us now say that an argument is globally valid just in case, necessarily, if all the propositions that are (actually and contingently) the precisifications of its premises are true, then all the propositions that are (actually and contingently) the precisifications of its conclusion are true. This new definition—which we shall stick with in what follows—allows arguments constituted by sentences to count as globally valid.

But even so, neither Argument D nor Argument D* is globally valid. For it is possible for all the propositions that are (actually and contingently) the precisifications of each argument's premise to be true even if all the propositions that are (actually and contingently) the precisifications of each argument's conclusion are false. This is because it is possible for Harry to be bald even if no one speaks English, and so even if the sentence 'Harry is bald' does not exist, and so even if that sentence is not true. Again, Harry's baldness does not necessitate that any given word has any particular meaning, and so Harry's baldness does not necessitate that 'Harry is bald' means that Harry is bald, and so Harry's baldness does not necessitate the truth (i.e., supertruth) of 'Harry is bald'.

[24] Every modally valid argument is constituted by propositions (Ch. 1, §IV). No argument constituted by propositions is logically valid (§§II–III). So no modally valid argument is logically valid.

More importantly, neither Argument D nor Argument D* is logically valid. This is because the truth of the premises of a logically valid argument guarantees the truth of its conclusion (§IV). But, for each of Argument D and Argument D*, the truth of its premise does not guarantee the truth of its conclusion. This is because Harry's being bald does not guarantee that the sentence 'Harry is bald' even exists, much less exists and means that Harry is bald; and so it does not guarantee that the following is true: 'Harry is bald' is true.[25]

You might respond that the following argument—Argument D**—is globally valid:

Harry is bald and 'Harry is bald' is an English sentence in context of use C.
Therefore,
'Harry is bald' is true in context of use C.

[25] The truth of the premises of a logically valid argument guarantees the truth of its conclusion. There are ways to make the guarantee more precise. My way of doing so—in terms of expressing a modally valid argument (§IV)—is not available to the supervaluationist. This is because my way presupposes that each premise and each conclusion of a logically valid argument expresses a single proposition.

The most obvious way for the supervaluationist to make the guarantee more precise is to take that guarantee to be a matter of global validity. Neither Argument D nor Argument D* is globally valid.

The supervaluationist might take the guarantee to be a matter of 'local validity'. An argument is locally valid just in case, for any uniform way of precisifying its premises and conclusion, those precisifications themselves constitute a modally valid argument. Neither Argument D nor Argument D* is locally valid. This is because Harry's being bald does not necessitate that the sentence 'Harry is bald' exists, much less exists and means that Harry is bald.

The supervaluationist might take the guarantee to be along these lines: For all possible worlds W, if the premises of an argument are true *at* W, then its conclusion is true *at* W. Argument's D's and D*'s conclusions are not true *at* all worlds *at* which their premise is true; for, unlike their premise, their conclusions are not true *at* any world in which there are no English sentences.

And perhaps supervaluationists will be forced to say that the corresponding conditional—assuming Harry is borderline bald—fails to be supertrue.

Moreover, in light of points made above, perhaps we should give 'DEF' a new definition. (Or, if you prefer, perhaps we should clarify how the original definition should be understood, once we add that propositions are the fundamental bearers of truth and falsity.) Let us say that 'DEF S' is true if and only if all the propositions that are (actually and contingently) the precisifications of S are true. Then we can take the following argument, Argument D*, to be globally valid after all:

Harry is bald.
Therefore,
DEF (Harry is bald)

But—since Harry is borderline bald—'If Harry is Bald, then DEF (Harry is bald)' is not true (supertrue).

The global validity of Arguments D** and D* does not fully rehabilitate the Major Objection. For Arguments D** and D* save the Major Objection only if they are logically valid.

Argument D** is clearly not logically valid. This is because logical validity is a matter of form (§I), and Argument D** does not have a logically valid form. (Look at it.) Moreover, supervaluationists can, and should, deny that Argument D* is logically valid. For supervaluationists can and should deny that 'DEF'—now defined in terms of the truth of the propositions that are actually and contingently the precisifications of a sentence—is a genuine logical operator. This denial does not violate classical logic. For classical logic has no DEF operator.

Of course, there are logics that go beyond classical logic, including, for example, logics that have modal operators and logics that have tense operators. So consider a logic that has the DEF operator. Supervaluationists should say that any such logic is thereby mistaken. (Recall that a logic can be mistaken (§V).)

They can then conclude that Argument D*—though perhaps logically valid by the lights of a mistaken logic—is not really logically valid.

You might think that the claim that any logic that uses the DEF operator is thereby mistaken is a cost of supervaluationism, and so counts against supervaluationism. I do not agree. To begin to see why, consider A. N. Prior's (1960) 'tonk' operator. According to a logic that has the tonk operator, the following holds for any sentences S and S*: S-tonk-S* is a logical consequence of S, and S* is a logical consequence of S-tonk-S*. Logical consequence is transitive. So, according to a logic that has the tonk operator, any sentence is a logical consequence of any other sentence.

Suppose, for reductio, that 'tonk' is a genuine logical operator. Then any sentence is a logical consequence of any other sentence. But it is false that any sentence is a logical consequence of any other sentence. So taking 'tonk' to be a genuine logical operator has unacceptable logical results. So 'tonk' is not a genuine logical operator. So any logic with the tonk operator is a mistaken logic. This all seems right. And there is no 'cost' to insisting that a logic that has a tonk operator is thereby mistaken. Insisting that a logic that has a tonk operator is thereby mistaken does not 'count against' anything.

Similarly, the supervaluationist should argue as follows. Suppose, for reductio, that 'DEF' is a genuine logical operator. Then we must reject conditional proof (etc.). But conditional proof (etc.) should not be rejected. So taking 'DEF' to be a genuine logical operator has unacceptable logical results. So 'DEF' is not a genuine logical operator. So any logic with the DEF operator is a mistaken logic. This is no more (or less) costly than denying that 'tonk' is a genuine logical operator. Supervaluationists prone to sloganeering can add: DEF is tonk.

Supervaluationists can and should deny that 'DEF' is a genuine logical operator. So supervaluationists can and should deny that Argument D* is logically valid. This illustrates how supervaluationists can and should block the Major Objection. Finally, note that supervaluationists who block the Major Objection in this way can and should accept certain obvious modal (but not logical) principles involving propositions. For example, these supervaluationists can and should insist that if an argument with proposition *p* as its sole premise and proposition *q* as its conclusion is modally valid, then, necessarily, if proposition *p* is true then proposition *q* is true.

VIII. Kripke's Puzzle

Propositions never constitute arguments that are logically valid (§§II–III). An obvious upshot of this is that propositions do not have logical form. For if propositions did have logical form, then they would constitute logically valid arguments. For example, a proposition that had the logical form of the conjunction of two propositions would be the logical consequence of those two propositions.

So propositions do not have logical form. So it is false, for example, that one proposition is literally the negation of another, or that one proposition is literally the conjunction of two others, and so on. Of course, sentences express propositions (Ch. 1, §V), and sentences have logical form (§§I–III). But this no more implies that propositions have logical form than it implies that propositions are grammatical.[26]

[26] You might say that propositions have logical form, but only derivatively, in virtue of the logical form of the sentences that express them. But this seems to me infelicitous. For I think that the following two sentences express the same proposition: 'Either it is not raining or it is not snowing' and 'It is false that it is both raining and snowing'. And I think it is infelicitous to say that a single proposition is, even 'derivatively', both a disjunction and also the negation of a conjunction. Moreover—and more importantly—'derivative logical form' is not logical form. For propositions never constitute logically valid arguments (§§II–III). But if propositions had logical form, they would constitute logically valid arguments.

Being contradictory is a matter of logical form. So no proposition is logically contradictory and no proposition logically contradicts another proposition. (Of course, contradictory sentences express propositions and a sentence that expresses a proposition can contradict another sentence that expresses a proposition.) So we should not be surprised to find that believing a proposition and also believing that proposition to be false does not automatically commit one to believing anything logically contradictory.

'Cicero is an orator' has the logical form *a is F*. 'It is not the case that Tully is an orator' has the logical form *it is not the case that b is F*. A sentence of the form *a is F* does not logically contradict a sentence of the form *it is not the case that b is F*. So the sentence 'Cicero is an orator' does not logically contradict the sentence 'It is not the case that Tully is an orator'. So—and this is the absolutely standard thing to say here—an agent who accepts both of those sentences does not thereby believe anything logically contradictory.

Again, an agent who accepts both the sentence 'Cicero is an orator' and also the sentence 'It is not the case that Tully is an orator' does not thereby believe anything contradictory. This is so even if the sentence 'Cicero is an orator' and the sentence 'Tully is an orator' express the same proposition. So this is so even if that agent thereby both believes the proposition *that Cicero/Tully is an orator* and also believes that proposition to be false. So believing a proposition and also believing that proposition to be false does not imply having logically contradictory beliefs.

Peter accepts the sentence 'Smith is a doctor' and accepts the sentence 'It is not the case that Smith is a physician' (§III). Peter accepts a sentence of the form *a is F* and accepts a sentence of the form *it is not the case that a is G*. He does not thereby believe anything logically contradictory. And all of this stands even though 'Smith is a physician' and 'Smith is a doctor' express the same proposition. So all of this stands even though Peter believes the proposition *that Smith is a doctor/physician* and also believes it to be false.

With all of this in mind, consider the case of Kripke's (1979) Pierre. Raised in France on British propaganda, Pierre came to believe—as he still puts it—'*Londres est jolie*'. Learning English in a London slum years later, he came to believe—again, as he still puts it—'London is not pretty'. Pierre does not know that '*Londres*' and 'London' refer to the same city.

Kripke (1979, 257) says: 'So we must say that Pierre has contradictory beliefs, that he believes that London is pretty *and* he believes that London is not pretty.' Kripke immediately adds that there are 'insuperable difficulties' with Pierre's having contradictory beliefs, since:

> We may suppose that Pierre . . . is a leading philosopher and logician. He would *never* let contradictory beliefs pass . . . And surely anyone, leading logician or no, is in principle in a position to notice and correct contradictory beliefs if he has them . . . (1979, 257)

Kripke emphasizes that Pierre is a logician. Given the arguments of this chapter, Pierre's logical expertise lies in the realm of sentences. So let us grant—for the sake of argument—that Pierre would never accept two sentences that logically contradict each other.

In the case Kripke describes, Pierre does not accept the first of these contradictory English sentences: 'London is pretty' and 'London is not pretty'. Moreover, I do not think that there is any logical contradiction among the sentences that Pierre does accept. One reason is that '*Londres est jolie*' and 'London is not pretty' use different names for London, just as 'Cicero is an orator' and 'It is not the case that Tully is an orator' use different names for Cicero.

Of course, Pierre does believe both the proposition *that London is pretty* and also the proposition *that London is not pretty*. Moreover, Pierre believes and also believes to be false the proposition *that London is pretty*. But all of this is merely to have beliefs that are not all possibly true. This is not—for reasons made clear above—to believe anything contradictory. So to the extent that Kripke's puzzle is generated by Pierre the *logician* having *contradictory* beliefs, this chapter's point that logic is in the realm of sentences dissolves Kripke's puzzle.[27]

IX. Conclusion

An argument is *modally valid* just in case, necessarily, if its premises are true, then its conclusion is true. An argument is *logically valid* just in case it preserves the truth of its premises in virtue of its form. This chapter has defended some claims about the relationship between modal validity and logical validity. For example, this chapter has argued that logically valid arguments are not themselves modally valid, but do express modally valid arguments.

I accept this chapter's claims about the relationship between modal validity and logical validity mainly because of the arguments explicitly given in this chapter directly for those claims. But those claims are further recommended by their salutary implications. For example, if those claims are correct, supervaluationists can block a major objection to their view, and all of us can solve Kripke's puzzle involving Pierre.

[27] Kripke thinks there is a second puzzle here, arguing that we can get from Pierre's having the relevant beliefs to an outright contradiction. But his argument turns on the 'Strong Disquotation Principle' (1979, 249). And I think that Kripke's Pierre is a clear counterexample to that principle (cf. Salmon, 1986, 132); so too is the case involving Peter (§III). Moreover, I deny that Kripke's Paderewski case involves logically contradictory beliefs; in particular—and for the sorts of reasons outlined in the footnote near the end of §I—I say that the sentence 'Paderewski is a musician' logically contradicts the sentence 'It is not the case that Paderewski is a musician' only in a context of use in which the occurrences of 'Paderewski' are appropriately linked.

3

PROPOSITIONS ARE NOT SETS OF POSSIBLE WORLDS

The claim that propositions are sets of possible worlds is one of the two leading accounts of the nature of propositions. This chapter opposes that account. Chapters 4 and 5 attack the other leading account. In the course of criticizing these two leading accounts, we shall reach a variety of conclusions that I shall later rely on when defending my own account of the nature of propositions (Ch. 6).

I. Properties, Propositions, and Possible Worlds

Some hold that each proposition is the set of possible worlds in which that proposition is true. For short, some hold that each proposition is a set of possible worlds. David Lewis gives this argument for that account of propositions:

> I identify propositions with certain properties—namely, with those that are instantiated only by entire possible worlds. Then if properties generally are the sets of their instances, a proposition is a set of possible worlds. (1986a, 53)

This brief argument merits detailed examination. For it is one of the few explicit arguments in the literature for the claim that propositions are sets of possible worlds (see §§II–III below for more such arguments). Moreover, Lewis is not alone in defending this sort of argument; Robert Stalnaker, for example, defends more or less the same argument.[1] And, finally, this argument touches on a variety of themes relevant to the idea that propositions are sets of possible worlds.

Here is Lewis's argument again:

(1) Properties are sets of their instances.
(2) Propositions are properties.
(3) Possible worlds are the (only) instances of propositions.
Therefore,
(4) Propositions are sets of possible worlds.

I do not think that Lewis would (or should) find all of my objections below to this argument convincing. In particular, as I shall note, Lewis can resist my objections to this argument's first premise. Even so, I shall raise those objections, and others. For the question here is not whether this argument fits with Lewis's overall system. It is, instead, whether this argument is a good reason for us to conclude that propositions really are sets of possible worlds. And I say that this argument is not a good reason for that conclusion, since—I shall argue—all three of its premises are false.

Suppose, for reductio, that, necessarily, properties are sets of their instances. Let set S be an arbitrarily chosen property. Then, necessarily, S is the set of its instances. So, necessarily, something is a member of S if and only if it is an instance of S. Sets have their members essentially. So S has its members

[1] Here is Stalnaker:

Since the extension of a one-place predicate is a class of individuals, the intension of a predicate—the property it expresses—is a function from possible worlds into classes of individuals. And if one takes the extension of a sentence to be a truth value, then the intension of a sentence—the *proposition* it expresses—. . . may be thought of as a set of possible worlds: the set of worlds in which the sentence expressing the proposition denotes the value true. (1976, 79–80)

essentially. So S has its instances essentially. S is an arbitrarily chosen property. So the above result generalizes. So all properties have their instances essentially.

But some properties have some of their instances contingently. For example, I am contingently an instance of *being an American*. So our assumption for reductio is false. So it is not the case that, necessarily, properties are sets of their instances. So (1)—which says that properties are sets of their instances—is not necessarily true. But if (1) is true, then (1) is necessarily true. This is the first reason to deny (1).[2]

Suppose that everything that has a kidney has a heart. And vice versa. Then the set of instances of *having a kidney* has exactly the same members as does the set of instances of *having a heart*. So the set of instances of *having a kidney* is identical with the set of instances of *having a heart*. So if a property is the set of its instances, then the property *having a kidney* is identical with the property *having a heart*. But *having a kidney* is not identical with *having a heart*. This is the second reason to deny (1).

This second reason to deny (1) is familiar. The standard reply—a reply offered in defense of (1)—is that properties are sets of their possible instances (Montague, 1969, 163; Lewis, 1986a, 55). Defenders of the standard reply will say that *having a kidney* is not identical with *having a heart* because there are possible instances of *having a kidney* that lack a heart, and vice versa.

I am possibly an instance of, for example, the property *being an Englishman*. But defenders of the standard reply will not say that I am thereby a member of the set of that property's 'possible instances'. For they think that the members of that set really are instances of that property. (Recall that they are defending premise (1), the claim that properties are sets of their instances.) And I am not an instance of *being an Englishman*.

[2] Lewis (1986a, 51–2) can resist this reason to deny (1). His way of doing so turns on, first, there being merely possible instances of properties and, second, counterpart theory. See my discussion of merely possible instances of properties below.

So a 'possible instance' of a property—as understood by defenders of the standard reply—is not something that is possibly an instance of that property. Rather, a 'possible instance' of a property is either an actual entity that is an instance of that property or a merely possible entity that is an instance of that property.

The standard reply is successful only if there are merely possible entities that have hearts and other merely possible entities that have kidneys. More generally, the standard reply is successful only if, for every property, there are merely possible entities that really do have that property.[3] So the standard reply is successful only if there are merely possible entities that are—with respect to the sorts of properties they exemplify—just like actual entities.

Lewis has the resources to defend the standard reply. For Lewis (1986a) says that, for each way everything could be—past, present, and future—there is a universe in which things are that way. Moreover, Lewis says that the denizens of these other universes, some of which are just like actual entities, are merely possible. So Lewis believes in merely possible entities that are—with respect to the sorts of properties they exemplify—just like actual entities.

Not everyone agrees with Lewis. For some object that, even if there is a universe for each way everything could be, the denizens of those universes are not *merely possible* (see, e.g., van Inwagen, 1986). Others object that it is false that there is a universe for each way everything could be (see, e.g., almost everyone). I find both of these objections persuasive. So I deny that there are merely possible entities that are just like actual entities. So I stand by my second reason for denying (1).

[3] Well, for almost every property. The standard reply can allow for there to be no merely possible instances of properties that are essentially exemplified by necessarily existing entities.

Premise (2) says that propositions are properties.[4] Each proposition represents things as being a certain way, and as a result has a truth-value (Ch. 1, §IV). No property has a truth-value. So no property represents things as being a certain way, not in the way that propositions do. So no property is a proposition. So (2) is false.

As we shall see (§V), some philosophers say that sets represent things as being a certain way in virtue of how those sets are 'interpreted'. No one explicitly says this about properties (even though, as we have seen, some take properties to be sets). Nevertheless, suppose—just for the sake of argument—that we have interpreted the property *being red* to represent dogs as barking. (Dogs bark. So add that *being red* is true.) This would block my above objection to (2), the objection that no property is a proposition because no property represents things as being a certain way.

But this does not block a related objection. For it is surely possible for *being red* to have not been interpreted to represent dogs as barking, and even possible for it to have not been interpreted at all. So it is contingent that *being red* has been interpreted to represent dogs as barking. So *being red* only contingently represents dogs as barking. So *being red* does not essentially represent dogs as barking. There is nothing special in this regard about *being red*. No property essentially represents things as being a certain way (cf. Jubien, 2001 and King, 2007a, 136). But each proposition not only represents things as being a certain way, but also essentially represents things as being that way (Ch. 1, §IV). So—even if we actually have interpreted some properties to represent things as being a certain way—no property is a proposition. So (2) is false.[5]

[4] Montague (1969, 163), van Inwagen (2004, 131 n. 17; 2006, 454), and Speaks (2014), among others, join Lewis in endorsing this premise.

[5] I suspect that there is no way to interpret a property to represent things as being a certain way without the result that that property represents things as being

Only properties are instantiated. So only properties have instances. As we have just seen, propositions are not properties. So propositions do not have instances. So there are no instances of propositions. So premise (3)—the premise that possible worlds are the instances of propositions—is false.

Set this objection to (3) aside. That is, suppose, just for the sake of argument, that propositions are properties. Even so, possible worlds seem to be the instances—and in some cases the only instances—of some properties that are obviously not propositions, properties such as *being self-identical* and *being a possible world*. So being instantiated by a possible world does not automatically make a property a proposition. So I think that—even if propositions have instances—the burden of proof is on those who claim that possible worlds are the instances of propositions. Unless there is a good argument for that claim, we should not accept premise (3).

Here is what Lewis says in support of that claim:

> A proposition is said to *hold* at a [possible] world, or to be *true at* a [possible] world. The proposition is the same thing as the property of being a [possible] world where that proposition holds... (1986a, 53–4; see also Lewis, 1973, 46–7)

Lewis's reasoning seems to require not only that propositions are true (or false) at possible worlds, but also that propositions are not true (or false) simpliciter. For if propositions are true (or false) simpliciter, then I see no way for Lewis to get the result that each proposition 'is the same thing as the property of being a [possible] world where that proposition holds'. And that result

that way in virtue of how it is related to something else that represents things as being that way. Suppose my suspicion is correct. If a property—or a set (see §V) or a structured proposition (see Ch. 4, §V)—represents things as being a certain way in virtue of how it is interpreted, then that property (set, etc.) only derivatively represents things as being that way. But propositions fundamentally represent things as being a certain way (Ch. 1, §V). This is another reason to conclude that if a property (set, etc.) represents things as being a certain way in virtue of how it is interpreted, then that property (set, etc.) is not a proposition.

is Lewis's reason for thinking that propositions are instantiated by possible worlds.

But I object that propositions are not only true (or false) at possible worlds, but also true (or false) simpliciter. Here are two defenses of this objection. First, propositions are the premises and conclusions of modally valid arguments, and the premises and conclusions of modally valid arguments are true (or false) simpliciter (see Ch. 1, §§I–II). Second, consider the proposition *that there exist some flying pigs*. That proposition's truth conditions are satisfied in some possible worlds and not in others. So I agree that that proposition is true at some possible worlds and false at others. But I also add that it is false simpliciter. (Moreover, Lewis's modal realism implies that there exist some flying pigs—and so Lewis himself should say that *that there exist some flying pigs* is true simpliciter.)

II. Necessarily Equivalent Propositions

Fermat's Last Theorem (FLT) is necessarily true.[6] So FLT is true in all possible worlds. So the proposition *that dogs bark* is true in all and only those possible worlds in which the proposition *that dogs bark and FLT is true* is true. So the set of possible worlds in which *that dogs bark* is true is identical with the set of possible worlds in which *that dogs bark and FLT is true* is true. So if propositions are sets of possible worlds, the proposition *that dogs bark* is identical with the proposition *that dogs bark and FLT is true*.

More generally, the thesis that propositions are sets of possible worlds has the result that *necessarily equivalent* propositions are identical. (For all propositions p and q, p is necessarily equivalent to q if and only if, necessarily, p has the same truth-value as q.)

[6] FLT states that the following equation has no non-zero integer solutions for x, y, and z where $n > 2$: $x^n + y^n = z^n$.

Many take this result to constitute an objection—the most common objection—to that thesis (see §IV). But not Robert Stalnaker. On the contrary, that result seems to be his main reason for endorsing that thesis. Stalnaker says:

> The picture of a rational agent deliberating is a picture of a man who considers various alternative possible futures, knowing that the one to become actual depends in part on his choice of action. The function of desire is simply to divide these alternative courses of events into the ones to be sought and the ones to be avoided ... The function of belief is simply to determine which are the relevant alternative possible situations ... If this is right, then the identity conditions for the objects of desire and belief are correctly determined by the possible-world account of propositions. (1976, 81; see also Stalnaker, 1987, 24)

Stalnaker argues that necessarily equivalent objects of desire and belief are identical. And he takes the objects of desire and belief to be propositions. Thus he concludes that necessarily equivalent propositions are identical. This conclusion rules out the most prominent competitors to propositions-as-sets-of-possible-worlds (see Ch. 4, §I). But it does not rule out—indeed, it is a result of—propositions-as-sets-of-possible-worlds. Thus Stalnaker concludes that propositions are sets of possible worlds.

Or perhaps I should say, instead, that Stalnaker concludes only that propositions can be modeled by sets of possible worlds. For he says that a proposition 'may be thought of' as a set of possible worlds (Stalnaker, 1976, 80). This might be a natural way to say that propositions can be modeled by sets of possible worlds, but would be a misleading way to say that propositions really are sets of possible worlds.

Moreover, Stalnaker says that the thesis that propositions are sets of possible worlds is 'equivalent' to the thesis that propositions are functions taking possible worlds to truth-values (Stalnaker, 1976, 80). But sets of possible worlds are not functions taking possible worlds to truth-values. On the other hand, sets of possible worlds and such functions might be equally good (or bad) ways to model propositions. All of this further suggests that Stalnaker has modeling in mind.

But let us not be concerned with whether Stalnaker means only to model propositions or instead to give an account of their nature. For the question here is not whether Stalnaker himself is committed to the claim that propositions really are sets of possible worlds. It is, instead, whether Stalnaker's argument should convince us that propositions really are sets of possible worlds. And there are three reasons that it does not convince me.

First, the claim that necessarily equivalent propositions are identical supports the thesis that propositions are sets of possible worlds in part by ruling out the most prominent competitors to that thesis (see Ch. 4, §I). But, as Chapters 4 through 6 will make clear, I do not think that ruling out those most prominent competitors should lead us to conclude that propositions are sets of possible worlds.

Second, propositions-as-sets-of-possible-worlds is not the only account of propositions that accommodates the identity of necessarily equivalent propositions. Here is another such account: No proposition is a set; rather, every proposition is a simple abstract object, with neither parts nor members; and each such proposition is identical with every proposition that is necessarily equivalent to it. As Chapter 6 will make clear, this is the account that I would accept if I came to believe that necessarily equivalent propositions are identical.

Third, as we shall see in Section IV, I think that some necessarily equivalent propositions are not identical. And I am not persuaded by Stalnaker's argument to the contrary. This is partly because I reject Stalnaker's functionalism about belief and desire. And it is partly because—so I have argued elsewhere (Merricks, 2009a)—desire is not a propositional attitude.[7]

[7] Stalnaker seems to offer one more argument for the thesis that propositions are sets of possible worlds. Here it is: 'the possible-worlds theory... defines propositions independently of language. If desires and beliefs are to be understood

III. Ockham's Razor

Here is the Ockham's razor argument: We believe in possible worlds. We believe in set-theoretic constructions out of things we believe in. For the sake of ontological parsimony, if we can take propositions to be entities to which we are already committed, we ought to do so. So propositions are sets of possible worlds.[8]

The premises of the Ockham's razor argument imply—at most—that propositions are some set-theoretic construction or other out of possible worlds. Those premises do not imply that propositions are exactly one such construction. And sets of possible worlds are just one such construction. (For other such constructions, see §V.) This is my first objection to the Ockham's razor argument.

My second objection builds on a controversial claim that I shall defend below (§VII): Possible worlds are themselves propositions. The Ockham's razor argument begins with a commitment to possible worlds. Since possible worlds are themselves propositions, the Ockham's razor argument begins with a commitment to propositions. Given that beginning, no

in terms of their role in the rational determination of action, then their objects have nothing essential to do with language' (1976, 82). I agree with Stalnaker that propositions are independent of language (see esp. Chs 1 and 6). But this does not imply that propositions are sets of possible worlds.

[8] King (2011) and Moore (1999) take this to be a standard argument for propositions-as-sets-of-possible-worlds. And I think that Lewis would find this argument attractive. For he says:

> If we believe in possible worlds and individuals, and if we believe in set-theoretic constructions out of things we believe in, then we have entities suited to play the role of properties. (1986a, 50)

Lewis then builds on this, getting from properties-as-sets-of-their-instances to propositions-as-sets-of-possible-worlds by way of the argument discussed above (§I). But note that the passage just quoted could have its final word, 'properties', replaced by the word 'propositions' without any loss (or gain) in plausibility.

gain in parsimony is made by identifying propositions with sets of possible worlds (that is, with sets of propositions).

My third objection to the Ockham's razor argument begins with a parody of that argument: We believe in electrons; for the sake of ontological parsimony, if we can take propositions to be entities to which we are already committed, we ought to do so; so propositions are electrons. Propositions-as-electrons is not an unparsimonious offense to the razor. Even so, the parody should not convince us that propositions are electrons. This is because there are good reasons to deny that propositions are electrons. (For example, electrons lack truth-values; see also Ch. 6, §I.) The moral of the parody is that if there are good reasons to deny that propositions are sets of possible worlds, then the Ockham's razor argument should not convince us that propositions are sets of possible worlds. And I shall offer a number of such reasons (§§IV–VII).[9]

IV. More on Necessarily Equivalent Propositions

The thesis that propositions are sets of possible worlds implies that necessarily equivalent propositions are identical (§II). This leads to the most common objection to that thesis. One way—not the usual way—to present this objection is simply to take as a premise the claim that two particular necessarily equivalent propositions are not identical (see, e.g., Bealer, 1998). Here is an example. Premise: The proposition *that dogs bark* is not identical with the proposition *that dogs bark and FLT is true*. So not all necessarily equivalent propositions are identical. So propositions are not sets of possible worlds.

[9] Some might hold that propositions ought to be reduced to other entities, entities that we already believe in. My objections to the Ockham's razor argument can easily be turned into objections to a parallel argument driven by reductive motivations, even if those motivations differ from the desire for parsimony.

Another way—the usual way—to present the most common objection starts with the claim that one can believe a given proposition without believing every necessarily equivalent proposition (see, e.g., King, 2007a, 2–3; Richard, 1990, 7–16; Soames, 1987). Here is an example. One can know about dogs without knowing that FLT is true. Let A be such a person. The proposition *that dogs bark* is believed by A. But the proposition *that dogs bark and FLT is true* is not believed by A. So *that dogs bark* is not identical with *that dogs bark and FLT is true*. So propositions are not sets of possible worlds.

A third and final way—my preferred way—to present the most common objection turns on how propositions represent things as being. Here is an example. The proposition *that dogs bark and FLT is true* represents dogs as barking and FLT as being true. The proposition *that dogs bark* does represent dogs as barking, but does not represent FLT as being true. So those propositions differ in how they represent things as being. So *that dogs bark and FLT is true* is not identical with *that dogs bark*. So propositions are not sets of possible worlds.

A similar argument can be run with an example from Chapter 1 (§IV). The propositions *that 2+1=3* and *that all dogs are dogs* are necessarily true. So they are necessarily equivalent. But those propositions differ in what they are about. One of them is about integers (and not about dogs) and the other is about dogs (and not about integers). And those propositions differ in how they represent things as being. One of them represents the sum of 2 and 1 as being 3 and the other represents every dog as being a dog. So the proposition *that 2+1=3* is not identical with the proposition *that all dogs are dogs*. So propositions are not sets of possible worlds.

Defenders of the thesis that propositions are sets of possible worlds have replies to each of these ways of presenting the most common objection: They can deny the premise that says that *that dogs bark* is not identical with *that dogs bark and FLT is true*. They can claim that A does believe the proposition *that dogs bark and FLT is true*, but under the guise associated with 'Dogs bark' and not under the guise associated with 'Dogs bark and FLT is true' (cf. Ch. 2, §§II–III; Stalnaker, 1976, 87–91; Williamson, 2007, 66–7). And they can claim that *that dogs bark* does represent FLT as being true and that *that 2+1=3* is about dogs.

My own view is that their replies are not compelling, especially their final reply. So my own view is that the most common objection to the thesis that propositions are sets of possible worlds is persuasive, especially when presented in the third and final way. So I conclude that propositions are not sets of possible worlds.

V. Sets and Representing Things as Being a Certain Way

No book on set theory claims that certain sets are true. I think that this is because no set is true. Or false. So no set represents things as being a certain way (in the way that propositions do, in the way that gives truth conditions to the entity that thus represents). Because no set is true or false and because no set represents things as being a certain way, no set is a proposition (cf. Plantinga, 1987, 207–8; Soames, 2014, 32). So propositions are not sets. So propositions are not sets of possible worlds.

But suppose—just for the sake of argument—that each set of possible worlds does represent things as being a certain way. Then there must be an explanation of how each set of possible worlds manages to do this.[10] Defenders of *structured propositions* typically claim that a proposition's structure and constituents explain how that proposition manages to represent things as

[10] The claim that if a set of possible worlds represents things as being a certain way, then there must be an explanation of how that set manages to do this, is uncontroversial. Even so, for reasons that will then be apparent, I shall defend this claim in Ch. 6 (§III).

being a certain way (see Ch. 4, §V). With this in mind, you might claim that the structure and members of a set of possible worlds explain how that set manages to represent things as being a certain way. But I object. For I deny that the structure and members of any set—and so of any set of possible worlds—would explain how that set manages to represent things as being a certain way (cf. Jubien, 2001; King, 2007a, 8).

Moreover, suppose—just for the sake of argument—that each set of possible worlds does represent things as being a certain way because of its structure and members. Suppose, for example, that the set of possible worlds in which dogs bark represents dogs as barking because of that set's structure and members. And suppose that this is why the proposition *that dogs bark* is that set of possible worlds. All of this implies that the proposition *that dogs bark* is a particular set if and only if that set represents, because of its structure and members, dogs as barking.

There are many sets that are—as far as their structure and members go—as qualified to represent dogs as barking as is the set of possible worlds in which dogs bark. There is the set of ordered pairs whose first member is a possible world and whose second member is a truth-value; in particular, the second member is *true* if and only if the first member is a possible world in which dogs bark, otherwise it is *false*. And there is a similar set of ordered pairs, but whose first member is a truth-value and whose second member is a possible world.[11] And there is the set whose sole member is the set of all possible worlds in which dogs bark. And so on.

[11] There are competing alleged reductions of sets of ordered pairs to sets of unordered sets (cf. Forrest, 1986b, 90–1 and Armstrong, 1986, 87). So each set of ordered pairs here leads to two or more unordered sets that, as far as their structure and members go, are as suited to represent dogs as barking as is the set of possible worlds in which dogs bark.

The proposition *that dogs bark* is a particular set if and only if that set represents dogs as barking because of its structure and members. We have just seen that there are many other sets that are, as far as their structure and members go, as qualified to represent dogs as barking as is the set of possible worlds in which dogs bark. So if the proposition *that dogs bark* is identical with the set of possible worlds in which dogs bark, then that proposition is also identical with those many other sets. Thus we get the absurd conclusion that those many other sets are identical with each other. This absurd conclusion is the result of our above supposition for the sake of argument, the supposition that a set of possible worlds represents things as being a certain way because of its structure and members. So I conclude that it is false that the structure and members of a set of possible worlds would explain how that set manages to represent things as being a certain way.[12]

Moreover, suppose (bizarrely) that exactly one of the sets that represents dogs as barking because of its structure and members is identical with the proposition *that dogs bark*. And even suppose (conveniently) that that set is the set of possible worlds in which dogs bark. These suppositions would block my above argument from the claim that a set of possible worlds represents things as being a certain way because of its structure and

[12] Moore (1999) makes a similar objection. And this objection to propositions-as-sets-of-possible-worlds parallels Benacerraf's (1965) objection to numbers as sets. Benacerraf's critics often reply that it is indeterminate which of the many competing sets is a given number (see, e.g., Wright, 1983; Katz, 1996; Maddy, 1981; and McGinn, 1984). Similarly, defenders of propositions-as-sets-of-possible-worlds might respond that it is indeterminate which set is identical with the proposition *that dogs bark*. But this response is an odd—and even self-defeating—response for a defender of propositions-as-sets-of-possible-worlds; for if this response is correct, then it is not determinately the case that propositions are sets of possible worlds. Besides, I think this response is not correct; I think this partly because the 'indeterminacy' here seems to be a novel—and dark—sort; it is not, for example, the sort of indeterminacy associated with vagueness or with Quinean indeterminacy of translation (see Merricks, 2003a).

members to the absurd conclusion that many distinct sets are identical with each other. But even granting—only for the sake of argument—these suppositions, there is still a problem for the claim that a set of possible worlds represents things as being a certain way because of its structure and members.

For even granting these suppositions, it is still the case that if a set of possible worlds represents (for example) dogs as barking because of that set's structure and members, then—for the reasons noted above—there are many other sets that do so too. I do not deny that there are non-linguistic and non-mental entities that represent things as being this way or that (see Chs 1 and 6). But I think it is false that for each way things are represented as being, many non-linguistic and non-mental entities represent things as being exactly that way. So, again, I conclude that it is false that the structure and members of a set of possible worlds would explain how that set manages to represent things as being a certain way.

Some philosophers say that a set can represent things as being a certain way because of how that set is interpreted.[13] Suppose, for the sake of argument, that they are right. It is contingent just how—and even whether—a given set is interpreted. So if a set of possible worlds represents things as being a certain way because of how it is interpreted, then that set of possible worlds contingently represents things as being that way. But if a proposition represents things as being a certain way, then that proposition essentially represents things as being that way (Ch. 1, §IV). So if a set of possible worlds represents things as being a certain way because of how it is interpreted, then sets of possible worlds are not propositions.

Moreover, suppose that how a set represents things as being is entirely a matter of how we interpret that set. Then we could interpret the set of possible worlds in which A loves B so that, as

[13] See, for example, Quine (1969), Lewis (1986a, 144–5), and Heller (1998). See Merricks (2003a) for discussion.

a result of that interpretation, that set represents A as loving B. But by the same token we could, instead, interpret the unit set of 37 so that, as a result of that interpretation, that set represents A as loving B. And likewise for any other set. I think this shows that representation-by-interpretation undermines the thesis that propositions are sets of possible worlds. For that thesis surely requires sets of possible worlds to be especially qualified—and certainly more qualified than the unit sets of integers—to be propositions.

If a set of possible worlds is a proposition, then that set must represent things as being a certain way. If a set of possible worlds represents things as being a certain way, then there must be an explanation of how that set does so. The literature suggests only two such explanations. The first involves that set's structure and members. The second turns on how that set is interpreted. I have argued that both of these alleged explanations are unacceptable. I do not believe there is another, better, explanation to be had. So I conclude that propositions are not sets of possible worlds.

VI. Possible Worlds as Universes

My objections to propositions-as-sets-of-possible-worlds have—so far—been neutral with regard to the nature of possible worlds. But if propositions are sets of possible worlds, then there are possible worlds. And if there are possible worlds, then they have a nature. So let us now consider how the thesis that propositions are sets of possible worlds fares given this or that account of the nature of possible worlds.

Let us start with David Lewis's (1986a) account, according to which—as noted in Section I—a possible world is a universe. As also noted in Section I, I deny that there is a universe for each way everything could be, past, present, and future. So, given Lewis's account of possible worlds, I deny that there are

possible worlds. So, given Lewis's account of possible worlds, I deny that there are sets of possible worlds. Propositions are sets of possible worlds only if there are sets of possible worlds. Thus my first reason for saying that, given Lewis's account of possible worlds, propositions are not sets of possible worlds.

Given Lewis's account of possible worlds, each possible world exists in—that is, is located in or is a part of—only one possible world, itself. So, given Lewis's account of possible worlds, there is no possible world in which all the members of a set of possible worlds exist. So, given Lewis's account of possible worlds, there is no possible world in which a set of possible worlds exists. So, given Lewis's account of possible worlds, sets of possible worlds do not possibly exist. (The exceptions that prove the rule: sets of possible worlds with exactly one member.) Again, given Lewis's account of possible worlds, sets of possible worlds are impossible entities.

Lewis believes that there are sets of possible worlds. But I do not think he would dispute my argument for the conclusion that, given his account of possible worlds, sets of possible worlds are impossible entities. For here is what Lewis says about 'trans-world individuals', which he takes to be single individuals that have parts located in various possible worlds:

> It is possible for something to exist iff it is possible for the whole of it to exist. That is, iff there is a world at which the whole of it exists. That is, iff there is a world such that, quantifying only over parts of that world, the whole of it exists. That is, iff the whole of it is among the parts of some world. That is, iff it is part of some world—and hence not a trans-world individual; trans-world individuals are therefore *impossible* individuals. (1986a, 211)

Lewis believes that trans-world individuals exist. But he thinks that they are impossible.

Given Lewis's account of possible worlds, sets of possible worlds are impossible entities. Lewis believes that there are some impossible entities. I do not. Indeed, the claim that some impossible entities exist strikes me as absurd. So I say that, given Lewis's account of possible worlds, there are no sets of possible worlds. And if there are no sets of possible worlds, then propositions are not sets of possible worlds. So, given Lewis's account of possible worlds, propositions are not sets of possible worlds.

Here is a related point. Pretend that it is coherent to say that an impossible entity exists. Even so, it is surely incoherent to say that an impossible entity exists necessarily.[14] So if sets of possible worlds are impossible entities, then sets of possible worlds do not exist necessarily. But propositions exist necessarily (Ch. 1, §IV; §VII below; Ch. 5, §II). So, again, given Lewis's account of possible worlds, propositions are not sets of possible worlds.

We saw above that Lewis claims that trans-world individuals are impossible and also exist. But, perhaps because he knows that this claim will strike some as absurd, he adds:

> ...it would be...easy to give 'possible individual' a more inclusive sense. We could say that an individual exists at a world iff, quantifying only over parts of that world, *some part* of that individual exists—that way, the trans-world individuals would count as possible. (1986a, 211)

Similarly, let us now say that a set of possible worlds possibly exists just in case *some member* of that set exists in a possible world.[15] Then, even given Lewis's account of possible worlds,

[14] Lewis would agree. According to Lewis (1986a), an entity is impossible just in case it fails to exist in any possible world. And an entity is necessary just in case it exists in all possible worlds. So, according to Lewis, if something is both impossible and necessary, then it exists in no possible worlds and exists in all possible worlds.

[15] Lewis might not like this. He says:

> I take it that the part–whole relation applies to individuals, not sets. Then no set is in any world in the sense of being a part of it. Numbers, properties, propositions, events—all these are sets, and not in any world...Even a sequence of possible individuals all from the same world is not, strictly speaking, itself in that world... (1983, 40)

All of this seems to create an extra hurdle for the thesis that propositions are sets of possible worlds. I shall ignore this extra hurdle.

sets of possible worlds come out as possibly existing. So they are not impossible entities. So Lewis's 'more inclusive' sense of 'possible individual' blocks one of my objections above, the objection that turns on the claim that, given Lewis's account of possible worlds, sets of possible worlds are impossible entities.

But his more inclusive sense of 'possible individual' does not block the objection that turns on the claim that, given Lewis's account of possible worlds, sets of possible worlds do not exist necessarily. Nor does the correlative 'more inclusive' sense of 'necessary individual', which applies to a set just in case some member or other of that set exists in every possible world. For, given Lewis's account of possible worlds, a set of possible worlds does not have some member or other that exists in every possible world. So—even given the more inclusive sense of 'necessary individual'—sets of possible worlds do not come out as existing necessarily. (The exception that proves the rule: the set of all possible worlds.) But propositions do exist necessarily. So, again, given Lewis's account of possible worlds, propositions are not sets of possible worlds.

Lewis says:

> Let us say that an individual exists *from the standpoint of* a world iff it belongs to the least restricted domain that is normally—modal metaphysics being deemed abnormal—appropriate in evaluating the truth at that world of quantifications. I suppose that this domain will include all individuals in that world; none of the other individuals; and some, but not all, of the sets. There will be many sets that even exist from the standpoint of all worlds, for instance the numbers. Others may not; for instance, the unit set of a possible individual might only exist from the standpoint of the world that the individual is in. (1983, 40)

Lewis thinks that some sets exist from the standpoint of every possible world. But not all sets. In particular, he seems to think that if a set's members do not exist from the standpoint of every possible world, then that set does not exist from the standpoint of every possible world. And merely possible individuals—including possible worlds themselves—do not exist from the standpoint of every possible world ('modal metaphysics being deemed abnormal'). So sets of possible worlds do not exist from the standpoint of every possible world.[16]

Perhaps you want to be more inclusive than Lewis with respect to what exists from the standpoint of every possible world. So perhaps you say that an individual 'exists from the standpoint of every possible world' just in case that individual belongs to the least restricted domain that is appropriate in evaluating the truth at every possible world of completely unrestricted quantifications. Then, given Lewis's account of possible worlds, you can say that possible worlds and sets of possible worlds exist from the standpoint of every possible world.

You could claim that existing from the standpoint of every possible world—given your more inclusive definition—is sufficient for existing necessarily. And this claim, given Lewis's account of possible worlds, implies that sets of possible worlds exist necessarily. But this claim, given Lewis's account, also implies that you and I—along with every other possible individual—exist necessarily. So this claim is not plausible.

I suppose you could claim that thus existing from the standpoint of every possible world *and being a set of possible worlds* is sufficient for existing necessarily. This claim implies that sets of possible worlds exist necessarily, even given Lewis's account of possible worlds. And this claim does not imply that you or I exist necessarily, not even given Lewis's account. But this claim is not principled, at least not when combined with a

[16] Lewis takes the property *having a kidney* to be a set that has members that do not exist from the standpoint of the actual world (§I). So Lewis must say that that property does not exist from the standpoint of the actual world. But surely the property *having a kidney* belongs to the least restricted domain that is normally appropriate in evaluating the truth at the actual world of quantifications. I conclude that Lewis's notion of existing from the standpoint of a possible world cannot be consistently combined with his account of properties.

rejection of the implausible claim that existing from the standpoint of every possible world is sufficient for existing necessarily.

Given Lewis's account of possible worlds, there is no plausible and principled way to defend the claim that sets of possible worlds exist necessarily.[17] So I conclude that, given Lewis's account, it is false that sets of possible worlds exist necessarily. But propositions exist necessarily. So, once again, given Lewis's account of possible worlds, propositions are not sets of possible worlds.

I think that when a name refers to an entity, it does so 'directly'. So I think that when a sentence using a name expresses a proposition, it expresses a proposition that is directly about a particular entity. Let a *singular proposition* be a proposition that is directly about a particular entity (see Ch. 5, §I). My final reason for denying that propositions are sets of possible worlds, at least given Lewis's account of possible worlds, focuses on singular propositions.

Pretend that Starbuck actually exists and is actually brave. The sentence 'Starbuck is brave' expresses a singular proposition. So *that Starbuck is brave* is a singular proposition. According to the thesis that propositions are sets of possible worlds, the singular proposition *that Starbuck is brave* is the set of all possible

[17] John Divers (1999) would disagree. For Divers argues that defenders of Lewis's account of possible worlds should say that 'exists necessarily' just means *exists* when predicated of sets of possible worlds. Divers would take this to be a principled reason to say that, given Lewis's account of possible worlds, sets of possible worlds exist necessarily but you and I do not. But I think that the claim that 'exists necessarily' sometimes just means *exists* is not plausible; and if this claim is not plausible, then this claim does not yield a plausible defense of the view that, given Lewis's account of possible worlds, sets of possible worlds exist necessarily. Moreover, I would argue that Divers only defends the view that the Lewisian should adopt a semantics according to which, if sets of possible worlds exist, then the sentence 'Sets of possible worlds exist necessarily' is true; and this, I would also argue, is not to defend the view that—given Lewis's account of possible worlds—if sets of possible worlds exist, then they exist necessarily.

worlds in which Starbuck exists and is brave. But given Lewis's account of possible worlds, Starbuck exists in only a single possible world, namely, the actual world.[18] So Lewis's account of possible worlds combined with the thesis that propositions are sets of possible worlds implies that the singular proposition *that Starbuck is brave* is the unit set of the actual world.

By parity of reasoning, Lewis's account of possible worlds combined with the thesis that propositions are sets of possible worlds implies that each and every true singular proposition about an actually existing entity is identical with the unit set of the actual world. This has the result, for example, that the proposition *that Starbuck is brave* is identical with the proposition *that Smith is a doctor*. More generally, this has the result that each true singular proposition about an actually existing entity is identical with every true singular proposition about an actually existing entity. This result is obviously false. So, given Lewis's account of possible worlds, singular propositions are not sets of possible worlds.

Given Lewis's account of possible worlds, singular propositions are not sets of possible worlds. But if propositions are sets of possible worlds, then singular propositions—being propositions—are sets of possible worlds. Thus my final reason for concluding that, given Lewis's account of possible worlds, propositions are not sets of possible worlds.

(Lewis himself would resist this final reason by denying that if propositions are sets of possible worlds, then singular propositions—being propositions—are sets of possible worlds. For Lewis does not think that all propositions are sets of possible worlds. (Or, as he would put it, he does not think

[18] This argument presupposes that Lewis's account of possible worlds implies counterpart theory. If you believe that Starbuck is a trans-world individual with parts in various possible worlds, then run this argument with a singular proposition about one of those parts. But whatever you believe, do not believe that all possible worlds in which Starbuck exists 'overlap' at Starbuck, that is, have the whole of Starbuck as a shared part (see Lewis, 1986a, 198–209).

that sets of possible worlds play all the propositional 'roles'.) For example, Lewis (1986a, 57–9) would take the singular proposition *that Starbuck is brave* to be the ordered pair <Starbuck, *bravery*>.[19])

VII. Possible Worlds as Abstract Objects

Given Lewis's account of possible worlds, the thesis that propositions are sets of possible worlds is false (§VI). I doubt that this will trouble most defenders of that thesis, since few philosophers—and so few defenders of that thesis—endorse Lewis's account. Instead, most defenders of propositions-as-sets-of-possible-worlds will take possible worlds to be abstract objects of one sort or another.

Some take possible worlds to be *maximal properties*. A property F is maximal just in case, for each proposition *p*, either, necessarily, if F is exemplified then *p* is true or, necessarily, if F is exemplified then *p* is false.[20] Only a universe can exemplify a maximal property. So, according to this view, only a universe can exemplify a possible world. And this view adds that

[19] Do not attempt to out-Lewis Lewis here by trying to salvage the claim that singular propositions are sets of possible worlds by way of counterpart theory. For example, do not claim that the singular proposition *that Starbuck is brave* is the set of all possible worlds in which Starbuck *or one of Starbuck's counterparts* is brave. For which objects count as Starbuck's counterparts turns on which of Starbuck's features are salient in the relevant context. So which set of possible worlds counts as the set of worlds containing Starbuck or one of those counterparts turns on which of Starbuck's features are salient in the relevant context. So there is no such set as *the* set of possible worlds in which Starbuck or one of her counterparts is brave.

[20] If you think some propositions can be neither true nor false, just add a third disjunct: necessarily, if F is exemplified, then *p* is neither true nor false. The above definition counts a property that could not possibly be exemplified as maximal; only maximal properties that are possibly exemplified are alleged to be possible worlds; my discussion to follow will be implicitly restricted to those maximal properties that are possibly exemplified.

the *actual world* is the one and only possible world—that is, the one and only maximal property—exemplified by our universe. Defenders of this view include Robert Stalnaker (2003, 7; 2012, 8–14), Peter Forrest (1986a), John Bigelow and Robert Pargetter (1989), and Jeffrey King (2007b, 447).[21]

I shall argue that those who think that propositions are sets of possible worlds should reject the claim that possible worlds are maximal properties. My argument begins by recalling two of the arguments discussed above for the thesis that propositions are sets of possible worlds. One of those arguments has as a premise the claim that properties are sets of their instances (§I). The other is the Ockham's razor argument (§III); those motivated by the Ockham's razor argument should also be motivated by a similar argument to conclude that properties are sets of their instances. Moreover, I think that anyone who endorses the thesis that propositions are sets of possible worlds should find at least one of the two arguments just noted attractive. So I conclude that those who take propositions to be sets of possible worlds should take properties to be sets of their instances.[22]

Suppose that properties are sets of their instances. Add that a possible world is a maximal property. Only a universe can exemplify a maximal property. So—assuming that no two universes exemplify the same maximal property—we get the result that each possible world is the unit set of a universe. A set exists only if its members exist. So there are only as many possible worlds as there are universes.[23] I assume that there is not a

[21] They do not all describe this view in the way I do. For example, Stalnaker, Forrest, and King—unlike me—use the word 'world' for both a possible world and also for a universe, and use the expression 'actual world' to denote our universe.

[22] This conclusion can be combined with Section I's argument for the claim that properties are not sets of their instances to yield another objection to propositions-as-sets-of-possible-worlds.

[23] Suppose we do not assume that no two universes exemplify the same maximal property. Even so, a universe cannot exemplify more than one maximal property. So we get the result that there are either as many possible worlds as there are universes or fewer possible worlds than there are universes.

universe for each way everything could be. So there are not as many possible worlds (i.e., unit sets of universes) as there are ways everything could be. (Presumably, there is just one universe and so just one possible world.) But there is supposed to be a possible world for each way everything could be. So I conclude that if properties are sets of their instances, then possible worlds are not maximal properties.[24]

As argued above, those who think that propositions are sets of possible worlds should take properties to be sets of their instances. But we have just seen that if properties are sets of their instances, then possible worlds are not maximal properties. So those who think that propositions are sets of possible worlds should deny that possible worlds are maximal properties.

I said above that only a universe can exemplify a maximal property. This seems fairly plausible, at least assuming that a universe is 'everything' and a maximal property is 'a way everything could be'. But you might claim that a maximal property can be exemplified by something (or some things) other than a universe. Suppose you are right. Even so, it is still the case—no matter what entity or entities are taken to exemplify maximal properties—that if properties are sets of their instances, then possible worlds are not maximal properties.

To see why I say this, assume that possible worlds are maximal properties. Then the actual world is—no matter what does the exemplifying—the maximal property that is exemplified. And the merely possible worlds are—no matter what does the

[24] In defending a version of Section I's argument for the claim that propositions are sets of possible worlds, Stalnaker (1976, 80) says: 'the intension of a predicate—the property it expresses—is a function from possible worlds into classes of individuals.' This claim, combined with the view that possible worlds are maximal properties, implies that a possible world is a function from possible worlds into unit classes of universes (which are the individuals that exemplify possible worlds). This has not only implications akin to those just noted in the text, but also the uncomfortable result that a possible world is a member of (an ordered pair that is) a member of itself (see discussion below of the Axiom of Regularity).

exemplifying—those maximal properties that could have been exemplified, but are not. There are merely possible worlds. So there are unexemplified maximal properties. So there are unexemplified properties. So there are properties that do not have instances. So properties are not sets of their instances. Thus our assumption that possible worlds are maximal properties has the result that properties are not sets of their instances. So if properties are sets of their instances, then possible worlds are not maximal properties.

As argued above, those who think that propositions are sets of possible worlds should take properties to be sets of their instances. But we have just seen (again) that if properties are sets of their instances, then possible worlds are not maximal properties. So defenders of the thesis that propositions are sets of possible worlds should deny that possible worlds are maximal properties. Defenders of that thesis must seek a different account of the nature of possible worlds.

Here is a final thought about the claim that possible worlds are maximal properties. On the one hand, I think that only the most expansive accounts of properties should countenance maximal properties; so I think that if the most expansive accounts of properties are false, then there are no maximal properties.[25] On the other hand, the major motivation for expansive accounts of properties seems to be the claim that properties are sets of their instances (cf. Lewis, 1986a, 59–60); but—as emphasized above—that claim implies that there is at most one maximal property. And, of course, if there are no maximal properties, or instead just one, then possible worlds are not maximal properties.

Robert Adams takes a possible world to be a set of propositions. More precisely, Adams (1974, 225) takes a possible world to be: 'a set which has as its members one member of every pair of

[25] I reject the most expansive accounts; see, for example, Merricks, 2003b, 734–6.

mutually contradictory propositions, and which is such that it is possible that all of its members be true together'.[26] And Adams (1974, 225–6) takes the actual world to be the possible world all of whose members are true; that is, he takes the actual world to be the set of all true propositions.

If possible worlds are sets of propositions, then propositions are not sets of possible worlds. To see why, assume for reductio both (a) propositions are sets of possible worlds and (b) possible worlds are sets of propositions. Given (a), proposition *p* is the set of possible worlds in which *p* is true. Given (b), each possible world in which *p* is true has *p* as a member. So, given (a) and (b), proposition *p* is a set each of whose members are sets that have *p* as a member.

So, given (a) and (b), some sets are members of members of themselves. Standard set theory includes the Axiom of Regularity. One result of that axiom is that no set is a member of a member of itself. I assume that propositions-as-sets-of-possible-worlds should be consistent with standard set theory. So I conclude that the combination of (a) and (b) has an unacceptable implication. So the combination of (a) and (b) is unacceptable. So I say that if (b) is true, then (a) is false. In other words, I say that if possible worlds are sets of propositions, then propositions are not sets of possible worlds.

The claim that propositions are sets of possible worlds is itself a claim about what propositions *are*. That is, it is an account of the *nature* of propositions. If possible worlds are

[26] More precisely still, Adams calls such a set a 'world-story'. He then analyzes claims about possible worlds into claims about 'world-stories'. For example, he analyzes *there is a possible world in which p* as *the proposition p is a member of some world-story* (Adams, 1974, 225).

Because propositions do not have logical form (Ch. 2, §VIII), there are no 'mutually contradictory' propositions. Let us assume that Adams can work around this by tweaking his account of possible worlds. (One option involves pairs of propositions that could be expressed by mutually contradictory sentences. Another option involves pairs of propositions such that it is impossible that both be true even though each is possibly true.)

themselves sets of propositions, then that account turns out to say that propositions are certain sets of sets of—wait for it—propositions. So if possible worlds are themselves propositions, then that account of the nature of propositions is circular. (Compare it to this account of the nature of knowledge: S knows that *p* just in case *p* is a member of the set of things that S knows.) Such circularity is not acceptable. This is my second—and final—reason for saying that if possible worlds are sets of propositions, then propositions are not sets of possible worlds.[27]

Believers in propositions routinely reason as follows: Dogs bark; therefore, there is the (true) proposition *that dogs bark*. There are no flying pigs; therefore, there is the (false) proposition *that there are flying pigs*. More generally, believers in propositions routinely assume—at the very least—both of the following: If things are a certain way, there is a (true) proposition that is true just in case things are that way. And if things are not a certain way, there is a (false) proposition that is true just in case things are that way.[28]

[27] Happily for defenders of the thesis that propositions are sets of possible worlds, there is a reason—independent of that thesis—to deny that possible worlds are sets of propositions. Taking possible worlds to be sets of propositions seems to lead to a familiar Cantorian set-theoretic paradox; see Grim (1984; 1988) and Bringsjord (1985). But less happily for defenders of the thesis that propositions are sets of possible worlds, Jubien (1988, 307) argues that that same paradox directly undermines that thesis.

[28] Believers in propositions typically assume something stronger. They typically assume that if things are (are not) a certain way, then there is a true (false) proposition that represents things as being exactly that way. (Those who discuss the aforementioned Cantorian paradox seem to make this stronger assumption; see, for example, Plantinga and Grim (1993, 288) and Menzel (1986, 70–1).) But Pruss and Rasmussen (2015) argue that the wholly unqualified claim that if things are a certain way, then there is a true proposition that represents things as being exactly that way is part of what leads to a version of Russell's paradox. (The assumptions relied on in the text do not threaten us with this paradox, which is why I rely on them, as opposed to the stronger assumption discussed in this note.)

Now consider the way *everything* is. Reasoning as believers in propositions routinely do, I conclude that there is a proposition that is true just in case that is how things are. So that proposition is true. And that proposition necessitates the proposition *that dogs bark*. Moreover, that proposition necessitates that the proposition *that there are flying pigs* is false. More generally, for every proposition *p*, that proposition necessitates *p* or necessitates that *p* is false. So let us say that that proposition is *maximal*.[29]

Given the above routine reasoning, there is a true maximal proposition. And given that reasoning there is also, for each way everything is not, a false maximal proposition. Some of those false maximal propositions are possibly true. One standard approach to possible worlds—more or less the approach defended by Alvin Plantinga in *The Nature of Necessity*—takes possible worlds to be possibly true maximal propositions.[30] And it takes the actual world to be the true maximal proposition.[31]

[29] Proposition *p* necessitates proposition *q* just in case, necessarily, if *p* is true, then *q* is true. Proposition *p* necessitates that proposition *q* is false just in case, necessarily, if *p* is true, then *q* is false. If you think some propositions can be neither true nor false, then say that a proposition *p* is maximal just in case, for every proposition *q*, *p* necessitates *q* or necessitates that *q* is false or necessitates that *q* is neither true nor false.

[30] Plantinga (1974) says that possible worlds are maximal 'states of affairs', adding that these 'states of affairs' might be propositions (1974, 45; see also Plantinga, 1987, 192). NB: I shall use the expression 'states of affairs' in Chapters 4 and 6, but I shall not mean what Plantinga does by that expression.

[31] Above I said that the major motivation for expansive accounts of properties seems to be the claim that properties are sets of their instances. But given how believers in propositions routinely reason, one might charge that believers in properties routinely reason in a parallel way, a way that motivates maximal properties. That is, one might charge that believers in properties claim that for each way things are (and for each way things are not), there is a property to the effect that things are that way (or are not that way). But that claim is false. Here is one reason that I say this. The property of *being a horse* is non-self-exemplifying. (Sorry, Plato.) That is one way that property is. Now consider all the properties that are that way. It is false that all those properties are that way—i.e., non-self-exemplifying—in virtue of exemplifying a property to the effect that things

Let us assume that propositions never change in truth-value. (But see below.) Given that assumption, I think that maximal possibly true propositions are as good a candidate for possible worlds as one could want. Moreover, with respect to ontological parsimony, possible-worlds-as-maximal-possibly-true-propositions has a marginal cost of zero for those of us who accept that for each way things are or could be, there is a proposition that is true (false) just in case things are (are not) that way. So I conclude that if there are possible worlds, then possible worlds are maximal possibly true propositions. Assume that there are possible worlds, if only to give the thesis that propositions are sets of possible worlds a fighting chance. Then possible worlds are maximal possibly true propositions.

Possible worlds are maximal possibly true propositions. So propositions are not sets of possible worlds. To see why, assume for reductio both (a) propositions are sets of possible worlds and (b*) possible worlds are propositions. Given (b*), possible world Beta is a proposition. So, given (a), Beta is a set of possible worlds. That is, given (a), Beta is the set of possible worlds *in which Beta is true*. Since Beta is itself a possible world, Beta is true in only one possible world, namely, itself.[32] So Beta is the unit set of Beta.

are that way. For such a property would be exemplified by everything that did not exemplify itself. (So it would exemplify itself and not exemplify itself.)

Here is a similar charge: If *p* is a maximal proposition, then there is the property of *being such that p is true*, which is a maximal property. First Reply: I do not think *p*'s existence implies that there is the property of *being such that p is true*. Second Reply: Defenders of propositions-as-sets-of-possible-worlds should not take a property such as *being such that p is true* to be a possible world, and not just for the reasons noted in my earlier discussion of maximal properties and possible worlds. For suppose they did. Then they must say that *p*—being maximal—is a set with one possible world as a member, which possible world is *being such that p is true*. More generally, they must say that each maximal proposition is the unit set of the property of being such that that proposition is true. This is not an appropriately informative account of the nature of those propositions.

[32] A proposition *p* is *true in* a possible world (i.e., a maximal proposition) *W* just in case, necessarily, if *W* is actual (i.e., true), then *p* is true.

The combination of (a) and (b*) has the result that Beta is the unit set of Beta. So it has the result that Beta is a member of itself. As noted above, standard set theory includes the Axiom of Regularity. And, as also noted above, one result of that axiom is that no set is a member of a member of itself. A second, and similar, result of that axiom is that no set is a member of itself. So I conclude that the combination of (a) and (b*) has an unacceptable implication. So the combination of (a) and (b*) is unacceptable. But possible worlds are propositions. So (b*) is true. So we should deny (a). So we should conclude that propositions are not sets of possible worlds.

Moreover, the thesis that propositions are sets of possible worlds is intended to tell us what propositions *are*. That is, it is an account of the *nature* of propositions. Possible worlds are themselves certain propositions. So that account turns out to say that propositions are certain sets of—wait for it—propositions. So that account is objectionably circular. So I conclude that propositions are not sets of possible worlds.

So far in this section, I have assumed that propositions do not change in truth-value. I have done this because the standard view among philosophers nowadays seems to be that propositions do not and even cannot change in truth-value.[33] But my own view is that some propositions can, and do, change in truth-value (see Merricks, 2007, 74–5). I think, for example, that the proposition *that A sits* can change in truth-value. (Of course, the proposition *that A sits at time t* cannot change in truth-value).

Possible worlds are propositions of a certain sort. A possible world's being actual just is its being true. Add that the possible world that is the actual world always was and always will be the

[33] For an overview of the contemporary controversy over whether some propositions change in truth-value, see Brogaard (2012, 1–12). The ancient view was that some propositions do change in truth-value; at least, this was the view of the Stoics (see Bobzien, 2003, 87); see also Aristotle, *Categories* 4a, 24–6 [1984, 7].

actual world. Then the proposition that is the actual world always was and always will be true. So the actual world does not necessitate any propositions that did or will change in truth-value, even though some such propositions are true. So the actual world is not maximal *simpliciter*, but instead—I add—maximal *with respect to propositions that do not change in truth-value*. More generally, I conclude that possible worlds are not maximal simpliciter, but instead are maximal only in the qualified way just noted (see Merricks, 2007, 74–80).

The claim that possible worlds are possibly true propositions that are maximal only in this qualified way does not negatively impact my above two objections to propositions-as-sets-of-possible-worlds. For those objections can be run with equal strength whether propositions are maximal simpliciter or instead, as I believe, maximal only with respect to propositions that do not change in truth-value. But taking possible worlds to be maximal only in this qualified way does lead to a new objection to the thesis that propositions are sets of possible worlds.

Here it is. Possible worlds are propositions. So a proposition is true in a possible world just in case, necessarily, if that possible world is actual (i.e., true), then that proposition is true. Because possible worlds are maximal only with respect to propositions that do not change in truth-value, no proposition that changes in truth-value is true in (i.e., necessitated by) a possible world. If a proposition is a set of possible worlds, then that proposition is the set of possible worlds in which it is true. So no proposition that changes in truth-value is a set of possible worlds. But some propositions do change in truth-value. So not all propositions are sets of possible worlds. This completes my final argument for the claim that if possible worlds are propositions of some sort, then propositions are not sets of possible worlds.[34]

[34] Suppose the proposition *that A sits* changes in truth-value. Pretend that there is a possible world in which A sits for all eternity. That possible world does

(This final argument suggests parallel arguments against the thesis that propositions are sets of possible worlds combined with taking possible worlds to be properties, and combined with taking possible worlds to be sets of propositions. Here is how those parallel arguments begin: If possible worlds are properties, they must not be maximal simpliciter, but instead maximal only with regard to propositions that do not change in truth-value. And: If possible worlds are sets of propositions, they are sets all of whose members are propositions that do not change in truth-value.)

Suppose that some propositions change in truth-value and also that possible worlds are maximal only with respect to propositions that do not change in truth-value. Propositions that change in truth-value can be the premises and conclusions of modally valid arguments. (Consider: A sits; therefore, A sits.) But, as we saw above, such propositions are not true *in* any possible worlds. Nor are such propositions—for basically the same reason—true *at* any possible worlds.[35] These points constitute another objection to the claim, considered in Chapter 1 (§III), that modal validity should be defined in terms of truth *at* possible worlds. They also constitute an objection to defining modal validity in terms of truth *in* possible worlds. All of this is one reason that I did not even mention possible worlds when defining *modal validity* (see, e.g., Ch. 1, §I).

Of course, those who accept my claim that possible worlds are not maximal simpliciter can say that there are some other propositions—propositions that are not possible worlds—that

necessitate *that A sits*. For ease of exposition, I ignore these odd (and ultimately irrelevant) sorts of possible worlds. (No one thinks both that some propositions can change in truth-value and also that each such proposition is the set of possible worlds in which it is eternally true.)

[35] A proposition is true *at* a possible world just in case that proposition has truth conditions and, necessarily, if that possible world were actual, then those truth conditions would be satisfied (see Ch. 1, §III).

are maximal simpliciter. We might call such propositions 'possible world states'.[36] (Along similar lines, some might say that maximal properties are possible world states, or that certain sets of propositions are possible world states.) And some might react to the objection I have just raised to understanding modal validity in terms of possible worlds by exchanging an account of modal validity in terms of possible worlds for one in terms of possible world states. Likewise, some might react to my above final argument for the claim that if possible worlds are propositions of some sort, then propositions are not sets of possible worlds, by saying that propositions are sets of possible world states.

I do not know whether exchanging possible worlds for possible world states would bother those who originally claimed that modal validity is to be understood in terms of truth *at* possible worlds. And I doubt that it would bother those who originally claimed that propositions are sets of possible worlds. But whether it would bother them or not, this exchange will not be of much help to those who originally claimed that propositions are sets of possible worlds. For aside from the final argument that traded on propositions that change in truth-value, this section's arguments against combining propositions-as-sets-of-possible-worlds with various accounts of possible worlds can easily be transformed into arguments against combining propositions-as-sets-of-possible-world-states with parallel accounts of possible world states.

At any rate, I believe that some propositions change in truth-value. As a result, I believe that the best account of the nature of possible worlds says that possible worlds are propositions that are maximal only with respect to propositions that do not change in truth-value. So I wanted to explicitly note how this bears on modal validity and also how it might lead some to

[36] I called them 'abstract times' in Merricks (2007, 127).

claim that propositions are sets of possible world states (as opposed to possible worlds). But I shall set these issues aside for the rest of this book, and pretend that possible worlds are maximal simpliciter. And below I shall return to the thesis that propositions are sets of possible worlds (as opposed to possible world states).

As noted above, believers in propositions routinely reason as follows: Dogs bark; therefore, there is the (true) proposition *that dogs bark*. Most believers in propositions do not think that it is merely contingent that if dogs bark, then there is the (true) proposition *that dogs bark*. Rather, they think that this is how things must be. They think that, necessarily, if dogs bark, then there is the (true) proposition *that dogs bark*. And they think that, necessarily, if it is not the case that dogs bark, then there is the (false) proposition *that dogs bark*.

Necessarily, dogs bark or it is not the case that dogs bark. Thus the way believers in propositions routinely reason leads to the conclusion that *that dogs bark* exists necessarily (cf. Ch. 5, §VII). More generally, the way in which believers in propositions routinely reason leads to the conclusion that propositions exist necessarily. This is a new argument for the conclusion that propositions exist necessarily, an argument in addition to those given in Chapter 1 (§IV).

Here is a second new argument for the conclusion that (at least some) propositions exist necessarily: Possible worlds exist necessarily; possible worlds are a certain sort of proposition; so propositions (of the relevant sort) exist necessarily. If you do not accept my account of the nature of possible worlds, you will not be persuaded by this second new argument for the necessary existence of (at least some) propositions. And, more importantly, you will not be persuaded by the above arguments based on my account of possible worlds for the conclusion that propositions are not sets of possible worlds.

But you should not yet—not even by your own lights—dismiss the overall reasoning against propositions-as-sets-of-possible-worlds prosecuted in this section and the previous. For that overall reasoning highlights the fact that if propositions really are sets of possible worlds, then possible worlds really do exist, and so really are entities of one sort or another. Reflecting on this fact can reveal new problems for the thesis that propositions are sets of possible worlds, problems that even those who reject my account of possible worlds should acknowledge.

For example, you might react to the above discussion of various accounts of the nature of possible worlds by dismissing the whole project of earnestly seeking the true account of what possible worlds really are. There are two reasons you might react in this way. First, you might hold that—while talk of possible worlds can perhaps serve as a useful heuristic—possible worlds do not really exist, and so they have no nature to be discovered. But then you do not believe that there really are possible worlds. So you should not believe that there really are sets of possible worlds. So you may not believe that propositions are sets of possible worlds.

Second, you might react in this way because your view is that there are many different sorts of entities that are all equally good candidates to bear the label 'possible worlds', and so seeking out the single correct account of the nature of possible worlds is at best quixotic. But suppose your 'equally good candidates' just are those entities put forward by the standard accounts of possible worlds. Then each of your candidates—so I have argued above—creates serious problems for the thesis that propositions are sets of possible worlds. In order to sidestep those problems, your many candidates will have to be candidates other than those discussed above.

Moreover, if there are many different sorts of entities that are all equally good candidates to bear the label 'possible worlds', then there are many equally good candidates to bear the label 'sets of possible worlds'. And so—if propositions are sets of possible worlds—there are many equally good candidates to be this or that proposition. This strengthens the objections to propositions-as-sets-of-possible-worlds emphasized in Section V, objections turning in part on the many equally good candidates (so far as their structure and members are concerned) to be this or that proposition.

There is only one way to resist the overall reasoning against propositions-as-sets-of-possible-worlds presented in this section and the previous, and to do so without strengthening the objections of Section V. It is to show, first, that there is a single best account of the nature of possible worlds and, second, that this account can be combined with the thesis that propositions are sets of possible worlds without creating any new problems for that thesis. (So this single best account must not be one of the accounts discussed above, since those accounts do create new problems.)

I do not think that defenders of the thesis that propositions are sets of possible worlds can successfully resist the overall reasoning against propositions-as-sets-of-possible-worlds presented in this section and the previous. And it is not merely because I cannot see what account of the nature of possible worlds they could offer that would not create new problems for that thesis. It is also because I think that there is a single best account of the nature of possible worlds, according to which possible worlds are propositions of a certain sort; and that account—like all the standard accounts—does create new and even fatal problems for the thesis that propositions are sets of possible worlds.

VIII. Conclusion

There are surprisingly few explicit arguments for the conclusion that propositions really are sets of possible worlds. This chapter has examined those arguments, and argued that they fail. So this chapter concludes that the claim that propositions are sets of possible worlds is unmotivated. Moreover, so this chapter has argued, there are a number of compelling objections to the claim that propositions are sets of possible worlds. So this chapter concludes that propositions are not sets of possible worlds.

4

AGAINST STRUCTURED PROPOSITIONS

CHAPTER 3 opposed the claim that propositions are sets of possible worlds, one of the two leading accounts of the nature of propositions. The other leading account endorses *structured propositions*. This chapter argues that the standard motivations for structured propositions fail. Moreover, this chapter and Chapter 5 give reasons to reject structured propositions.

I. What Are Structured Propositions?

The *Stanford Encyclopedia*'s entry on 'Structured Propositions' says:

> To say that propositions are structured is to say something about the nature of propositions. Roughly, to say that propositions are structured is to say that they are complex entities, entities having parts or constituents, where the constituents are bound together in a certain way. (King, 2011)

This description of structured propositions is absolutely standard. And it says important things about the nature of structured propositions.

But this standard description is not (nor is it intended to be) a full answer to the question: 'What are structured propositions?'

This is because sets of possible worlds satisfy this standard description. That is, sets of possible worlds are 'complex entities', having constituents (possible worlds) that are bound together in a certain way (set-theoretically). But sets of possible worlds are not structured propositions. For propositions-as-sets-of-possible-worlds is a competitor to, not a version of, structured propositions.

Here is one reason that the thesis that propositions are sets of possible worlds is not a version of structured propositions. That thesis rules out numerically distinct but necessarily equivalent propositions (Ch. 3, §§II and IV). But structured propositions allow for numerically distinct but necessarily equivalent propositions. Indeed, defenders of structured propositions regularly claim that structured propositions are superior to propositions-as-sets-of-possible-worlds because they are more 'fine-grained' in just this way (see, e.g., Soames, 1987; Richard, 1990, 7–16; King, 2007a, 2–3; and King, 2011).[1]

Mark Richard says:

> Someone might observe that, even if the structure of a ['that'-clause] is reflected in the individuation of propositions, it doesn't follow that the propositions themselves have any structure at all. They might, for all that, turn out to be Twinkies—so long as, for example, no Twinkie named by *that A and B* is named by *that not A*. (1990, 34)

Taking Richard's example for my own purposes, note that the claim that structured propositions are more fine-grained than

[1] All defenders of structured propositions agree that some necessarily equivalent propositions are not identical. But there is disagreement about exactly how fine-grained structured propositions are supposed to be. For example, some think that no one structured proposition could be expressed by two sentences differing in syntax (see, e.g., Lewis, 1986a, 57; Richard, 1990, 8; Braun, 1993, 461; King, 2007a); but others think that sentences with different syntax can express the same proposition (see, e.g., Frege, 1892b; Collins, 2007). For another example, some think that 'Cicero is an orator' and 'Tully is an orator' express the same proposition (see, e.g., King, 2007a; Soames, 1987; Salmon, 1986); but others think they express different propositions (see, e.g., Richard, 1990; Stanley, 2011).

sets of possible worlds does not rule out the view that each proposition is a Twinkie. More importantly, that claim is consistent with any account of the nature of propositions that permits some necessarily equivalent propositions to be distinct. So the claim that structured propositions are more fine-grained than sets of possible worlds does not tell us what structured propositions *are*.

Structured propositions are more fine-grained than propositions-as-sets-of-possible-worlds. Defenders of structured propositions will insist that this is not a brute fact. As we shall see in Section V, they will insist that there is something about the nature of structured propositions that explains *why* they are more fine-grained than propositions-as-sets-of-possible-worlds. But nothing mentioned above explains this.

So what exactly *are* structured propositions? And *why* are they more fine-grained than sets of possible worlds? There are a number of useful ways to answer these two questions. My way of answering them begins with the theory of propositions defended by Bertrand Russell in 1903.

II. Russell 1903

Suppose—just for the sake of argument—that when you sit there exists not only you and the property *sitting*, but also the *state of affairs* of your exemplifying that property. More generally, suppose that when an object exemplifies a property there is the state of affairs of that object's exemplifying that property. Suppose also that there are states of affairs involving two or more things being related to each other, such as A's being related by *loving* to B.

Some states of affairs are spatially located and causally efficacious. For example, the state of affairs of your sitting is located just where the sitting you is located. And that state of affairs can cause certain effects, such as a chair's reclining. And states of affairs have parts. For example, your sitting has both you and *sitting* as parts. And the state of affairs of A's being related by *loving* to B has A, B, and *loving* as parts.[2]

In 1903, Bertrand Russell thought that propositions were states of affairs. For Russell describes the proposition *that A differs from B* just as I would describe the state of affairs of A's differing from B:

> Consider, for example, the proposition '*A* differs from *B*.' The constituents of this proposition, if we analyze it, appear to be only *A*, difference, *B*. Yet these constituents, thus placed side by side, do not reconstitute the proposition. The difference, which occurs in the proposition, actually relates *A* and *B*, whereas the difference after analysis is a notion which has no connection with *A* and *B*. (1903, 49; see also Russell, 1903, 139–40)

Russell here takes the proposition *that A differs from B* to be identical with the state of affairs of A's differing from B. *That A differs from B* would be true if the state of affairs of A's differing from B existed. With this in mind, I describe Russell's 1903 account of propositions—or, for short, Russell 1903—as the view that each proposition is identical with the state of affairs that makes that proposition true.

Recall that propositions are the objects of belief (Ch. 1, §V). So when I believe that A loves B, I believe the proposition *that A loves B*. So—according to Russell 1903—I believe a certain chunk of the world, namely, A's standing in the *loving* relation to B. Something similar goes for believers and beliefs generally. Thus Russell's 1903 account of propositions delivers direct realism about belief. This is the first virtue of Russell 1903.[3]

[2] States of affairs are also called 'events' and—because of Russell's post-1903 usage (e.g., 1918–19)—'Russellian facts'.

[3] G. E. Moore's 'The Refutation of Idealism' appeared in 1903. Just as Russell 1903 takes states of affairs to be the objects of belief, so Moore takes similar entities to be the contents of our perceptual experience (see esp. Moore, 1903, 451–3). Thus Moore defends a direct realism about perception that parallels Russell's direct

There is a second virtue of Russell 1903. Russell 1903 implies an elegant account of what it is for a proposition to be true. Recall that his account takes each proposition to be identical with the 'truthmaking' state of affairs for that proposition. (For example, his account takes the proposition *that A loves B* to be identical with the state of affairs of A's standing in the *loving* relation to B.) Hence his account seems to imply that, for a proposition, to be true is to exist. Elegant indeed.

In Chapter 1 (§IV), I concluded that propositions essentially represent things as being a certain way. A key premise in my argument for that conclusion was that a proposition's truth conditions are a result of how that proposition represents things as being. I stand by that conclusion, and by my argument for it. But Russell 1903 can resist that argument. For Russell 1903 implies that a proposition is true just in case it exists. So defenders of Russell 1903 can deny that a proposition is true just in case things are as that proposition represents things as being. And this in turn allows them to deny that each proposition essentially represents things as being a certain way.

This is a third virtue of Russell 1903. To see why this is a virtue, recall that—so I argued (Ch. 3, §V)—propositions-as-sets-of-possible-worlds founders in part because a set of possible worlds fails to essentially represent things as being a certain way. Moreover, as I shall argue in this chapter, many present-day accounts of structured propositions fail because they fail to meet the demand that a proposition essentially represents things as being a certain way. Thus Russell 1903—because it does not need to meet that demand—can sidestep what I believe to be among the most serious objections to current accounts of the nature of propositions.[4]

realism about belief. I hazard that it is no coincidence that these colleagues published parallel views in the same year.

[4] I think that the only views that can join Russell 1903 in sidestepping such objections are those that identify a proposition with its truthmaker. For I think

What binds the constituents of a structured proposition together into a single entity, a proposition? Can the very same constituents constitute two distinct propositions? These are questions about the 'unity of the proposition'. The fourth virtue of Russell 1903 is that it answers these questions. For example, it says that A, B, and *loving* constitute one proposition (= state of affairs) in virtue of A's standing in the *loving* relation to B. Moreover, those very same constituents constitute a distinct proposition in virtue of B's standing in the *loving* relation to A.

Perhaps I should describe this fourth virtue in the following way. Russell 1903 reduces the above questions about the unity of the proposition—questions faced only by defenders of structured propositions—to questions about what it is for an object to exemplify a property, or what it is for an object to stand in a relation to an object. Russell 1903 does not answer these latter questions. But these are questions everyone must face, or at least everyone who believes that objects have properties and stand in relations.

Russell 1903 has so many virtues! But it also has fatal flaws. Suppose that A loves B. Then there is the state of affairs of A's standing in the *loving* relation to B. But had A not loved B, that state of affairs would not have existed. So that state of affairs exists contingently. Russell 1903 implies that that state of affairs is the proposition *that A loves B*. So Russell 1903 implies that the proposition *that A loves B* exists contingently. But all propositions exist necessarily (Ch. 1, §IV; Ch. 3, §VII; Ch. 5, §II). So Russell 1903 is false.

And suppose that A does not love B. Then there is no state of affairs of A's standing in the *loving* relation to B. Then, given Russell 1903, the proposition *that A loves B* does not exist. More generally, Russell 1903 rules out the existence of false propositions.

that that identification delivers the only principled way to deny that a proposition is true just in case things are as that proposition represents things as being.

(Recall that, given Russell 1903, a proposition is true just in case it exists.)

Russell—even in 1903—seems to recognize that Russell 1903 ill accommodates false propositions. He says:

> [There is a] sense of assertion, very difficult to bring clearly before the mind, and yet quite undeniable, in which only true propositions are asserted. True and false propositions alike are in some sense entities, and are in some sense capable of being logical subjects; but when a proposition happens to be true, it has a further quality, over and above that which it shares with false propositions, and it is the further quality which is what I mean by assertion in a logical as opposed to a psychological sense. (1903, 49)[5]

I am not certain what Russell's 'further quality' is supposed to be. Perhaps it is *existence* (cf. Russell, 1903, 449–50; but also see Russell, 1903, 467). Or perhaps it is the property *being true* (cf. Russell, 1904a, 523–4). Or perhaps it is something else.[6]

At any rate, Russell 1903 rules out the existence of false propositions. But Chapter 1 showed that there really are propositions, and that propositions are, among other things, the fundamental bearers of truth *and falsity*. So, again, Russell 1903 is

[5] And consider this passage from Russell's *Theory of Knowledge*:

> Our disbelief in [the reality of false propositions] may be reinforced by asking ourselves what kind of entity a false proposition could be. Let us take some very simple false proposition, say '*A* precedes *B*,' when in fact *A* comes after *B*. It seems as though nothing were involved here beyond *A* and *B* and 'preceding' and the general form of the dual complexes. But since *A* does not precede *B*, these objects are not put together in the way indicated by the proposition. It seems, therefore, that nothing which actually is composed of these objects is the proposition; and it is not credible that anything further enters into the proposition. (1913 [1984, 109–10])

This passage is discussed by Ian Proops (2011, 199). Proops (2011, 200) suggests a way to resist this argument. But Proops's way is not available to Russell 1903.

[6] Even after abandoning his 1903 account of the nature of propositions, Russell continued to find false propositions particularly troublesome. For example, in 1907 Russell articulates (but neither affirms nor rejects) the thesis that there are no false propositions, but there are true ones. Russell later comes to reject the existence of all propositions—but he still takes false propositions to be especially objectionable (see, e.g., Russell, 1912, 124 and 1918–19 [1985, 87]).

false. But Russell 1903 is still a nice example of what structured propositions are supposed to be. Moreover, Russell 1903 delivers an instructive way to characterize structured propositions as they are defended today.

Start with the Russell 1903 account of the nature of propositions. Then replace what it says about the unity of the proposition with something else. That is, agree with Russell 1903 about the constituents of this or that proposition, but disagree with Russell 1903 about what unites those constituents into a proposition. (For example, agree that the constituents of the proposition *that A loves B* are A, *loving*, and B, but deny that what unites them into that proposition is A's standing in the *loving* relation to B.) Those who understand structured propositions in more or less this way are 'neo-Russellians'. They include, among others, David Kaplan (1975; 1989), Nathan Salmon (1986, 1), David Lewis (1986a, 57ff.), Scott Soames (1987), David Braun (1993), and Jeffrey King (2007a, 76). Most present-day defenders of structured propositions are neo-Russellians.

There are also 'neo-Fregeans'. Neo-Fregeans join neo-Russellians in replacing what Russell 1903 says about the unity of the proposition with something else. But neo-Fregeans depart from Russell 1903 in one more way, taking the Fregean *sense* of a name to be a constituent of a proposition where Russell 1903 and neo-Russellians take the referent of that name to be a constituent. Gareth Evans (1982), John McDowell (1994, 104–7), and Jason Stanley (2011), among others, are neo-Fregeans.[7]

[7] So neo-Fregeanism is a view about structured propositions. (Outside this book, 'neo-Fregeanism' often names a view about the ontology of mathematical entities.) Frege's own view is that the constituents of propositions include not just the senses of names, but also the senses of 'concept words' (see Ch. 2, §III and Frege, before 1895). I reject neo-Fregeanism in part for the reasons that I rejected Fregeanism about names in Chapter 2 (§§II–III). (I admit to the artificiality of distinguishing Fregeanism about names from neo-Fregeanism; even so, I take the first as a thesis about how fine-grained certain propositions are, and the second as a version of structured propositions that would, among other things, explain that fine-grainedness.)

Further emendations of Russell 1903 lead to further versions of structured propositions. There are versions that take propositions to have as constituents not just Fregean senses of names, but also Fregean senses of predicates (see, e.g., Frege, before 1895, and Chalmers, 2011, esp. 613–15). There are versions that take some propositions to have both the referent and also the sense of a name as a constituent (see, e.g., Church, 1956, 8 n. 20). And we shall consider versions that endorse constituents unimagined by Russell or Frege (see, e.g., §VI's discussion of 'Zip').

All of this allows us to say what structured propositions *are*. Structured propositions are what you get when you start with Russell 1903 and stay there, or amend Russell 1903 in the sorts of ways described above.[8] And this characterization of what structured propositions are explains *why*—if propositions are structured—some necessarily equivalent propositions are numerically distinct.

A single example will do. All defenders of structured propositions should say that the proposition *that dogs bark* has (something along the lines of) the properties *being a dog* and *barking* as constituents. And all defenders of structured propositions should also say that the proposition *that dogs bark and FLT is true* has as its constituents all the constituents of *that dogs bark*, and more besides, including, for example, some mathematical properties. And if *that dogs bark and FLT is true* has more constituents than does *that dogs bark*, then the proposition *that dogs bark and FLT is true* is not identical with the proposition *that dogs bark*.

[8] There are limits to the emendations you may make. You no longer have structured propositions if you 'amend' Russell 1903 by saying that the only constituents of propositions are possible worlds, or by saying that propositions lack constituents entirely.

III. Logical Form

There are three standard motivations for structured propositions. The first motivation turns on claims about logical form (see, e.g., Salmon, 1989b, 332 n. 4).[9] There are various ways we could present this motivation. I shall present it as two arguments. Here is the first argument: Propositions have logical form. If propositions have logical form, then propositions are structured. Therefore, propositions are structured. Therefore, there are structured propositions.

Here is the second argument: Some arguments with propositions as their premises and conclusions are logically valid by the lights of predicate logic. An argument is logically valid if and only if that argument's conclusion is true in all models in which its premises are true. The models for predicate logic apply to arguments with propositions as their premises and conclusions only given structured propositions (cf. Turner, 2005). Therefore, there are structured propositions.

Both of these arguments are unsound. The first argument is unsound because propositions do not have logical form (Ch. 2, §VIII). The second argument is unsound because no argument constituted by propositions is logically valid, not even by the lights of predicate logic (Ch. 2, §§II–III). So I conclude that the first standard motivation for structured propositions—the motivation based on logical form—fails.

IV. Language is Compositional

Perhaps this is your first encounter with the sentence: 'Unicorns vomit'. Even so, you know what that sentence means.

[9] Keller and Keller (2014, 314) say: 'The Compositionality Argument, along with the argument from logical form, is one of the two sturdiest pillars supporting Structured Propositionalism.' I discuss the compositionality argument in the next section.

This is because you know what 'unicorns' and 'vomit' mean, and you understand that when they are put together as above they yield a sentence that means: Unicorns vomit.

All of this suggests that the sentence 'Unicorns vomit' has the meaning that it does because of its structure and the meanings of 'unicorns' and 'vomit'. Indeed, let us assume—for the sake of argument and idiomatic sentences aside—that the meaning of a sentence is always explained by a combination of the meanings of the words in that sentence and the structure of that sentence.

Let us assume, in other words, that language is *compositional*.[10] The second standard motivation for structured propositions is the claim that language's being compositional somehow leads to structured propositions (see, e.g., Frege, 1914 [1979, 225], 1923 [1977, 55], and undated letter to Jourdain [1980, 78–80]; Cresswell, 1985, 25–7; and Davidson, 2001, 57).

The meaning of a sentence is explained by a combination of the meanings of the words in that sentence and the structure of that sentence. But surely that alone does not—not without further argument—compel us to believe that propositions exist. (If so, I could just exchange Chapter 1 for the claim that language is compositional!) And if language's being compositional does not automatically compel us to believe that there are propositions, then it does not automatically compel us to believe that there are structured propositions.

Of course, one might argue that language's being compositional leads, perhaps surprisingly, to the conclusion that there are propositions, and even to the conclusion that there are structured propositions. With this in mind, consider these remarks from Frege:

[10] My rough characterization of what it is for language to be compositional is good enough for our purposes. But see Szabó (2000) for discussion of the controversies over more precise characterizations—and indeed over whether English and other natural languages really are compositional.

It is remarkable what language can achieve. With a few sounds and combinations of sounds it is capable of expressing a huge number of thoughts [i.e., propositions], and, in particular, thoughts which have not hitherto been grasped or expressed by any man. How can it achieve so much? By virtue of the fact that thoughts have parts out of which they are built up. And these parts, these building blocks, correspond to groups of sounds, out of which the sentence expressing the thought is built up, so that the construction of the sentence out of parts of a sentence corresponds to the construction of a thought out of parts of a thought. And as we take a thought to be the sense of a sentence, so we may call a part of a thought the sense of that part of the sentence which corresponds to it. (1914 [1979, 225])

Frege's remarks suggest two related arguments. Here is the first: A structured proposition's constituents and structure would explain how that proposition manages to represent things as being a certain way. This allows us to explain how the meaning of a sentence's constituent words and its structure result in that sentence's expressing a structured proposition that represents things as being a certain way.[11] And this allows us to explain why language is compositional. Because structured propositions allow us to explain why language is compositional, we should conclude that there are structured propositions.

Here is the second: Language is compositional. So how a sentence represents things as being is explained by that sentence's constituent words (and what they mean) and that

[11] I agree with Frege that if language is compositional, then which proposition a sentence expresses is explained by the meaning of that sentence's constituent words and that sentence's structure. This is because language's being compositional implies that how a sentence represents things as being—and so which proposition that sentence expresses (Ch. 1, §V)—is explained by the meaning of that sentence's constituent words and that sentence's structure. Of course, a sentence expresses a proposition only in a context of use (Ch. 1, §V). Perhaps this implies—in light of our assumption that language is compositional—that a sentence's constituent words have particular meanings, or that a sentence has a given structure, only in a context of use. Or perhaps it implies that my rough characterization of language's being compositional is not good enough after all, and we should expand it to explicitly address contexts of use.

sentence's structure. So how a sentence represents things as being is explained by its constituents and its structure. This coheres elegantly with the claim that how a proposition represents things as being is explained by its constituents and its structure. And a structured proposition's constituents and structure would explain how that proposition manages to represent things as being a certain way. So we should conclude that there are structured propositions.

Many defenders of propositions-as-sets-of-possible-worlds will say that how a proposition (which they take to be a set of possible worlds) represents things as being is explained by that proposition's constituents (that is, its members) and structure (see Ch. 3, §V). So I suspect that many defenders of propositions-as-sets-of-possible-worlds will object that the above two arguments inspired by Frege's remarks do not deliver the conclusion that there are structured propositions, as opposed to propositions-as-sets-of-possible-worlds.

But I am not a defender of the thesis that propositions are sets of possible worlds. So I shall develop a different objection to those above two arguments. Both of those arguments presuppose that a structured proposition's constituents and structure would explain how that proposition manages to represent things as being a certain way. But I shall argue that a structured proposition's constituents and structure would not explain how that proposition manages to represent things as being a certain way (§§VI–X). That argument—assuming it is successful—will undermine both of the above two arguments. And I believe that that argument—assuming it is successful—will block the motivation for structured propositions based on language's being compositional.

V. Structured Propositions and Explaining Representation

Ray Buchanan (2012, 3) says: 'To say that a proposition is structured is to say that it is a complex with constituents, the identity and arrangement of which determine its truth-conditions.' A proposition has its truth conditions because of how it represents things as being (Ch. 1, §IV). So I think that Buchanan would take a structured proposition's representing things as being a certain way to be explained by that proposition's constituents and structure ('arrangement').

David Braun says:

> Our intuitions concerning *aboutness* and *what is said* are among the strongest motivations for the structured proposition theory. The proposition I express by uttering 'Bush is taller than Reagan' is about Bush, and Reagan, and the relation of being-taller-than. The structured proposition view recognizes this in a straightforward way, for on this view, Bush, Reagan, and the relation of being-taller-than are constituents of the proposition I express. Thus *what I say* is *about* those items. But obviously the proposition I express could not be a mere aggregate, or set, consisting of these three items, for if it were, the proposition expressed by 'Bush is taller than Reagan' would be the same as that expressed by 'Reagan is taller than Bush'... The theory of structured propositions holds that there is something more, namely, a *structure*. (1993, 461)

I think that Braun would join Buchanan in taking a structured proposition's constituents and structure to explain how that proposition manages to represent things as being a certain way.

Buchanan and Braun are not alone. All defenders of structured propositions seem to agree that a proposition's constituents and structure explain how that proposition manages to represent things as being a certain way. And belief in an explanation of this sort is the third standard motivation for structured propositions.[12] Indeed, I take belief in this sort of explanation to

[12] Some might say that this third motivation ought to be stated in terms of explaining a proposition's *having certain truth conditions*, as opposed to explaining its *representing things as being a certain way*. But how a proposition represents things as being is prior to its truth conditions (Ch. 1, §IV); so a proposition's constituents and structure would explain that proposition's having certain truth conditions only by way of explaining how that proposition manages to represent things as being a certain way. Besides, my arguments below against the claim that a proposition's

be the main motivation for structured propositions (cf. King, 2007a, 6 and 2011; Jubien, 1991, 266–7; and Salmon, 1989b, 332–3).[13]

Again, defenders of structured propositions agree that a proposition's constituents and structure explain how that proposition manages to represent things as being a certain way. But defenders of structured propositions disagree about whether a proposition's constituents and structure *fully* explain how that proposition manages to represent things as being a certain way. For some have taken structured propositions to represent things as being a certain way at least partly because of the cognitive activity of agents (cf. Ch. 3, §V).

But the view that a proposition represents things as being a certain way because of our cognitive activity can threaten, rather than support, structured propositions. To begin to see why I say this, consider David Lewis's remarks about a view along these lines. Lewis says:

> The ersatzer who presents his worldmaking language must still stipulate how it is interpreted... A real number could serve as a name for itself, but it could equally well serve as a name for itself plus seventeen. I could be my own name, but alternatively I could be yours; or I could be put to some other use in a language, say as a punctuation mark. (1986a, 146)

Suppose that we have interpreted the ordered set <A, *loving*, B> to represent A as loving B. Presumably, and with Lewis's remarks in mind, that is not the only way we could have interpreted that

constituents and structure would explain how that proposition manages to represent things as being a certain way could easily be adjusted to (and in some cases already do) take aim directly at the claim that a proposition's constituents and structure would explain that proposition's having certain truth conditions.

[13] The view that nothing—not their constituents, not their structure, not anything—explains how a structured proposition manages to represent things as being a certain way undercuts the main motivation for structured propositions. So it is no surprise that not a single defender of structured propositions endorses this view. But for reasons that will then be apparent, I shall return to—and raise new objections to—this view in Chapter 6 (§III).

set. I suppose we could have interpreted that set to represent C as hating D. And, for that matter, I suppose we could have also interpreted the ordered set <C, *hating*, D> to represent A as loving B.

These observations illustrate a general point. A proposition's representing things as being a certain way because of how we interpret that proposition has the result that how a proposition represents things as being could fail to be intuitively correlated with that proposition's constituents. But that result threatens structured propositions. For all defenders of structured propositions will insist that at least some of a structured proposition's constituents must be intuitively correlated with how that proposition represents things as being. For example, all defenders of structured propositions will reject the claim that the constituents of *that A loves B* are exactly C, D, and *hating*.

So the claim that a proposition represents things as being a certain way because of how it is interpreted can threaten, rather than support, structured propositions. And some accounts that give our cognitive activity a role in explaining how a proposition manages to represent things as being a certain way really do succumb to this threat, such as the sort of account Lewis has in mind in the passage quoted above.[14]

There is a second potential problem with the claim that each proposition represents things as being a certain way at least in part because of what we do. To begin to see that problem, recall from Chapter 3 (§VII) that believers in propositions routinely assume that if dogs bark, then there is the (true) proposition *that dogs bark*. And if pigs do not fly, then there is the (false) proposition *that pigs fly*. More generally, believers in propositions typically assume both of the following: If things are a

[14] But there are ways to guard against this threat. For example—and as will be clear in Section IX below—the way in which King (2007a, 127–36; 2009) takes a structured proposition's representing things as being a certain way to depend on our cognitive activity is not vulnerable to this threat.

certain way, there is a (true) proposition that is true just in case things are that way. And if things are not a certain way, there is a (false) proposition that is true just in case things are that way.

Pretend for the moment that there is a proposition that represents dogs as barking only because of our cognitive activity. Even so, it is hard to see how our limited cognitive activity could have done its part to deliver, *for every way things are and for every way things are not*, a proposition that is true just in case things are exactly that way. All of this constitutes a second potential problem with the claim that each proposition manages to represent things as being a certain way only because of, at least in part, our cognitive activity.[15]

Let us turn to a third problem with that claim, and to my principal reason for rejecting any account that gives our cognitive activity a role in explaining how a proposition manages to represent things as being a certain way. Pretend that a structured proposition *p* represents things as being a certain way at least in part only because of what we do. Let us add that *p* essentially represents things as being that way. Then it follows that *p* exists only if we engage in the relevant activity. Our engaging in the relevant activity is a contingent matter. So all of this implies that *p* exists contingently. And some defenders of the claim that structured propositions represent things as being a certain way in virtue of our cognitive activity—for example, King (2007a, 128–36)—explicitly endorse this implication.

[15] King (2014, 57–8) argues that he can avoid this second potential problem. In Soames, 2010 (103–7) and in Soames, 2014 (91–124), each proposition is a type whose tokens are mental events. It is not clear to me whether the relevant types have constituents. So it is not clear to me whether Soames's account here is a version of structured propositions. So it is not clear to me that this account is directly relevant to this chapter. But it is still worth noting that Soames (2014, 102–3) agrees that this account has the result that there is not a proposition that, for every way things could be (or even for every way things are), is true just in case things are exactly that way. (He is not bothered by this result, but only because he thinks that a proposition can be true even if it does not exist; I deny that a proposition can be true without existing (see Ch. 5, §VII).)

Again, pretend that a structured proposition *p* represents things as being a certain way at least in part only because of what we do. But let us add that *p* does not exist contingently, but rather necessarily. Even so, our actions are contingent. So all of this implies that *p* does not essentially represent things as being a certain way (cf. Ch. 3, §V). I think that this implication should be accepted by, for example, those who defend the sort of view Lewis discusses above.

Suppose structured propositions represent things as being a certain way at least in part only because of what we do. Then, as we have just seen, either structured propositions exist contingently or structured propositions do not essentially represent things as being a certain way. Either result is unacceptable. This is because propositions exist necessarily (Ch. 1, §IV; Ch. 3, §VII; Ch. 5, §II) and each proposition essentially represents things as being a certain way (Ch. 1, §IV). So I conclude that if there are structured propositions, then how a structured proposition represents things as being is not even partly explained by what we do.[16]

As already noted, it is uncontroversial among defenders of structured propositions that there is an explanation of how each proposition manages to represent things as being a certain way, and that that explanation involves that proposition's

[16] My focus here is on structured propositions. But the argument just given supports the conclusion that no proposition—structured or otherwise—represents things as being a certain way even partly in virtue of what we do. And I suspect that there is no way to explain how a proposition manages to represent things as being a certain way in terms of our cognitive activity without having the result that that proposition represents things as being that way in virtue of how it is related to something else that represents things as being that way. (And this is a result of King's (2007a) and Soames's (2010, 2014) accounts of how a proposition represents things as being a certain way; see Ch. 6, §V.) Suppose my suspicion is correct. Then the claim that a structured proposition represents things as being a certain way partly because of what we do implies that that proposition only derivatively represents things as being that way. This gives us another reason to deny that claim, since propositions fundamentally represent things as being a certain way (Ch. 1, §V).

constituents and structure. The only controversy here, among defenders of structured propositions, is over whether that explanation also involves what we do. I have argued that it does not. So I conclude that if there are structured propositions, then how a structured proposition represents things as being is fully explained by that proposition's constituents and structure.

There are structured propositions only if how a structured proposition represents things as being is fully explained by that proposition's constituents and structure. But—so the rest of this chapter will argue—a structured proposition's constituents and structure would not fully explain how that proposition manages to represent things as being a certain way. This implies that there are no structured propositions. It also blocks the third and main motivation for structured propositions. And it also—see the end of Section IV—blocks the second motivation for structured propositions, which turned on language's being compositional.

VI. Set-Theoretic Accounts of the Unity of the Proposition

David Lewis says:

> If it is central to the role you associate with 'proposition' that there should be some sort of quasi-syntactic structure . . . then sets of worlds will not do. But more complicated set-theoretic constructions . . . can serve instead . . . Corresponding to an atomic predication in which the subject and predicate have as semantic values an individual A and a property P, we have as meaning the pair <A, P>. This is a structured subject-predicate proposition . . . It is true iff the individual A has the property P, otherwise false. (1986a, 57)

Nathan Salmon (1986), Mark Richard (1990, 62–3), M. J. Cresswell (1985), and many others join Lewis in seeming to take structured propositions to be ordered sets. So these many philosophers seem to think a proposition's structure is to be understood set-theoretically. In other words, these many philosophers seem to endorse set-theoretic accounts of the unity of the proposition.

In fact, a quick overview of the literature can make set-theoretic accounts appear to be the orthodoxy among defenders of structured propositions. One could even get the impression that the view that there are structured propositions just is the view that propositions are ordered sets. But we should be careful here. Michael Jubien (2001), Jeffrey King (2011), and Stephen Schiffer (2003, 16) all think that many apparent endorsements of set-theoretic accounts of the unity of the proposition really only endorse the claim that structured propositions can be modeled by sets. (Jubien, King, and Schiffer think this in large part because they find set-theoretic accounts so implausible.)

So perhaps some (or most or all) of the many who seem to endorse set-theoretic accounts of the unity of the proposition are really only endorsing a claim about modeling.[17] So perhaps set-theoretic accounts of the unity of the proposition are not as dominant as they can seem. Even so, our topic is the nature of propositions. So this section will focus on the thesis that a proposition really is a set and that a proposition's constituents really are its members.[18] And I have three objections to that thesis.

[17] Some philosophers—e.g., Almog (1986, 233 n. 18) and Soames (2014, 29–30)—explicitly say both that they use ordered sets to model propositions and also that propositions are not really ordered sets.

[18] For ease of exposition, I shall talk as if set-theoretic accounts of the unity of the proposition imply that the constituents of a proposition are its members. But those accounts can allow the constituents of a proposition to be members of the members (of the members . . .) of that proposition. With this in mind, note that set-theoretic accounts typically take propositions to be ordered sets and also that some take ordered sets to be reduced to non-ordered sets; for example, Kuratowski (1921) proposes reducing <a,b> to {a,{a,b}}. (Unsurprisingly, there are competing alleged reductions of ordered sets to unordered sets, which reinforces my third objection in this section.) None of my objections to set-theoretic accounts turn on their taking a proposition's constituents to be its members, as opposed to the members of its members (etc.).

In Chapter 3 (§V) I objected to the claim that propositions are sets of possible worlds as follows. No set is true. And no set is false. So no set represents things as being a certain way. Because no set is true or false and because no set represents things as being a certain way, no set is a proposition. This same objection applies to the claim that structured propositions are sets. Thus my first objection to set-theoretic accounts of the unity of the proposition.

Put aside my first objection. So suppose that some sets do represent things as being a certain way. If such sets are structured propositions, then how each such set represents things as being must be fully explained by its constituents and structure (§V). That is, how each such set represents things as being must be fully explained by its members and structure. But—and here I repeat another point from Chapter 3 (§V)—no set represents things as being a certain way solely in virtue of its members and structure. This is my second objection to set-theoretic accounts of the unity of the proposition.

Here is a possible reply to this second objection. Take the proposition *that A loves B* to be the set whose members are A, *loving*, B, and a special abstract object, named 'Zip'. That set essentially represents A as loving B. That set does this because of how Zip works. There is no explanation of Zip's working in this way.

This reply takes Zip to have unexplained powers relevant to representation. So this reply should not satisfy defenders of structured propositions. For they believe that there is a full explanation of how each proposition manages to represent things as being a certain way, an explanation in terms of that proposition's constituents and structure. So I set Zip aside. And I stand by my second objection.

Here is my third objection. The ordered set <A, *loving*, B> is neither a better nor a worse candidate for being the proposition *that A loves B* than is, for example, <B, *loving*, A> or <A, B, *loving*>. More generally, there will be many ordered sets that are all equally good candidates to be any given proposition (cf. Bealer, 1998, 6–7; Jubien, 2001; King, 2007a, 7–8; Schiffer, 2003, 16). But the ordered set that is that proposition must be the best candidate for being that proposition. So it is false that any one ordered set is that proposition. A parallel point holds for unordered sets.

Look at it this way. The main motivation for structured propositions is the hope that such a proposition's constituents and structure will explain how that proposition manages to represent things as being a certain way (§V). So two sets are equally good candidates to be (for example) the structured proposition *that A loves B* just in case the structure and members of each such set are equally good at explaining how that set represents A as loving B. The third objection succeeds because there is no set whose structure and members better explain how that set represents (for example) A as loving B than do the structure and members of every other set. (For more on issues relevant to this third objection, see Ch. 3 (§V).)

VII. The Merely Mereological Account of the Unity of the Proposition

Structured propositions are not sets (§VI). Only sets have members. So structured propositions do not have members. So a structured proposition's constituents are not its members. So let us consider the claim that a structured proposition's constituents are its parts. In fact, let us consider the *merely mereological* account of the unity of the proposition, which says that there is no more to the unity of the proposition—and so no more to a proposition's structure—than a proposition's having its constituents as parts.[19]

[19] NB: I use 'mereological' to mean *having to do with parthood*. As I use it, 'mereological' does not suggest—and I most definitely reject (see Merricks,

I think that many defenders of structured propositions would be happy to say that a structured proposition's constituents are its parts. But I do not think that any of them would endorse the merely mereological account. Even so, I am going to raise four objections to that account. For those objections will illustrate that the unity of the proposition demands more than just that the constituents of a given proposition compose (that is, are the parts of) a single entity. Also, displaying the shortcomings of the merely mereological account will motivate states of affairs accounts of the unity of the proposition, to which I shall turn in Section IX.

A human body does not have a truth-value. So a human body does not represent things as being a certain way. So a human body does not represent the cells that compose it as being a certain way. So it does not follow from certain objects' composing some entity that that entity represents those objects (or anything else) as being a certain way.

Suppose—just for the sake of argument—that exactly A, B, and *loving* compose an entity. Again, it does not follow from certain objects' composing some entity that that entity represents those objects as being a certain way. So it does not follow from A, B, and *loving*'s composing an entity that that entity represents A or B or *loving* as being a certain way. So the entity composed of A, B, and *loving* does not represent A as loving B in virtue of its being composed of A and B and *loving*.[20]

Add that there is no more to the structure of that entity than its being composed of A, B, and *loving*. Then that entity does not represent A as loving B in virtue of its structure and parts.

2001)—the particular theory of parthood called 'Mereology' and associated with Leonard and Goodman (1940).

[20] The same would go for the entity composed of exactly *loving* and the Fregean senses of 'A' and 'B'. If you disagree—if you object that Fregean senses would make all the difference here—then you must explain how they would do so. If you protest that there is no such explanation, then your Fregean senses are on a par with Zip (see below).

And so that entity does not represent A as loving B in virtue of its structure and constituents. So that entity is not the structured proposition *that A loves B*. For if the proposition *that A loves B* is a structured proposition, then it represents A as loving B in virtue of its structure and constituents (§V).

Defenders of the merely mereological account cannot enrich the structure of the entity composed of exactly A, *loving*, and B in the hopes of delivering the proposition *that A loves B*. For the merely mereological account of the proposition says that there is no more to a proposition's structure than its having its constituents as parts. Nor would adding further parts to that entity seem to make that entity represent A as loving B in virtue of its structure and parts. But that entity—or something relevantly just like it—is as close as the merely mereological account can get to delivering the structured proposition *that A loves B*. So the merely mereological account cannot deliver that proposition. This is my first objection to the merely mereological account of the proposition.

My first objection turns on the claim that it does not follow merely from certain objects' composing some entity that that entity represents those objects (or anything else) as being a certain way. But some might resist that claim, despite my motivation for it above in terms of a body and its cells. For some might reply that if the part in question is a special object—and not just a cell (or A or *loving*)—then that entity's having that object as a part does imply that that entity represents things as being a certain way.

Let Zip be a special object of the imagined sort. And consider the reply that the entity composed of A, *loving*, B, and Zip essentially represents A as loving B. That entity does this because that is how Zip works. There is no explanation of Zip's working in this way. This reply adds that the object composed of A, *loving*, B, and Zip is the proposition *that A loves B*. And this reply concludes that the merely mereological account can, once armed with Zip, deliver the proposition *that A loves B* after all.

This reply to my first objection endows Zip with unexplained powers relevant to representation. So this reply should not satisfy those who defend structured propositions. For they believe that there is a full explanation of how a proposition manages to represent things as being a certain way, an explanation in terms of that proposition's constituents and structure. So I set Zip aside. And I stand by my first objection.

Given structured propositions, the proposition *that A loves B* has the same constituents as the proposition *that B loves A*. Given the merely mereological account of the unity of the proposition, those constituents are parts. Thus the merely mereological account tells us that *that A loves B* has exactly the same parts as *that B loves A*. Moreover, on the merely mereological account, the parts of *that A loves B* are united in exactly the same way—namely, only by composing something—as are the parts of *that B loves A*.

I think that, for all *x* and for all *y*, if *x* and *y* have exactly the same parts united in exactly the same way, then *x* is identical with *y*.[21] Suppose I am right. Then the merely mereological account of the unity of the proposition implies that the proposition *that A loves B* is identical with the proposition *that B loves A*. But that implication is false. Thus my second objection to the merely mereological account.

Again, suppose that the proposition *that A loves B* has exactly the same parts, united in exactly the same way, as the proposition *that B loves A*. Then *that A loves B* and *that B loves A* are exactly alike with regard to their constituents and structure. If a proposition is structured, then that proposition represents things as being a certain way in virtue of its constituents and

[21] You should agree even if you think that a statue is not identical with, but has all the same parts as, the lump of clay that 'constitutes' that statue. For you should say that those parts compose a statue in virtue of being united in one way but that they compose a lump in virtue of being united in a different way (see Sutton, 2012).

structure (§V). So we get the result that *that A loves B* and *that B loves A* are exactly alike in how they represent things as being. But that result is false. (For example, the former proposition represents A as loving B, but the latter does not.) Thus my third objection to the merely mereological account.

My second and third objections presuppose that—given the merely mereological account of the unity of the proposition—*that A loves B* and *that B loves A* are alike with regard to their structure and parts. Defenders of the merely mereological account cannot deny that they are alike with regard to their structure, since the only structure those defenders countenance for propositions is mereological. But those defenders might try to resist my second and third objections by denying that those two propositions are alike with regard to their parts.

For example, they might say that *that A loves B* has as parts A, *loving*, B, and the empty set; moreover, they might add, *that B loves A* has as parts only A, *loving*, and B. And there are a variety of other ways for them to claim that *that A loves B* fails to have exactly the same parts as *that B loves A*. But I object that any such difference between the parts of *that A loves B* and *that B loves A* would be objectionably arbitrary.

To better understand this objection, recall that the main motivation for structured propositions is the idea that a proposition's constituents and structure explain how that proposition manages to represent things as being a certain way (§V). It is false that the object composed of A, *loving*, B, and the empty set has parts and structure that better explain how that object manages to represent A as loving B than does the object composed of only A, *loving*, and B.

More generally, it is false that the object composed of A, *loving*, B, and some fourth part has parts and structure that better explain how that object manages to represent A as loving B than does every other object. And that is why it is objectionably arbitrary to claim that the object composed of A, *loving*, B, and that fourth part is the proposition *that A loves B*, but no other object is.[22]

My fourth objection presupposes that parthood is transitive. Suppose that the proposition *that A loves B* has A as a constituent. Given the merely mereological account, constituency is parthood. So, given the merely mereological account, the proposition *that A loves B* has A as a part. Since parthood is transitive, the proposition *that A loves B* has every part of A as a part. This includes cell C, which is one of the cells that compose A.

Frege would have found the claim that the proposition *that A loves B* has cell C as a part to be absurd on its face.[23] I do not. Even so, there is a problem with that claim given the merely mereological account of the unity of the proposition. For a structured proposition is supposed to represent things as being a certain way in virtue of its constituents and structure (§V). Given the merely mereological account of the proposition, this implies that *that A loves B* represents things as being a certain way in virtue of having as parts those entities that it does have as parts. But then it is hard to see how that proposition could represent A as being a certain way—which it is supposed to do simply in virtue of having A as a part—but not also

[22] Perhaps you think that *that A loves B* is composed of A, *loving*, B, and, for example, the state of affairs of *A's loving*. But this state of affairs is no better at leading to the relevant explanation than is the state of affairs of *B's being loved*. Moreover, *B's being loved* would not exist if no one loved B; nor would *A's loving* exist if A loved no one. But surely it must be possible for the proposition *that A loves B* to exist (and be false) even if A is unloving and B unloved.

[23] See Frege's undated letter to Jourdain [1980, 79]. In that letter, Frege takes constituency to be parthood, and parthood to be transitive. And he takes examples like the one just noted in the text to show that material objects are not the constituents of propositions. Others draw different morals from the same sort of example. For example, Hawthorne and Manley (2012, 14–15) assert that this sort of example shows that constituency is not parthood, and Gilmore (2014) takes this sort of example to call for a revision in our understanding of parthood. But I think that examples like the one in the text show only that the merely mereological account of the unity of the proposition is problematic (and also—see Ch. 5, §I—that *direct aboutness* cannot be analyzed as constituency).

represent cell C as being a certain way—which it is not supposed to do at all (cf. Keller, 2013). This is my fourth objection to the merely mereological account, at least to versions of it that allow constituents of propositions to have parts.[24]

Some might respond that the proposition *that A loves B* does represent cell C as being a certain way. For example, they might respond that it represents cell C as being a part of someone who loves B. I find their response implausible. Moreover, suppose, for reductio, that their response is correct. Cell C is contingently a part of A. So cell C is contingently a part of *that A loves B*. The proposition *that A loves B* would not have represented cell C as being any way at all if cell C had not been a part of that proposition. So the proposition *that A loves B* contingently represents cell C as being a certain way. But if a proposition represents things as being a certain way, then that proposition essentially represents things as being that way (see Ch. 1, §IV). So our assumption for reductio is false.

I have raised four objections to the merely mereological account of the unity of the proposition. Those objections show that the merely mereological account of the unity of the proposition has unacceptable implications for the proposition *that A loves B*. So that account is itself unacceptable.

Those four objections can easily be adapted to show that the merely mereological account has unacceptable implications for a variety of other propositions as well. The first objection can show this for all propositions. The second and third can show this for any two or more structured propositions that would have exactly the same constituents, such as, for example, *that A is to the left of B* and *that B is to the left of A*. The fourth can show this for any structured proposition that would have

[24] One natural, but mistaken, reply to this fourth objection is to say that a structured proposition represents things as being a certain way only because of its parts *that are not themselves parts of parts of that proposition*. To see that this is mistaken, consider the proposition *that cell C is a part of A*.

constituents that have parts, and which does not represent those parts as being a certain way. Because of these four objections, I reject the merely mereological account of the unity of the proposition.

VIII. More on Logical Form

The merely mereological account of the unity of the proposition fails (§VII). The set-theoretic account also fails (§VI). So one might be tempted to say that a proposition's constituents are neither parts nor members of that proposition. With this in mind, consider the following speech:

> Propositions have logical form. And I define 'structure' and 'constituents' in terms of the logical form of propositions. First, I count logical form as a kind of structure. So it is trivial that if a proposition has logical form, then it has structure. Second, it is trivial that if a proposition has logical form, then it has constituents. For example, suppose that proposition *p* has the logical form *q or r*. Then *p* thereby has *q* and *r* as constituents.

I think that George Bealer would endorse this speech. At any rate, the view affirmed in this speech is largely inspired by his work (see, e.g., Bealer, 1998). And the view affirmed in this speech is one we should take seriously.

But the view affirmed in this speech is not a version of what I am calling structured propositions. Again, the view affirmed in this speech is not the sort of view described at the end of Section II. Relatedly, the 'constituents' of the view affirmed in this speech are not the sort of constituents associated with (what I am calling) structured propositions. For the 'constituents' mentioned in this speech do not need to be united to result in a proposition. So the view endorsed in this speech does need an answer to the question of the unity of the proposition. (Thus this speech does not contain an answer to the question of the unity of the proposition.)

Because the view affirmed in this speech is not a version of (what I am calling) structured propositions, the arguments I give in this chapter and Chapter 5 against structured propositions do not touch the view affirmed in this speech. Nevertheless, I do reject that view. And I do have arguments against it. They are the arguments of Chapter 2 (§§II–III and §VIII), arguments for the conclusion that propositions do not have logical form.

IX. States of Affairs Accounts of the Unity of the Proposition

Scott Soames says:

> Propositions are, I think, best conceived as abstract, structured complexes, the constituents of which are objects and (n-place) properties. To say that certain constituents make up a complex is to say that, in the complex, the constituents stand in certain relations to one another. The complex is, in effect, *the standing of the constituents in those relations*. So, a proposition is an entity in which its constituent parts stand in certain relations to one another . . . for example . . . the proposition that Fido is brown is a complex entity in which *Fido and the property of being brown stand in a certain relation R*. (2008, 326; emphasis added)

Soames's 'complexes' are our states of affairs. So Soames (in his 2008) takes propositions to be states of affairs.[25]

Let R be the sentential relation that relates 'Rebecca' to 'swims' so that 'Rebecca' and 'swims' make up the sentence 'Rebecca swims'. And let R* be the relation that relates the

[25] Soames only briefly sketches his 2008 account of propositions, and seems to set it aside fairly quickly, endorsing a different account in his 2010 and 2014. Even so, I am focusing on his 2008 account in this section. This is because that account is clearly an account according to which propositions are states of affairs, and so nicely illustrates the approach to the unity of the proposition considered in this section.

semantic values of any lexical items that are themselves related by R. For example, suppose Rebecca is the semantic value of 'Rebecca' and the property *swimming* is the semantic value of 'swims'. Then—because 'Rebecca' is related by R to 'swims'—Rebecca herself is related by R* to the property *swimming*. Jeffrey King (2007a, 29ff.) takes the proposition *that Rebecca swims* to be the state of affairs of Rebecca's being related by R* to *swimming*.[26] More generally, King (2007a) takes propositions to be states of affairs.

The state of affairs of Rebecca's being related by R* to *swimming* exists even if the sentence 'Rebecca swims' is false. So King can say that the proposition *that Rebecca swims* exists even if that proposition is false. So King can accommodate false propositions. So can Soames. In this way (and obviously to their credit) King and Soames differ from Russell 1903, despite their joining Russell 1903 in taking propositions to be states of affairs.

Let R_3 be the three-part sentential relation that relates (in this order) 'A' to 'loves' to 'B' so that those terms constitute the sentence 'A loves B'. R_3 is also the relation that relates (in this order) 'B' to 'loves' to 'A' so that they constitute the sentence 'B loves A'. And let R_3* be the relation that relates the semantic values of any lexical items that are related by R_3. On King's account, *that A loves B* is the state of affairs of R_3*'s relating (in this order) A to *loving* to B; and *that B loves A* is the numerically distinct state of affairs of R_3*'s relating (in this order) B to *loving* to A (cf. King 2007a, 122–3).

So, given King's account, the proposition *that A loves B* has the same constituents as the proposition *that B loves A*: A, B, *loving*, and R_3*. But those propositions differ in how they are structured. In particular, they differ in the order in which A, B,

[26] More carefully, the state of affairs of Rebecca's being related by R* to *swimming* is King's first approximation of his official account of the proposition *that Rebecca swims*. But both King's first approximation and his more complicated official account take propositions to be states of affairs, which is what matters here.

and *loving* are related by R_3^*. This illustrates how states of affairs accounts of the unity of the proposition—unlike the merely mereological account—can accommodate distinct propositions that have the same constituents. It also illustrates the way in which states of affairs accounts are immune to analogues of my second and third objections to the merely mereological account (§VII).

Suppose that A is related by R* (in this order) to *loving* to B. It does not follow that cell C is related by R* (in any order) to *loving* to B, not even if cell C is a part of A. This illustrates how states of affairs accounts of the unity of the proposition are immune to analogues of my fourth objection to the merely mereological account (§VII). And it illustrates that states of affairs accounts are thus immune even if the constituents of a state of affairs are its parts and parthood is transitive.

But I think that states of affairs accounts are vulnerable to an analogue of my first objection to the merely mereological account. For starters, consider the state of affairs of a certain flowerpot's being blue. That state of affairs does not represent that flowerpot (or anything else) as being a certain way. In particular, that state of affairs does not represent that flowerpot as being a certain way *solely in virtue of that state of affairs's constituents and structure*. And so it goes—it seems to me—for all states of affairs, or at least for those alleged to be propositions.[27]

[27] If there are states of affairs, then there are mental states of affairs, including the state of affairs of an agent's believing that things are a certain way. You might think that that state of affairs—that mental event—represents things as being a certain way solely in virtue of its constituents and structure. (Soames (in his 2010 and 2014) seems to claim that mental events do thus represent; see Ch. 6 (§V) for discussion.) But no one would allege that such a state of affairs—itself a token mental event—is a proposition. That is why I said in the text that states of affairs that are *alleged to be propositions* do not seem to represent things as being a certain way solely in virtue of their constituents and structure.

Soames and King deny that a proposition represents things as being a certain way solely in virtue of that proposition's constituents and structure. So Soames and King deny that any state of affairs that is a proposition represents things as being a certain way solely in virtue of its constituents and structure. For example, Soames follows up the passage quoted above with the following:

How does it come about that this entity—Fido's standing in R to this property—*represents* Fido as being brown? The answer, I suggest, rests not on anything intrinsic to R itself, but on the interpretation we agents place on R. Our use of R is such that for Fido and the property *being brown* to stand in R is for Fido to be represented as being brown. Similarly for other cases. (2008, 326)

And consider King's idea that the proposition *that Rebecca swims* is the state of affairs of Rebecca's being related by R* to *swimming*. According to King, that state of affairs (exists and) represents Rebecca as swimming only because of linguistic conventions. In particular, that state of affairs (exists and) represents Rebecca as swimming only because of conventions to the effect that if 'Rebecca' is related by R to 'swims', then we get a sentence that represents Rebecca as swimming. These conventions are the result of the contingent cognitive activity of agents (see King, 2007a, 136).

As we saw in Section II, the Russell of 1903 could deny that a proposition represents things as being a certain way. And if a proposition fails to represent things as being a certain way, then it fails to represent things as being a certain way in virtue of its constituents and structure. For this reason, I think that the Russell of 1903 would join Soames and King in denying that a state of affairs that is a proposition represents things as being a certain way solely in virtue of its constituents and structure.

The above leading defenders of propositions-as-states-of-affairs would agree that no state of affairs is both a proposition and also represents things as being a certain way solely in virtue of its constituents and structure. I think they are correct. But, contra those leading defenders, I think that this shows that states of affairs accounts of the unity of the proposition fail. For I add that there are structured propositions only if a proposition's constituents and structure would yield a full explanation of how that proposition manages to represent things as being a certain way (§V).

Some might reply that whenever there is the state of affairs of an object's being related by *Zipping* to a property, then that state of affairs essentially represents that object as having that property. Nothing explains why *Zipping* works this way. That is just how *Zipping* works. And neither *Zipping*'s existence nor its holding between O and F depends on anything that agents do. This reply concludes that the proposition *that O is F* is the state of affairs of O's being related by *Zipping* to F.

This reply takes *Zipping* itself to have unexplained powers relevant to representation. So this reply, as far as explaining representation goes, is no better than the earlier Zip-based attempts to save the set-theoretic (§VI) and the merely mereological accounts of the unity of the proposition (§VII). So this reply should not satisfy defenders of structured propositions. For they believe that there is a full explanation of how each proposition manages to represent things as being a certain way, an explanation in terms of that proposition's constituents and structure. So I set *Zipping* aside.[28]

[28] Mark Johnston seems to endorse a *Zipping*-based account of the unity of the proposition, although he calls the relation in question 'predication', rather than (the admittedly unflattering) '*Zipping*'. Johnston says:

...we can identify the proposition that *a* is *F* as the predication of *F*-ness of *a*. We may think of that as a complex item built up from F-ness and a, by way of the relation of being predicated of...So what it is for the proposition that Aristotle liked dogs to exist is for liking dogs to be *predicated* of Aristotle...The obvious hitch is that the predication of *F*-ness of *a* may seem to be just the act of judging that *a* is *F*. But the objectivist must deny this...when I perform an act of predicating *F*-ness of some individual *a*, I thereby relate myself in judgment to an objective entity, the predication of *F*-ness of *a*. I judge true the predication of

There are structured propositions only if a proposition's constituents and structure fully explain how that proposition manages to represent things as being a certain way (§V). I do not think that any state of affairs that is alleged to be a proposition is such that its constituents and structure fully explain how that state of affairs manages to represent things as being a certain way. So I reject states of affairs accounts of the unity of the proposition.

X. Objections to Structured Propositions

Many philosophers think that there is a set whose members are exactly A and B and *loving*. Many philosophers think that there is an object composed of exactly A and B and *loving* (and their parts). And many philosophers think that, as long as some relation relates A and B and *loving*, there is the state of affairs of A and B and *loving* being thus related. Indeed, it is comparatively easy to articulate a theory that implies that A, B, and *loving* are united into a single entity, an entity such as a set, a whole, or a state of affairs.

But to complete this easy task is not to give a satisfactory account of the unity of the proposition, not even just for the proposition *that A loves B* (cf. King, 2009; Soames, 2010, 106–7). This is because a successful account of the unity of the proposition tells us what unites the relevant constituents not merely into some entity or other, but into a proposition. That is, it tells us what unites the relevant constituents into a necessarily existing entity that essentially represents things as being a certain way (Ch. 1, §IV). Moreover, given a successful account, those constituents together with the way in which they are united fully explain how that resulting entity manages to represent things as being that way (§V). In light

F-ness of *a*. But this predication of *F*-ness of *a* is just the proposition that *a* has *F*-ness. (2006, 684–5)

of the arguments of this chapter, I conclude that there is no successful account of the unity of the proposition.

I also conclude, more specifically, that there is no way to unite the constituents of a proposition so that the resulting structured proposition's constituents and structure would explain how that proposition manages to represent things as being a certain way. So structured propositions are not actually motivated by their supposed main motivation (§V) (or by language's being compositional (§IV)). Moreover, and more importantly, there are no structured propositions. For if there were, then each structured proposition's constituents and structure would explain how it manages to represent things as being a certain way (§V).

XI. Conclusion

This chapter has argued that the standard motivations for structured propositions fail. And this chapter has argued that if there are structured propositions, then how a proposition represents things as being is fully explained by that proposition's constituents and structure. But this chapter has also argued that a structured proposition's constituents and structure would not fully explain how that proposition manages to represent things as being a certain way. So this chapter concludes that there are no structured propositions. And Chapter 5 will present further arguments against (the most widely defended versions of) structured propositions.

5

SINGULAR PROPOSITIONS

CHAPTER 4 argued that structured propositions are unmotivated. More importantly, it argued that there are no structured propositions. This chapter will prosecute further objections to structured propositions. In particular, this chapter objects to the most widely defended versions of structured propositions, which claim that a *singular proposition* about an entity has that entity as a constituent.

I. The Received View

I deny that names are definite descriptions. And I deny that a name refers to an entity in virtue of expressing a property that that entity happens to have. Rather, I think that when a name refers to an entity, that name refers to that entity *directly* (cf. Plantinga, 1974, 137–44; Kripke, 1980, 22–70). So a sentence that uses a name is a sentence that is *directly about* the named entity (cf. Adams, 1981, 12; Plantinga, 1983, 2–3; Kaplan, 1989, 483).

A sentence represents things as being a certain way in virtue of expressing a proposition that represents things as being that way (Ch. 1, §V). So a sentence that is directly about an entity is directly about that entity in virtue of expressing a proposition that is itself directly about that entity (cf. §VII). So a proposition can be directly about an entity. Let a *singular proposition* be a proposition that is directly about an entity.[1]

The received view about singular propositions is that each singular proposition has the relevant entity—the entity that that proposition is directly about—as a constituent. In this chapter I shall argue that the received view is false. That is, I shall argue that a singular proposition does not have the relevant entity as a constituent. But before arguing for the falsity of the received view, I shall show that the received view is not trivial. I shall show this because the view that a singular proposition has the relevant entity as a constituent can be made to seem trivial. And no trivial view is false.

Some define 'singular proposition' as a proposition that has the relevant entity as a constituent (see, e.g., Crimmins and Perry, 1989; Jeshion, 2002; Armstrong and Stanley, 2011; and Fitch and Nelson, 2013). And of course it is trivial that a proposition that has an entity as a constituent has that entity as a constituent. Thus we have one way that the received view itself can seem to be trivial.

I do not define 'singular proposition' as a proposition that has the relevant entity as a constituent. Rather, and as already noted, I define 'singular proposition' as a proposition that is directly about an entity. And this definition of 'singular proposition' is widespread, endorsed by, among others, Alvin Plantinga (1979, 109), Robert Adams (1981, 6–7; 1986, 315), David Kaplan (1989, 483), Richard Cartwright (1998, 73), and Kit Fine (2007, 54).

But the point here is not that my definition of 'singular proposition' is better (or worse) or more (or less) widespread

[1] I believe that there are singular propositions. So do my targets in this chapter. But neo-Fregeans do not. For neo-Fregeans will say that a proposition expressed by a sentence using a name is not directly about the named entity, but rather about that entity via the sense of that name. They will presumably add that no proposition is directly about an entity. (Cf. Kaplan, 1989, 483.)

than the alternative definition in terms of having the relevant entity as a constituent. Rather, the point here is that given what I mean by 'singular proposition', it is not trivial that a singular proposition has the relevant entity as a constituent. For I say that it is not trivial that a proposition that is directly about an entity has that entity as a constituent. Thus I say that the received view itself is not trivial.

This is what I say. But some will still maintain that—even given what I mean by 'singular proposition'—the received view is trivial. For some define a proposition's being 'directly about' an entity as that proposition's having that entity as a constituent (see, e.g., Salmon, 2007 and Armstrong and Stanley, 2011). And given this definition of 'directly about', the sentence 'A proposition directly about an entity has that entity as a constituent' asserts the triviality that a proposition that has an entity as a constituent has that entity as a constituent.

But there are three reasons that defenders of the received view, in particular, should not define 'directly about' as *has as a constituent*. The first reason presupposes that constituency is parthood and that parthood is transitive.[2] The proposition *that A loves B* is directly about A. So the received view implies that A is a constituent of that proposition. Constituency is parthood. So the received view implies that A is a part of that proposition. Parthood is transitive. So the received view implies that each part of A, including cell C, is a part—that is, a constituent—of that proposition. So the received view implies that cell C is a constituent of that proposition (cf. Ch. 4, §VII).

If 'directly about' means *has as a constituent*, then the received view implies that the proposition *that A loves B* is directly about

[2] To say that constituency is parthood is not to endorse the merely mereological account of the unity of the proposition (Ch. 4, §VII). It is instead to say that—whatever else may unite the constituents of a proposition or be included in a proposition's structure—to be a constituent of a proposition just is to be a part of that proposition. (The literature on structured propositions standardly takes constituency to be parthood or set membership; for more on this, see §III.)

cell C. In other words, the received view implies that *that A loves B* is a singular proposition about cell C. But that implication is false. So if 'directly about' means *has as a constituent*, then the received view has a false implication. This is the first reason that defenders of the received view should deny that 'directly about' means *has as a constituent*.

No one who defends the received view believes that only singular propositions have constituents or that the only constituent of a singular proposition is the entity that that proposition is directly about. Rather, every defender of the received view also defends structured propositions more generally. So defenders of the received view all hold that every proposition has constituents. So if 'directly about' means *has as a constituent*, defenders of the received view must say that every proposition is *directly about* some entities or others. That is, they must say that every proposition is a singular proposition. But surely that result will not please defenders of the received view. This is the second reason that defenders of the received view should deny that 'directly about' means *has as a constituent*.

To begin to understand the third and final reason that defenders of the received view should deny that 'directly about' means *has as a constituent*, recall that structured propositions are motivated by the claim that a structured proposition's constituents and structure explain how that proposition manages to represent things as being a certain way (Ch. 4, §V). A proposition's being directly about an entity is partly a matter of its representing that entity (as opposed to some other entity) as being one way or another (more on this in §VII). So defenders of the received view should say that a proposition's being directly about an entity is at least partly explained by its having that entity as a constituent.

And this is just what they typically do say. For example, here is King:

I think that propositions *do* have constituents. This is mainly because I find the idea of 'simple fine grained propositions', fine grained propositions without constituents or parts, mysterious. What would make such a simple proposition be about, say, Paris, as opposed to Santa Monica? In virtue of what would it have the truth conditions it in fact enjoys? I cannot see that these questions have answers if propositions are held to be simple and fine grained. But it seems to me they should have answers. (2007a, 6)

King then immediately endorses the received view (2007a, 6–7), making it clear that he thinks that a proposition's having Paris as a constituent explains why that proposition is directly about Paris.[3]

So defenders of the received view should say that a singular proposition's having an entity as a constituent at least partly explains how that proposition manages to be directly about that entity. But they cannot sensibly say this if 'directly about' is defined as *has as a constituent*. For it is not sensible to say that a singular proposition's having an entity as a constituent at least partly explains how that proposition manages to have that entity as a constituent.

For the above three reasons, defenders of the received view should not define 'directly about' as *has as a constituent*. For these same three reasons—and assuming we all want to be as fair as possible to the received view—no one should define 'directly about' in this way. Rather, a proposition's being directly about an entity should be understood as analogous to a sentence that uses a name's being directly about the named entity. That is, to be directly about an entity is to be about that entity, but not in virtue of how that entity is 'given' (Fine, 2007, 54), and not in virtue of that entity's having this or that

[3] King says that the proposition in question is about Paris, but does not say explicitly that it is directly about Paris. But if that proposition were only indirectly about Paris—if it were, say, the proposition *that the southernmost city lived in by Pierre includes the Eiffel Tower*—King would not take it to have Paris itself as a constituent.

property (cf. Plantinga, 1979, 109; Adams, 1981, 6–7 and 1986, 315; Cartwright, 1998, 73).

It is not trivial that a singular proposition—given my definition of 'singular proposition'—has the relevant entity as a constituent. Again, it is not trivial that if a proposition is directly about an entity, then that entity is a constituent of that proposition. Again, it is not trivial that if a proposition is about an entity, but not in virtue of that entity's having this or that property, then that entity is a constituent of that proposition. Again, it is not trivial that when a sentence using a name expresses a proposition, then that proposition has the named entity as a constituent.

The received view is substantive. And it is false. I say this because of the arguments in this chapter against the received view. Those arguments are thereby arguments against any thesis that is committed to the received view. The most widely defended versions of structured propositions are neo-Russellian and are thus committed to the received view.[4] Hence this chapter presents arguments against the most widely defended versions of structured propositions, arguments in addition to those presented in Chapter 4.

II. Propositions Exist Necessarily

The proposition *that A loves B* represents A as loving B, and does so in a particular way, being directly about A (and, for that matter, being directly about B). Defenders of the received view

[4] Thus the received view's defenders include Kaplan (1975; 1989), Salmon (1986, 1), Lewis (1986a, 57ff.), Soames (1987), Braun (1993), and King (2007a, 76). Moreover, Russell (1903; 1904b; 1910–11)—a mere proto-neo-Russellian—consistently endorsed the received view, even while changing his mind about the sort of singular propositions we can grasp. (In 1903 and 1904b, Russell thought that we grasp singular propositions about Mont Blanc and other familiar objects; by 1910–11, he thought that the only singular propositions we grasp are about sense data.)

will insist that *that A loves B* must have A as a constituent in order to thus represent A as loving B. If a proposition represents things as being a certain way, then that proposition essentially represents things as being that way (Ch. 1, §IV). So I take the received view to imply that *that A loves B* has A as a constituent essentially.[5]

A proposition has certain constituents only if those constituents exist (see §VII). So if a proposition essentially has a contingently existing constituent, then that proposition itself exists contingently. Given the received view, the proposition *that A loves B* essentially has a contingently existing constituent, A (and, for that matter, B). So, given the received view, the proposition *that A loves B* exists contingently. More generally, the received view has the result that no proposition directly about a contingently existing entity exists necessarily.

This result should not be surprising. For defenders of the received view regularly insist that singular propositions about contingently existing entities do not exist necessarily (see, e.g., Pollock, 1985, 134–40; Salmon, 1987, 95; Soames, 2008, 319; Armstrong and Stanley, 2011). Even the ancient Stoics seem to have thought that if a proposition is directly about a contingently existing entity, then that proposition itself exists contingently (Bobzien, 2006).

So I have argued—and everyone seems to agree—that if the received view is true, then singular propositions about contingently existing entities do not exist necessarily. But, as I argued in Chapter 1 (§IV) and Chapter 3 (§VII), all propositions exist necessarily. Those arguments are my first reason for concluding that singular propositions about contingently existing entities exist necessarily. And this conclusion implies that the received view is false.

[5] I do not think that defenders of the received view must say that *that A loves B* has all its constituents essentially. Let cell C be a part of A. Defenders of the received view can claim that *that A loves B* has C as a constituent, but only contingently, since it is possible for A to exist without having C as a part.

I have a second reason for concluding that (at least some) singular propositions about contingently existing entities exist necessarily. That second reason begins by considering sentences that are themselves logically valid. This includes, for example, sentences that have the logical form *P or ~P* and *if P, then P*. Any argument that has a logically valid sentence as its conclusion will be a logically valid argument, regardless of which (proposition-expressing) sentences are its premises.

Every logically valid argument expresses a modally valid argument (Ch. 2, §IV). So any argument that has a logically valid sentence as its conclusion will express a modally valid argument, regardless of which (proposition-expressing) sentences are the premises of that logically valid argument, and so regardless of which propositions are the premises of that modally valid argument. So an argument that is logically valid in virtue of having a logically valid conclusion will express an argument that is modally valid, and is modally valid in virtue of its conclusion. An argument is modally valid just in case, necessarily, if its premises are true, then its conclusion is true (Ch. 1, §I). So the only sort of conclusion that, on its own, renders an argument modally valid is a necessarily true conclusion. So I conclude that logically valid sentences express necessarily true propositions.[6]

Consider the following sentence about an arbitrarily chosen contingently existing individual, Paul Hewson: 'Hewson exists or it is not the case that Hewson exists'. That sentence has the

[6] For reasons that are defended in Chapter 1 (§III), my conclusion here is not that logically valid sentences express propositions that are true *at* all possible worlds; it is, again, that logically valid sentences express necessarily true propositions.

Some analytic sentences express contingently true propositions, such as, for example, the sentence '"Snow is white" is true if and only if snow is white' (Ch. 1, § V). So—since all logically valid sentences express necessarily true propositions—we get the result that not all analytic sentences are logically valid. This same result was arrived at back in Chapter 2 (§III), but by a different route.

logical form *P or ~P*. So that sentence is logically valid. Logically valid sentences express necessarily true propositions. So the proposition that that sentence expresses is necessarily true. Necessarily, if a proposition is true, then that proposition exists (see §VII). So the proposition that that sentence expresses exists necessarily.

A sentence that uses a name expresses a singular proposition about the named entity (§I). So the sentence 'Hewson exists or it is not the case that Hewson exists' expresses a singular proposition about Hewson, who exists contingently. We have just seen that the proposition expressed by that sentence exists necessarily. So the sentence 'Hewson exists or it is not the case that Hewson exists' expresses a necessarily existing singular proposition about a contingently existing entity. So there is a necessarily existing singular proposition about a contingently existing entity.

The argument just given can easily be adapted to show that every logically valid sentence expresses a necessarily existing proposition. Thus this argument gives us a new reason to conclude that (at least many) propositions exist necessarily, a reason in addition to those of Chapters 1 (§IV) and 3 (§VII).

Moreover, and of particular interest in this chapter, this argument shows that every logically valid sentence that uses the name of a contingently existing entity expresses a necessarily existing singular proposition about that entity. For example, this argument shows not only that the sentence 'Hewson exists or it is not the case that Hewson exists' expresses a necessarily existing singular proposition about a contingently existing entity, but also that the sentence 'If Hewson exists, then Hewson exists' does as well. Thus this argument is my second reason for concluding that (at least some) singular propositions about contingently existing entities exist necessarily. And this conclusion implies that the received view is false.

III. Singular Propositions about Singular Propositions

Let 'Fred' be the name of the proposition *that 2+2=4*. Then the sentence 'Fred is true' expresses a singular proposition about *that 2+2=4*. Therefore, *that Fred is true* is a singular proposition about *that 2+2=4*. This illustrates that there are singular propositions about propositions. So there is some proposition *p* and some other proposition *q* such that *p* is a singular proposition about *q*.

Moreover, there is some proposition *p* and some other proposition *q* such that *p* is a singular proposition about *q* and *q* is a singular proposition about *p*. Here is one example. Jane uses the description 'the proposition that John entertains at *t*' to fix the reference of '*p*'. She then goes on to entertain, at *t*, the proposition *that p is true*. And John uses the description 'the proposition that Jane entertains at *t*' to fix the reference of '*q*'. He then goes on to entertain, at *t*, *that q is true*.[7]

Here is another example. Jane uses 'the first proposition expressed by John on Tuesday' to fix the reference of '*p*'. John uses 'the first proposition denied by Jane on Monday' to fix the reference of '*q*'. First thing Monday, Jane denies the proposition *that John's evidence justifies p*. First thing Tuesday, John expresses the proposition *that q is about cats*. Again, *p* is a singular proposition about *q*, and *q* is a singular proposition about *p*.

So there is some proposition *p* and some numerically distinct proposition *q* such that *p* is a singular proposition about *q* and *q* is a singular proposition about *p*. Assume that constituency is parthood. Then the received view implies that for some proposition *p* and some numerically distinct proposition *q*: *q* is a part

[7] Compare: 'Lincoln' does not mean the sixteenth president of the United States, not even if that description fixes the reference of 'Lincoln'. The idea that descriptions can fix the reference of a name, but are not the meaning of that name, can be found in Plantinga (1974, 38–9) and Kripke (1980, 55), among others.

of p and p is a part of q. But this implication is false. It is false because the following principle about parthood is true:

The Antisymmetry of Parthood: $(x)(y)$ If x is part of y and y is a part of x, then $x = y$.

Because the received view has the false implication just noted, the received view itself is false.

The argument just given turns on the Antisymmetry of Parthood. This principle is widely endorsed. But not universally. Some hold that a statue S is not identical with the lump of clay L that 'constitutes' that statue. Moreover, some even add that—though S is not identical with L—L is a part of S and S is a part of L (see, e.g., Thomson, 1998). Those who add this will reject the Antisymmetry of Parthood.

Those who reject the Antisymmetry of Parthood do so because they believe that there are cases of two numerically distinct objects that *wholly overlap* and are parts of each other. Even those who reject the Antisymmetry of Parthood would find the following case absurd: Lump of clay L* constitutes the bottom half of S, and so does not wholly overlap S; L* is not identical with S; L* is a part of S; *and S is a part of L**.

With this in mind, recall the example in which q is the proposition *that John's evidence justifies p* and p is the proposition *that q is about cats*. Given the received view, q is a part of p and p is a part of q. But, even given the received view, p has parts that q does not have and q has parts that p does not have. For example, given the received view, q has John himself as a part but p does not. So the received view implies that p and q are not identical and are parts of each other even though p and q *do not wholly overlap*. I say that the received view is no better than the absurd case of S and L*.

Someone might object as follows: Parthood is transitive. So all of q's parts are also parts of p, and so p has John himself as a part. More generally, the transitivity of parthood and the received view imply that p and q, in virtue of being parts of each other, have all the same parts. So *p* and *q* wholly overlap after all. So the case of *p* and *q* is no worse than the original case of the statue and lump as described by the foes of the Antisymmetry of Parthood, that is, the case of S and L.

This objection is mistaken. To begin to see why, return to the absurd case of S and L*: lump L* constitutes the bottom half of S; L* is not identical with S; L* is a part of S; *and S is a part of L**. The transitivity of parthood implies that S and L* have all the same parts—recall the claim that S is a part of L*—and so wholly overlap. But this does not show that the case of S and L* is no worse than the case of S and L. Instead, it shows that the case of S and L* leads to contradiction: S and L* have all the same parts (because parthood is transitive) and it is not the case that S and L* have all the same parts (because L* constitutes only the bottom half of S).

Proposition *p* is *that q is about cats* and proposition *q* is *that John's evidence justifies p*. Those two propositions differ in how they represent things as being. And defenders of the received view—being defenders of structured propositions—should insist that that difference is partly explained by those two propositions' having different parts. Parthood's being transitive does not undermine this point. Instead, parthood's being transitive shows that the received view leads to contradiction: *p* and *q* have all the same parts and it is not the case that *p* and *q* have all the same parts.

I believe the Antisymmetry of Parthood. So I stand by the original version of the above argument against the received view that traded directly on that principle. But even those who reject the Antisymmetry of Parthood ought to endorse a version of that above argument. For even they ought to agree that if two objects do not wholly overlap, then those objects are not parts of each other. And the received view implies that *that John's evidence justifies p* and *that q is about cats* do not wholly overlap and are parts of each other. So all of us—friends and foes of the Antisymmetry of Parthood alike—ought to reject the received view.

This section's argument against the received view has assumed that constituency is parthood. But some might deny that constituency is parthood. They might claim, instead, that constituency is set membership (see Ch. 4, §VI). But then the received view implies—see the above examples—that for some proposition *p* and some numerically distinct proposition *q*: *q* is a member of *p* and *p* is a member of *q*. Then *p* is a member of a member of itself. And so is *q*. But *p* cannot be a member of a member of itself. Nor can *q*. At least, as already noted in Chapter 3 (§VII), the Axiom of Regularity implies that no set is a member of a member of itself.

The literature on structured propositions takes constituency to be either parthood or set membership. And I cannot see what else a structured proposition's constituents could be, if not its parts or its members.[8] So I conclude that the received view implies that two numerically distinct propositions can either be parts of each other or be members of each other. Either way—and in light of this section's arguments—the received view is in serious trouble. So I conclude that the received view is false.

[8] More carefully, I cannot see what else a structured proposition's constituents could be if not its members, the members of its members (of its members . . .), its parts, the parts of its parts (of its parts . . .) (if parthood is transitive, this is just its parts), or some combination of these (such as a member of a member of one of its parts). The arguments in this section can easily be adapted to 'constituents' understood in any of these ways.

Some who defend a 'constituent ontology' might claim that a proposition's structure is itself a constituent—but not a part or a member (or a member of a part . . .)—of that proposition. That is beside the point. For no defender of the received view thinks that the individual that a singular proposition is directly about is itself that proposition's structure. Rather, all should agree that that individual is a part or a member (or a member of a part . . .) of that proposition.

IV. Singular Propositions about Individuals that No Longer Exist

Abraham Lincoln no longer exists. This leads to another argument against the received view:

(1) Lincoln does not exist.
(2) If Lincoln does not exist, then the proposition *that Lincoln does not exist* is true.
(3) The proposition *that Lincoln does not exist* is true. (1, 2)
(4) If a proposition is true, then that proposition exists.
(5) The proposition *that Lincoln does not exist* exists. (3, 4)
(6) If a proposition exists and has constituents, then its constituents exist.
(7) If the received view is true, then Lincoln is a constituent of the proposition *that Lincoln does not exist.*
(8) If the received view is true, then Lincoln exists. (5, 6, 7)
Therefore,
(9) The received view is false. (1, 8)

The above argument will not, to put it mildly, persuade everyone. As we shall see, premises (1), (2), and (4) are controversial. I do not know of anyone who objects to premise (6), but some could object, since some claim that an object can stand in a relation even if that object does not exist (see §VII). Only premise (7) is beyond question, but this is in virtue of its triviality.[9] So I hereby endorse an argument whose every premise is suspect, save the trivial one.

I think that premise (1)—Lincoln does not exist—is true. But *eternalists* will say that objects located at long-ago times are no

[9] *That Lincoln does not exist* is supposed to be a singular proposition about Lincoln. This is what makes premise (7) trivial. Or, if you prefer, this is what makes (7) a trivial addition to the argument, which purports to have already concluded, in (5), that *that Lincoln does not exist* exists.

less real than are objects located at faraway places.[10] So eternalists will say that, although Lincoln is not located at the present time, he is located at some past times, and so he exists. So eternalists will deny premise (1) of the above argument.[11]

Indeed, eternalists (e.g., Fitch, 1994) have even turned arguments just like the above argument on their head. That is, eternalists have said: The received view is true; there are true singular propositions about apparently long-gone entities; therefore, those entities really do exist. But I think that it is a mistake to turn the above argument on its head. For I think that it is much more plausible to deny the received view than it is to say that Lincoln really does exist.

That Lincoln does not exist is supposed to be a singular proposition about Lincoln. But some say that there cannot be singular propositions about entities that do not exist. If they are right, then—given that Lincoln does not exist—there is no such proposition as *that Lincoln does not exist*. If so, then—given that a proposition must exist to be true—it is not the case that *that Lincoln does not exist* is true. Thus we can see why premise (2) is controversial, the premise that says that if Lincoln does not exist, then the proposition *that Lincoln does not exist* is true.

But I say that even if Lincoln does not exist, there really is the singular proposition *that Lincoln does not exist*. To begin to see why I say this, consider the following story about a nineteenth-century journalist. While Lincoln is alive—and so while Lincoln exists—that journalist says: 'Lincoln debated a senator'. That journalist thereby expresses a singular proposition about Lincoln. In other words, that journalist thereby expresses a proposition that is directly about Lincoln. Everyone who believes in

[10] So too will defenders of the 'growing block' view of time. But I think that the growing block view should not be a live option; see Merricks, 2006a.

[11] If you think that Lincoln still exists as a disembodied soul, then let '*L*' be the body Lincoln had and run the above argument with the singular proposition *that L does not exist* in place of *that Lincoln does not exist*.

singular propositions—including defenders of the received view—should agree with this.

Our journalist keeps repeating, over and over, 'Lincoln debated a senator'. (Don't ask.) As he repeats this, his intentions to assert that Lincoln debated a senator remain the same. And each repeated utterance of 'Lincoln debated a senator' is just what it appears to be: a repeated utterance of the same sentence. And whatever relevant causal-historical chains link the word 'Lincoln' to Lincoln are maintained from utterance to utterance. And there is no change, during these repeated utterances, in any semantic laws that regulate how meaning supervenes on use. And there is no significant change in the use of 'Lincoln', 'debated', or 'senator'. And so on.

Given all this, it seems obvious that our journalist's repeated utterances of 'Lincoln debated a senator' remain unchanged in how they represent things as being. A sentence represents things as being a certain way in virtue of expressing a proposition that represents things as being that way (Ch. 1, §V). So the journalist keeps expressing the same proposition.

Our journalist started out expressing a singular proposition about Lincoln. So he keeps expressing that same singular proposition. But let us now add that after the journalist began repeating 'Lincoln debated a senator'—but before he stops—Lincoln is shot and dies. For the reasons noted above, the journalist is still—after Lincoln has died—expressing a singular proposition about Lincoln (*pace* Markosian, 2004, 65 n. 28). And this is so even if a dead Lincoln no longer exists.

The moral of this story is that we can express singular propositions about no-longer-existing entities. So there are singular propositions about no-longer-existing entities. And surely if we can express those propositions, we can use them in arguments, as in the main argument of this section.

None of this should be surprising. After all, the proposition expressed by the sentence 'Lincoln does not exist' is evidently about Lincoln. But it is not a non-singular proposition about

Lincoln, such as, for example, *that the sixteenth president of the United States does not exist* or *that the eventual signer of the Emancipation Proclamation debated a senator.* So the proposition expressed by 'Lincoln does not exist' must be a singular proposition about Lincoln, even if Lincoln is no more.

Or look at it this way. Lincoln's failing to exist is sufficient for the truth of *that Lincoln does not exist.* But the non-exemplification of a quality like *being the sixteenth president of the United States* is not sufficient for the truth of *that Lincoln does not exist.* Similarly, *that Lincoln does not exist* is false in a possible world if and only if Lincoln himself—as opposed to someone merely just like Lincoln—exists in that possible world. So *that Lincoln does not exist* is a singular proposition about Lincoln, even if Lincoln is long gone.

I have defended the claim that there are singular propositions about entities that no longer exist. But, as noted above, some endorse the conclusion that there cannot be singular propositions about non-existent entities. And they have arguments for that conclusion. I shall respond to those arguments. But not yet. This is because those arguments deliver objections not only to premise (2) above, but also to the second premise of each of the main arguments of the next two sections. Similarly, objections to premises (4) and (6) threaten parallel premises in the following two main arguments. I shall respond to all these objections (§VII), but only after we have all the affected arguments—and their objectionable premises—on the table.

V. Singular Propositions about Individuals that Never Exist

Nathan Salmon says:

Let us name the (possible) individual who would have developed from the union of [sperm] *S* and [egg] *E*, if *S* had fertilized *E* in the normal manner, 'Noman'. Noman does not exist in the actual world, but there are many possible worlds in which he (it?) does exist. (1987, 49–50; cf. Plantinga, 1985, 334)

This leads to another argument against the received view:

(A) Noman does not exist.
(B) If Noman does not exist, then *that Noman does not exist* is true.
(C) *That Noman does not exist* is true. (A, B)
(D) If a proposition is true, then that proposition exists.
(E) *That Noman does not exist* exists. (C, D)
(F) If a proposition exists and has constituents, then its constituents exist.
(G) If the received view is true, then Noman is a constituent of *that Noman does not exist.*
(H) If the received view is true, then Noman exists. (E, F, G)
Therefore,
(I) The received view is false. (A, H)

Some of the objections to this argument are (or are easily turned into) objections to the main argument in the previous section and to the main argument in the next section. Those objections will be considered below (§VII). For now, let us focus only on objections that apply to this section's main argument alone.

This section's main argument is built on the stipulation that 'Noman' is the name of the individual who would have developed from the union of S and E, had S fertilized E. Thus this section's main argument presupposes that there is a fact of the matter about which particular individual would have developed from the union of sperm S and egg E.[12] One might object

[12] Some deny that a human person is identical with his or her body. They might also deny that a person (as opposed to a body) would have developed from the union of S and E. Those deniers should run the above argument with a singular proposition about (not the person but) the body that would have developed from the union of S and E.

to this argument by denying that there is such a fact of the matter.[13]

Presumably, defenders of this objection will deny that there are any true counterfactuals to the effect that had some event occurred (that never actually occurs), then a certain entity (that never actually exists) would have existed. Otherwise, we could recast the argument so that it involves some non-existent entity other than Noman, an entity that would have existed, had such-and-such occurred.[14]

Unlike our imagined objectors, I think that there are some true counterfactuals of the relevant sort.[15] In particular, I think that, for certain sperms and certain eggs, there is a fact of the matter about which particular individual would have developed from their union. Let us assume that S and E are such a sperm and egg. And let us conclude that the first objection to this section's main argument is mistaken.

A second objection to this section's main argument focuses on this premise:

(G) If the received view is true, then Noman is a constituent of *that Noman does not exist.*

[13] Perhaps our objectors will add that 'Noman' is, in this regard, no better than Quine's (1953, 4) 'the possible bald man in that doorway'.

[14] Kaplan says:

Consider, for example, the completely automated automobile assembly line. In full operation, it is, at each moment, pregnant with its next product. Each component: body, frame, motor, etc., lies at the head of its own subassembly line, awaiting only Final Assembly. Can we not speak of the very automobile that would have been produced had the Ecologists Revolution been delayed another 47 seconds? (1973, 517 n. 19)

Let 'Otto' be the name of the automobile that would have been produced, had the Revolution tarried. This section's main argument can be run with Otto in place of Noman. See also Kripke, 2013, 39 n. 10.

[15] Some claim that all true counterfactuals must be 'grounded'. They might add that nothing could 'ground' which (actually non-existent) individual would have resulted from the occurrence of an event that never occurs. But I argue—see Merricks, 2007, 146–66—that there are many true and 'ungrounded' counterfactuals.

Here is that second objection: 'Noman' is a definite description. In particular, 'Noman' *just means* the individual who would have developed from the union of S and E. So 'Noman' is not a name. So 'Noman does not exist' does not express a singular proposition. So *that Noman does not exist* is not a singular proposition. But (G) is true only if *that Noman does not exist* is a singular proposition. So—the objection concludes—(G) is false.

This objection to premise (G) is mistaken. For 'Noman' does not mean the individual who would have developed from the union of S and E. To begin to see why, return to Hewson, our arbitrarily chosen contingently existing person, and consider the following speech:

> Let S* and E* be the sperm and egg whose union actually resulted in Hewson. There are distant possible worlds, however, in which the union of S* and E* results in someone else. Similarly, there are distant possible worlds in which the union of S and E results in someone other than Noman. As a result, there are possible worlds in which Noman is not the individual who would have developed from the union of S and E. Nevertheless, in all the nearest possible worlds in which S and E unite, Noman is the result. Thus if S and E had united, Noman would have been the result.

Origin essentialists will claim that if S* and E*'s union resulted in Hewson, then Hewson could not possibly have resulted from the union of a sperm and egg other than S* and E*. But origin essentialism does not threaten the above speech. For the above speech does not suggest that Hewson could have resulted from the union of a sperm and egg other than S* and E*. Nor does origin essentialism imply that S* and E* could not possibly have resulted in a person other than Hewson.

S* and E* did unite and did result in Hewson, and Hewson alone. But there are possible worlds in which S* and E* unite, and then undergo twinning. In a possible world in which S* and E* unite and undergo twinning, at least one of the resultant persons is not Hewson. So there seems to be no principled reason to resist the claim that in yet another possible world S* and E* unite, and result in that 'other person' alone.

By the same token, suppose that S and E, had they united, would have resulted in Noman, and Noman alone. Even so, there is a possible world in which S and E unite, undergo twinning, and result in two persons, at least one of whom is not Noman. So there seems to be no principled reason to deny the possibility that S and E unite and result in just that 'other person', or at least in some person other than Noman.

All this seems right to me. So the above speech seems right to me. At the very least, the above speech is defensible. But if the above speech clearly implied the possibility of a contradiction, then it would not be defensible. So the above speech does not clearly imply the possibility of a contradiction.

Suppose that 'Noman' did mean the individual who would have developed from the union of S and E. Then the above speech would clearly imply the possibility of a contradiction, clearly implying that there are possible worlds in which the individual who would have developed from the union of S and E is not the individual who would have developed from the union of S and E. But, again, the above speech does not clearly imply the possibility of a contradiction. So 'Noman' does not mean the individual who would have developed from the union of S and E.

More generally, 'Noman' is not a disguised definite description. So what is 'Noman'? The obvious answer—which I endorse—is that 'Noman' is a name. Let me offer some support for this obvious answer.

Suppose—just for this paragraph—that S and E will someday unite and result in a person. (The main argument of this section assumes that S and E never unite.) Then 'Noman' will have a referent. There are expressions other than names that will have referents. Definite descriptions and pronouns come to mind. But, as we have seen, 'Noman' is not a definite description. Nor is anyone likely to venture that 'Noman' is a pronoun. The obvious conclusion is that if 'Noman' will have a referent, then 'Noman' is now a name. I think that whether 'Noman' is now a name should not turn on what happens to S and E in the future. So I conclude that even if S and E never unite, 'Noman' is a name.

'Noman' is a name. But 'Noman' does not have a referent. So Noman does not refer to anything. In particular, 'Noman' does not refer to Noman because there is no Noman to be referred to. In this regard, 'Noman' resembles 'Lincoln'. That is, both 'Noman' and 'Lincoln' are names that stand in no *referring* (or *denoting* or *rigidly designating*) relation to anything.

'Noman' is a name. A proposition is singular if it is expressed by a sentence using a name (§I). So I conclude that the sentence 'Noman does not exist' expresses a singular proposition. So I think that *that Noman does not exist* is a singular proposition. So premise (G) of this section's main argument is true. Indeed, I think that all the premises of that argument are true. And that argument is valid. So I conclude that the received view is false.

Moreover, in light of the arguments of this section, I conclude that two additional widely assumed theses are false. The first is that one cannot grasp or express a singular proposition about an entity that never has existed and never will exist. The second is that one cannot grasp or express a singular proposition about an entity with which one is not in some sense acquainted. But even though they are false, something in the neighborhood of these two theses is correct. For example, I admit that the reasoning of this section allows us to really grasp and express the proposition *that Noman does not exist* only if we can grasp singular propositions about sperm S and egg E, which is most easily done if we are acquainted with sperm S and egg E. (Cf. Jeshion, 2002, 72–3.)[16]

[16] Thus—so that it may fully succeed in what it purports to do—this section has a laboratory component. I leave this to the reader.

VI. Possibly True Negative Existential Singular Propositions

Hewson exists contingently. So we have another argument against the received view:

(i) Possibly, Hewson does not exist.
(ii) Necessarily, if Hewson does not exist, then *that Hewson does not exist* is true.
(iii) Possibly, *that Hewson does not exist* is true. (i, ii)
(iv) Necessarily, if a proposition is true, then that proposition exists.
(v) Possibly, *that Hewson does not exist* exists and is true. (iii, iv)
(vi) Necessarily, if a proposition exists and has constituents, then its constituents exist.
(vii) If the received view is true, then, necessarily, if *that Hewson does not exist* exists, it has Hewson as a constituent.
(viii) If the received view is true, then, possibly, Hewson exists and *that Hewson does not exist* is true. (v, vi, vii)
(ix) Necessarily, if Hewson exists, then it is not the case that *that Hewson does not exist* is true.

Therefore,

(x) The received view is false. (viii, ix)

The above argument resembles an argument from Alvin Plantinga (1983). And objections to Plantinga's argument suggest objections to the above argument. Some of those objections are (or are easily turned into) objections to the arguments in the previous two sections. Those objections will be considered below (§VII).

Some might turn this section's main argument on its head. Some might argue that the received view has the result that premise (i)—possibly, Hewson does not exist—is false. So, they would conclude, Hewson exists necessarily. There is nothing special in this regard about Hewson. So those who would turn this section's main argument on its head would say that everything exists necessarily. But I think that the claim that you and I and everything else exists necessarily is not plausible (cf. Ch. 2, §V).

At the very least, that claim is less plausible than the denial of the received view. So I think that it is a mistake to turn the above argument on its head.[17]

Hewson actually exists. And he actually did develop from the union of sperm S* and egg E*. But S* and E* did not unite of metaphysical necessity. And so there is a possible world in which S* and E* exist but never unite. Indeed, there is some possible world in which: S* and E* exist; S* and E* never unite; Hewson never exists; and if S* and E* had united, Hewson would have developed from that union. Let W be such a possible world.

Philosophers in W are obviously not acquainted with Hewson, who does not exist in W. But suppose that some philosophers in W are acquainted with S* and E*, which do exist in W. Then those philosophers could say: 'Let "Noperson" name whomever would have developed from the union of S* and E*.' Then those same philosophers could also say: 'Noperson does not exist', thereby expressing the singular proposition *that Hewson does not exist.* (I suggest that they then parlay this into an argument against the received view.) These observations strengthen the argument of the previous section. For they help us to see how even though Noman does not exist and 'Noman' does not refer to anything, 'Noman does not exist' expresses the singular proposition *that Noman does not exist.*

VII. Objections Pertaining to Serious Actualism

Nathan Salmon says:

Socrates is long gone. Consequently, singular propositions about him, which once existed, also no longer exist. Let us call the

[17] Williamson (2002) both argues that the received view has the result that everything exists necessarily and also defends this result himself by way of the claim that, necessarily, a singular proposition about an entity exists only if that entity exists (see §VII).

no-longer-existing proposition that Socrates does not exist, 'Soc'.... [Soc's] present lack of existence does not prevent it from presently being true. (1998, 286; see also Salmon, 1987, 95)

Salmon thinks that some true propositions—in particular, some true singular propositions—do not exist. Scott Soames (2008, 319) and John Pollock (1985, 134–40), among others, agree with Salmon.

These philosophers would deny the following premises:

(4) If a proposition is true, then that proposition exists.
(D) If a proposition is true, then that proposition exists.
(iv) Necessarily, if a proposition is true, then that proposition exists.

As a result, these philosophers would reject all three of the main arguments from Sections IV through VI.

Serious actualism is the claim that, necessarily, an entity exemplifies a property or stands in a relation only if that entity exists. Salmon, Soames, and Pollock deny (4), (D), and (iv) in part because they reject serious actualism. But I endorse it. And I claim that, necessarily, a proposition is true only if that proposition exemplifies some property or other. (In particular, I think that a proposition is true only if that proposition exemplifies a property to the effect that it represents things as being a certain way (cf. Ch.1, §IV).) So I conclude that (4), (D), and (iv) are true.

In arguing against the existence of true negative existential singular propositions, Salmon, Soames, and Pollock assume that it is not possible for a proposition to exist and have an entity as a constituent if that entity does not exist. So I think they would endorse the following premises from the above arguments:

(6) If a proposition exists and has constituents, then its constituents exist.
(F) If a proposition exists and has constituents, then its constituents exist.
(vi) Necessarily, if a proposition exists and has constituents, then its constituents exist.

I find this mildly puzzling. For I am not sure why deniers of serious actualism would assume that an entity must exist in order to be a constituent of a proposition. But never mind. I do accept serious actualism. And, since a constituent of a proposition would stand in a relation to that proposition, serious actualism implies (6), (F), and (vi). So I conclude that (6), (F), and (vi) are true.[18]

Consider these premises from the main arguments of Sections IV through VI:

(2) If Lincoln does not exist, then *that Lincoln does not exist* is true.
(B) If Noman does not exist, then *that Noman does not exist* is true.
(ii) Necessarily, if Hewson does not exist, then *that Hewson does not exist* is true.

Some defenders of the received view will accept all these premises. (Unfortunately, those defenders of the received view who do accept these premises are those who reject serious actualism.) But some defenders of the received view—and even some who do not defend the received view—will oppose these premises.

I want to consider two different ways that one could oppose these premises. The first way just turns the main arguments of the three preceding sections on their heads. That is, the first way begins with the received view; it infers from this that a premise in each of the above three main arguments is false; it accepts all the premises other than (2) and (B) and (ii); so it concludes that each of (2) and (B) and (ii) is false.

This first way is an instance of the seasoned method of turning your opponent's modus ponens into your own modus tollens. I do not object to this method in general. But I do object to this instance of this method. Here is why. The received view

[18] Another reason—which is dialectically useless in this chapter—that I endorse (6) and (F) (and (vi)) is that since propositions do not (and cannot) have constituents, each of those premises has a (necessarily) false antecedent (see Ch. 6, §IV).

is motivated only if structured propositions are motivated. Chapter 4 argued that structured propositions are unmotivated. So the received view is unmotivated. As we shall see, (2), (B), and (ii) are motivated, at least for believers in propositions. So—when forced to choose between the received view and (2), (B), and (ii)—we should choose (2), (B), and (ii), not the received view.

Believers in propositions routinely reason as follows: If dogs bark, then the proposition *that dogs bark* is true (Ch. 3, §VII). If cats meow, then the proposition *that cats meow* is true. If unicorns do not exist, then the proposition *that unicorns do not exist* is true. And so on. I think that this sort of reasoning, reasoning that believers in propositions should find attractive, motivates the following:

(2) If Lincoln does not exist, then *that Lincoln does not exist* is true.
(B) If Noman does not exist, then *that Noman does not exist* is true.

Most believers in propositions do not reason in the way just described because they think, for example, that it is merely contingent that if dogs bark, then the proposition *that dogs bark* is true. Instead, they think that, necessarily, if dogs bark, then the proposition *that dogs bark* is true (Ch. 3, §VII). So I think that most believers in propositions are also motivated to accept:

(ii) Necessarily, if Hewson does not exist, then *that Hewson does not exist* is true.

Some defenders of the received view might object to the way I have just motivated (ii). And they might thus object even though they grant that it is not merely contingent that if Hewson does not exist, then *that Hewson does not exist* is true. For they might object that the relevant non-contingency is a matter of truth *at* all possible worlds.

That is, some defenders of the received view might object that the relevant non-contingency does not motivate (ii), but instead motivates:

(ii*) The following is true *at* all possible worlds: if Hewson does not exist, then *that Hewson does not exist* is true.

Unfortunately for those defenders, (ii*) is no more consistent with the received view than is (ii).

To see why I say this, consider the following:

The Conditional: If Hewson does not exist, then *that Hewson does not exist* is true.

A claim's truth conditions are a result of how that claim represents things as being (Ch. 1, §IV). The Conditional's antecedent represents Hewson as not existing, and so its antecedent is true just in case Hewson does not exist. On the other hand, the Conditional's consequent represents a certain entity—namely, the proposition *that Hewson does not exist*—as being true. (In fact, its consequent is directly about the proposition *that Hewson does not exist.*) So the Conditional's consequent is true just in case the proposition *that Hewson does not exist* is true.

A claim is true *at* a possible world just in case that claim actually has truth conditions, and those truth conditions are satisfied *in* that possible world (cf. Ch. 1, §III). So the Conditional is true *at* all possible worlds only if the actual truth conditions for its consequent are satisfied *in* all possible worlds *in* which the actual truth conditions for its antecedent are satisfied. So the Conditional is true *at* all possible worlds only if the proposition *that Hewson does not exist* is true *in* all worlds *in* which Hewson does not exist.

So (ii*)—which says that the Conditional is true *at* all worlds—is true only if all Hewson-less possible worlds are possible worlds *in* which the proposition *that Hewson does not exist* is true. A proposition is true *in* a world only if it exists *in* that world. So (ii*) has the result that *that Hewson does not exist* exists *in* all Hewson-less possible worlds. And that rules out the received view. This is why I said above that (ii*) is no more consistent with the received view than is (ii).

There is a second way to oppose premises (2), (B), and (ii). This second way does not just take the received view as a premise and then invert my earlier arguments, turning them into arguments against (2), (B), and (ii). (On the contrary, this second way is even consistent with the denial of the received view.) Instead, this second way builds on an argument with serious actualism as its centerpiece.

Here is Robert Adams:

> [A serious] actualist must deny that there are singular propositions about non-actual individuals. A singular proposition about an individual *x* is a proposition that involves or refers to *x* directly, and not by way of *x*'s qualitative properties or relations to another individual... But according to [serious] actualism a proposition cannot bear such a relation to any non-actual individual. (1981, 12)

And here is Timothy Williamson:

> A proposition about an item exists only if that item exists... how could something be the proposition that that dog is barking in circumstances in which that dog does not exist? For to be the proposition that that dog is barking is to have a certain relation to that dog, which requires there to be such an item as that dog to which to have the relation. The argument is quite general... (2002, 240–1)

Adams and Williamson are endorsing the same argument. Here is their argument, put in terms of a proposition's being 'directly about' an entity: Necessarily, if a proposition is directly about an entity, then that proposition stands in a relation to that entity. Given serious actualism, a proposition cannot stand in a relation to an entity that does not exist. Thus a proposition cannot be directly about an entity that does not exist. Therefore, Adams and Williamson conclude, there cannot be singular propositions about entities that do not exist. (See also Hawthorne and Manley, 2012, 9–10.)

Adams's and Williamson's argument delivers a second way to oppose (2), (B), and (ii). For suppose that their argument is sound. Then there cannot be singular propositions about entities that do not exist. Then—given serious actualism—singular propositions about entities that do not exist cannot be true. But (2) and (B) require singular propositions about entities that do not exist to be true, and (ii) requires the possibility of such a proposition's being true. (That is, (2), (B), and (ii) all require this if each of the main arguments of the preceding three sections has a true first premise.) Thus the second way to oppose (2), (B), and (ii).

Adams's and Williamson's argument turns on the following:

The Aboutness Assumption: Necessarily, if a proposition is directly about an entity, then that proposition stands in a relation to that entity.

If the Aboutness Assumption is false, then the argument given by Adams and Williamson is unsound. If their argument is unsound, then the second way of opposing (2), (B), and (ii)—and what I take to be the most serious challenge to (2), (B), and (ii)—is unsuccessful. For the remainder of this section, I shall argue that the Aboutness Assumption is false.

I did not merely assume that there are singular propositions about Lincoln and Noman. I argued that there are such propositions. One such argument involved the story of the nineteenth-century journalist (§IV). Another such argument turned on a true counterfactual about which individual would have resulted from the union of sperm S and egg E (§V). Similarly, this section motivated premises (2) and (B) and (ii), premises that lead to the result that there are or can be singular propositions about entities that do not exist.

Those arguments and those motivations are all good reasons to conclude that there can be singular propositions about entities that do not exist. So those arguments and those motivations give us good reasons to conclude that something must have gone wrong in Adams's and Williamson's argument for the conclusion that there cannot be singular propositions about non-existent entities. The Aboutness Assumption is (so I believe) the weak link in that argument.

Here is a similar point. There are singular propositions about contingently existing entities. And I have argued that certain singular propositions about contingently existing entities exist necessarily (§II). And I have given other arguments for the conclusion that all propositions exist necessarily (Ch. 1, §IV; Ch. 3, §VII). So, possibly, a singular proposition about a particular contingent entity exists even though that entity does not exist. This too gives us a good reason to think something must have gone wrong in Adams's and Williamson's argument to the contrary, and again I say it is the Aboutness Assumption.

Another line of argument against the Aboutness Assumption begins by recalling what it is for a proposition to be directly about an entity. This is for that proposition, first, to be about that entity and, second, for it not to be the case that that proposition is about that entity in virtue of that entity's having this or that property or being 'given' in this or that way, and so on (§I).

The second condition for being directly about an entity merely denies one explanation of the first condition; this denial does not imply a relation between proposition and entity. So if the Aboutness Assumption is correct, then it is the first condition for being directly about an entity—namely, a proposition's being about that entity—that implies that a proposition must stand in a relation to an entity that it is directly about. Conversely, if a proposition's being about an entity does not imply that that proposition stands in a relation to that entity, then the Aboutness Assumption is false.

The true non-singular proposition *that there are no carnivorous cows* is—in a perfectly evident way—about carnivorous cows. After all, its being thus about carnivorous cows is part of what differentiates it from, say, *that there are no hobbits*. (*That there are no hobbits* is about hobbits, not carnivorous cows.) It also explains why the non-existence of carnivorous cows results in the truth of *that there are no carnivorous cows*. Also, *that there are no carnivorous cows*'s being about carnivorous cows, and denying their existence, explains why that proposition would be false if carnivorous cows did exist.

Again, *that there are no carnivorous cows* is—in a perfectly evident way—about carnivorous cows. But no carnivorous cows exist. And serious actualism is true. So *that there are no carnivorous cows* does not stand in any relation to carnivorous cows. Therefore, the way in which *that there are no carnivorous cows* is about carnivorous cows does not imply that it stands in any relation to carnivorous cows. (Cf. Merricks, 2007, 32–3.)

That Hewson does not exist is about Hewson in this same perfectly evident way. For that proposition's being thus about Hewson is part of what differentiates it from, say, *that Lincoln does not exist*. (*That Lincoln does not exist* is about Lincoln, not Hewson.) Moreover, *that Hewson does not exist*'s being thus about Hewson, and denying his existence, explains why that proposition would be true if Hewson did not exist, and also why his existence makes that proposition false.

So *that there are no carnivorous cows* is about carnivorous cows. Being about carnivorous cows in this way does not imply standing in a relation to carnivorous cows. *That Hewson does not exist* is about Hewson in this same way. So being about Hewson in this way does not imply standing in a relation to Hewson. So being about Hewson does not imply standing in a relation to Hewson. So the Aboutness Assumption is false.

Here is a final argument against the Aboutness Assumption. Each proposition represents things as being a certain way. But, as we shall see in Chapter 6 (§II), I think that there is no explanation of how a proposition manages to do this. So I deny that a proposition's representing things as being a certain way is explained by that proposition's standing in a relation to some entity or entities. So I deny that a proposition's representing a particular entity as being a certain way is a matter of (or is analyzed as, or is reduced to, etc.) that proposition's standing in a relation to that entity.

I add that a proposition's being about a particular entity is explained by that proposition's representing that entity as being a certain way. This is because, so I claim, a proposition's being about a particular entity is a matter of (or is analyzed as, or is reduced to, etc.) that proposition's representing that particular entity as being some way or other. As just noted, a proposition's representing things as being a certain way is not a matter of (and is not analyzed as, etc.) that proposition's standing in a relation to what is thus represented. So a proposition's being about an entity is not a matter of (is not analyzed as, etc.) that proposition's standing in a relation to that entity. So I conclude that a proposition's being about an entity does not imply that that proposition stands in a relation to that entity.

Here is another way to articulate more or less this same point. I think that each proposition exemplifies a property to the effect that it represents things as being a certain way. This property is not a relation that that proposition stands in to something else. This property is, rather, a monadic but extrinsic property. (Monadic but extrinsic properties are familiar; consider *being the only object in the universe*; see Merricks, 2007, 52–3.) A claim regarding what a proposition is *about* is really a partial description of that proposition's property of representing things as being a certain way. So such claims do not automatically imply that a proposition stands in any relation—not even the relation *being about*—to anything. So, again, the Aboutness Assumption is false.[19]

[19] As we saw above, what a proposition is about partly explains what it would take for that proposition to be true, and for it to be false. Recall also that a proposition is true just in case things are how that proposition represents things as being, and false otherwise (see, e.g., Ch. 1, §IV). Given that a proposition's being about something is a matter of (is analyzed in terms of...) how that proposition represents things as being, it is unsurprising that both what a proposition is about

VIII. Conclusion

The most widely defended versions of structured propositions imply that an individual is a constituent of any singular proposition about that individual. This chapter has presented a variety of arguments for the falsity of that implication, and thus a variety of arguments against the most widely defended versions of structured propositions. In this way, this chapter supports Chapter 4's conclusion that we ought to reject structured propositions.[20]

and how that proposition represents things as being are tied to that proposition's truth conditions.

[20] Merricks (2012) is an ancestor of this chapter.

6

THE NATURE OF PROPOSITIONS

LET a feature be *distinctive* of propositions if it sets propositions apart from many or most or all other entities. For example, *being a fundamental bearer of truth or falsity* is a distinctive feature of propositions, but *being self-identical* is not. And let *an account of the nature of propositions* articulate the core distinctive features of propositions, that is, those distinctive features of propositions that explain all the other distinctive features of propositions. This chapter presents and defends my account of the nature of propositions.

I. An Account of the Nature of Propositions

Here is my account of the nature of propositions: A proposition is a necessary existent that essentially represents things as being a certain way. Chapters 1 (§IV) and 3 (§VII) and 5 (§II) defended the claim that propositions are necessary existents. Chapter 1 (§IV) also defended the claim that each proposition essentially represents things as being a certain way. So—as Chapters 1, 3, and 5 showed—propositions really do have the distinctive features explicitly attributed to them by my account.

My account of the nature of propositions says that each proposition essentially represents things as being a certain way.

If things are as a proposition represents things as being, then that proposition is true. If things are not as a proposition represents things as being, then that proposition is false. In this way, my account explains not only why a proposition has truth conditions, but also why—as we saw in Chapter 1 (§IV)—it has those truth conditions essentially.

As we shall see in Section II, my account of the nature of propositions has the result that propositions fundamentally represent things as being a certain way. An entity that fundamentally represents things as being a certain way is thereby a fundamental bearer of truth or falsity (Ch. 1, §V). So my account has the further result that propositions are fundamental bearers of truth and falsity. And, as Chapter 1 (§V) showed, propositions are indeed the fundamental bearers of truth and falsity.

Chapter 4 (§I) noted (but, alas, did not defend) the hypothesis that propositions are Twinkies. Chapter 3 (§III) presented (but did not endorse) an argument for the conclusion that propositions are electrons. My account says that each proposition exists necessarily. Twinkies exist contingently. So do electrons. So my account rules out propositions-as-Twinkies and propositions-as-electrons, along with other bizarre hypotheses about the nature of propositions. For example, because propositions exist necessarily, no proposition is a dog or an asteroid or a politician. More generally—because no physical entity exists necessarily—my account has the result that propositions are nonphysical.[1]

The best way to understand what it is to be abstract is to start with paradigms of abstractness. And I think that these include nonphysical necessarily existing propositions. Nonphysical

[1] You might think both that the universe is physical and also that it would have existed no matter what, even if it had been 'empty'. So you might think that the universe is a necessarily existing physical entity. But the universe is but one thing. There are more propositions than one. You should conclude that no propositions are physical.

necessarily existing propositions are as paradigmatically abstract as, say, pure sets. So, since my account implies that propositions are nonphysical and says that they exist necessarily, my account has the result that propositions are abstract.

As noted above, my account of the nature of propositions has the result that propositions are fundamental bearers of truth and falsity. In Chapter 1 (§V), I defended the claim that propositions' being fundamental bearers of truth and falsity implies that a belief's being true should be analyzed partly in terms of a proposition's being true. This in turn implies, so I argued, that propositions are the objects of belief. (See also Merricks, 2009a.) This is one role played by propositions.

Again, my account has the result that propositions are fundamental bearers of truth and falsity. This implies, so I argued in Chapter 1 (§V), that a sentence's being true (in a context of use) is analyzed as that sentence's expressing a true proposition (in that context of use). I also argued, trading on claims about what propositions are like, that the same proposition can be expressed by more than one sentence (Ch. 1, §VI). In all of this we have another role played by propositions.

My account of the nature of propositions has the result that propositions have certain features and play certain roles. Those features and roles are familiar. Here are a few representative remarks from the literature attesting to their familiarity:

> [T]he central tenets of the traditional theory of propositions... include the following: (1) propositions are the primary bearers of such properties as... truth and falsity; (2) they are mind-independent extra-linguistic abstract objects; (3) a belief state consists in a subject standing in the relation of believing to a proposition... (4) propositions are typically public: people commonly believe one and the same proposition... (5) propositions are what (literal utterances of declarative) sentences express... (Bealer, 1998, 1)

> Nowadays it's very common to think of... propositions [as] those occupants of Frege's 'third realm' that are the ultimate bearers of truth values and the objects of belief... On this Fregean picture, to

have a propositional thought, say a belief, is to stand in a certain special relation to a specific proposition. This proposition is either true or false, and gets to be so according to whether it accurately represents the world (or part of the world). (Jubien, 2001, 47)

For consider *propositions*. We have been assuming that when I believe, for example, that all men are mortal, then there is something I believe: the proposition *All men are mortal*... propositions are the things (whatever precisely their nature) that are fundamentally capable of being believed or disbelieved, that are true or false, and... are often and ordinarily taken to be paradigmatically abstract. (Plantinga, 1993, 114)

Again, here is my account of the nature of propositions: A proposition is a necessary existent that essentially represents things as being a certain way. My account says true things about propositions. And my account is elegant, being both simple and powerful. Its simplicity is evident. And it is powerful in that it explains—as we have seen above—why propositions have the further features and play the roles that propositions do (and are widely taken to) have and play.

II. Primitive Representation

An account of the nature of propositions articulates the core distinctive features of propositions. That is, an account of the nature of propositions articulates those distinctive features of propositions that explain the other distinctive features of propositions. My account of the nature of propositions explicitly claims that a proposition essentially represents things as being a certain way. Thus my account takes such representing to explain—but not be explained by—other features that are distinctive of propositions.

Essentially representing things as being a certain way is a distinctive feature of propositions. So I assume that if a proposition's essentially representing things as being a certain way were explained by anything at all, it would be explained by its other features that are themselves also distinctive of propositions. For example, most defenders of structured propositions would say not only that a proposition's essentially representing things as being a certain way is explained by a proposition's constituents and structure, but also that having such constituents and structure is itself distinctive of propositions.

So my account of the nature of propositions implies that a proposition's essentially representing things as being a certain way is not explained by that proposition's other distinctive-of-propositions features. But if a proposition's essentially representing things as being a certain way were explained by anything at all, it would be explained by its other features that are distinctive of propositions. So my account implies that there is no explanation of how a proposition essentially represents things as being a certain way. In other words, my account implies that each proposition *primitively* essentially represents things as being a certain way.[2]

My account implies that there is no explanation of how a proposition manages to represent things as being a certain way (and do so essentially). So a proposition's representing things as being a certain way is not explained by anything. So a proposition's representing things as being a certain way is not explained by how that proposition is related to something else that represents things as being that way. So a proposition does not represent things as being a certain way in virtue of being related to something else that represents things as being that way. To *fundamentally* represent things as being a certain way just is to represent things as being a certain way, but not in virtue of

[2] Lewis (1986a, 174–91) attacks primitive—or, as he calls it, 'magical'—representation. His attack turns on the assumption that for each true proposition ('element'), there is something (namely, 'the concrete world') that stands in the *making true* ('selection') relation to that proposition. But I have argued that this assumption is false (Merricks, 2007). (For other objections to Lewis's attack, see Jubien, 1991 and van Inwagen, 1986.)

being related to something else that represents things as being that way. Thus—as promised in Section I—my account has the result that propositions fundamentally represent things as being a certain way.[3]

You might accept my arguments for the conclusion that propositions exist necessarily and essentially represent things as being a certain way, yet still deny that any proposition primitively represents things as being a certain way. For you might believe that there is a successful explanation of how each proposition represents things as being a certain way. Because of the arguments of Chapters 3 and 4, I conclude that that explanation may not rely on the cognitive activity of agents and will not be a matter of a proposition's structure and constituents. But then I have no idea—not an inkling—of how such an explanation is supposed to go. This is why I endorse an account of the nature of propositions that implies that each proposition primitively represents things as being a certain way.

But maybe you do have an explanation of how a proposition would manage to represent things as being a certain way, an explanation that does not run afoul of the arguments of Chapters 3 and 4. Or maybe you conclude that even though you have no idea of how that explanation is supposed to go, there is still such an explanation out there to be found, an explanation that relies on neither our cognitive activity nor on a proposition's alleged constituents and structure. Fair enough. I wish you luck. And bid you *adieu*.

Or maybe you agree with me that there is no yet-to-be-discovered explanation of how each and every proposition manages to represent things as being a certain way. Even so,

[3] So primitively representing things as being a certain way implies fundamentally representing things as being a certain way. But not vice versa. For example, a defender of structured propositions could take propositions to fundamentally represent things as being a certain way, while also saying that each proposition's representing things as being a certain way is explained by its structure and constituents (Ch. 4, §V).

you might conclude that only some—but not all—propositions primitively represent things as being a certain way. For you might endorse the following view: Although each *atomic* proposition primitively represents things as being a certain way, there is an explanation of how a *complex* proposition manages to represent things as being a certain way. This explanation is at least partly in terms of that composite proposition's having atomic propositions as constituents that themselves represent things as being certain ways.

Here is an example to illustrate this view: The proposition *that dogs bark and A loves B* is a complex proposition. It has two atomic propositions as constituents, namely, the proposition *that dogs bark* and the proposition *that A loves B*. One of those constituents represents dogs as barking and the other represents A as loving B. And having those atomic propositions as constituents at least partly explains how that complex proposition manages to represent dogs as barking and A as loving B.

No set has a truth-value. So no set represents things as being a certain way. So the set whose members are you, me, and the proposition *that dogs bark* does not represent dogs as barking. Membership is a kind of constituency. So the set whose constituents are you, me, and the proposition *that dogs bark* does not represent dogs as barking. This shows that an entity's having a proposition as a constituent does not, all by itself, guarantee that that entity represents things as being a certain way, not even the way that its propositional constituent represents things as being.

To get an entity that not only has propositions as constituents, but also represents things as being a certain way—as it must if that entity is to be a proposition—those constituent propositions must be appropriately united. Thus the view we are here considering requires there to be a successful account of the unity of the proposition for complex propositions. And I think that one moral of Chapter 4's discussion of the unity of the proposition is that there is no successful account.

Moreover, suppose for the sake of argument that a given complex proposition has *that dogs bark* and *that A loves B* as its propositional constituents. That complex proposition might be *that dogs bark and A loves B*. But it also might be *that dogs bark or A loves B* or *that if dogs bark, then A loves B* or *that it is not the case that dogs bark and it is not the case that A loves B*, and so on.

So—supposing for the sake of argument that complex propositions do have propositional constituents—complex propositions with exactly the same propositional constituents can and do differ in how they represent things as being. So a complex proposition's propositional constituents do not—not on their own—explain how that complex proposition manages to represent things as being a certain way.

If a complex proposition does not primitively represent things as being a certain way, then there is an explanation of how that complex proposition manages to represent things as being that way. We have just seen that a complex proposition's propositional constituents alone cannot explain this. Presumably, the structure of a complex proposition is supposed to pick up the explanatory slack.[4] Again, this requires there to be a

[4] You might object that the explanatory slack will be picked up by non-propositional constituents of complex propositions, non-propositional constituents that—somehow—play roles correlated with 'not' and 'or' and 'and' and 'sheffer stroke' and so on; let these alleged constituents be: *negation* and *disjunction* and *conjunction* and *sheffer stroke* and so on. I have two responses.

First, the sentences that express propositions have logical form. So too do the that-clauses that name (so-called) complex propositions. But propositions themselves do not have logical form (Ch. 2, §VIII). And if propositions do not have logical form, it seems like *negation* and *disjunction* and *conjunction* and *sheffer stroke* are not even candidates to be constituents of propositions.

Second, suppose for the sake of argument that complex propositions have atomic propositions as constituents and also constituents such as *negation*, *disjunction*, and so on. Then it seems that the proposition *that if p then q* and the proposition *that if q then p* have all the same constituents. But those propositions differ in how they represent things as being. So the explanation of how each of those propositions manages to represent things as being a certain way cannot be solely in terms of its constituents. So, presumably, that explanation must also involve each proposition's structure.

successful account of the unity of the proposition for complex propositions. And, again, I think that one moral of Chapter 4 is that there is no successful account.

I conclude that each proposition primitively represents things as being a certain way. This goes for propositions like *that dogs bark and A loves B* just as much as it goes for propositions like *that dogs bark*. That conclusion was already implicit in my account of the nature of propositions. And that conclusion will play a central role in much of what follows in this chapter.

III. Double Standard?

There is (so I have argued) no successful explanation of how a set of possible worlds would manage to essentially represent things as being a certain way. This is one reason that I rejected propositions-as-sets-of-possible-worlds in Chapter 3 (§V). And no one (so I have argued) has successfully explained how a structured proposition would manage to essentially represent things as being a certain way. This is one reason that I rejected structured propositions in Chapter 4 (§X).

In thus rejecting those views, I was assuming that if a set of possible worlds or a structured proposition did essentially represent things as being a certain way, then there would be some explanation of how it manages to do so. Chapters 3 and 4 never even countenance the claim that sets of possible worlds or structured propositions primitively represent things as being a certain way. My own view of propositions, however, avails itself of primitive representation. So you might object that I have relied on an unacceptable double standard.

But I have not. For there are compelling reasons to deny that propositions-as-sets-of-possible-worlds primitively represent things as being a certain way. And there are compelling reasons to deny that structured propositions primitively represent things as being a certain way. But none of those reasons is a reason to deny that propositions-as-I-understand-propositions primitively represent things as being a certain way.

To begin to see why I say this, consider the thesis that propositions are sets of possible worlds. The best argument for that thesis is the 'Ockham's razor argument' (Ch. 3, §III). That argument is most compelling if its defenders can claim that those who believe in sets of possible worlds thereby believe in propositions of the sort endorsed by those who think that propositions are sets of possible worlds.

This most compelling version might succeed if a set of possible worlds manages to represent things as being a certain way in virtue of its members and structure. For then those who believe in a set with those members and that structure would thereby believe in a set that has all it takes to represent things as being a certain way. And so it seems fair to say that they would thereby believe in propositions of the sort endorsed by those who think that propositions are sets of possible worlds.

But those who believe in sets of possible worlds do not thereby believe in sets that primitively represent things as being a certain way. So they do not thereby believe in propositions of the sort endorsed by those who think that propositions are sets of possible worlds that primitively represent things as being a certain way. So adding primitive representation to the thesis that propositions are sets of possible worlds undermines the most compelling version of the best (least bad) argument for that thesis.[5]

Let us turn to structured propositions. The main motivation for structured propositions is the claim that there must be an explanation of how each proposition manages to represent

[5] Perhaps there is a version of the Ockham's razor argument that claims that parsimony dictates that we attribute *primitively representing things as being a certain way* to entities that we already believe to exist. But this gives us no parsimony-driven reason to attribute thus representing to sets of possible worlds in particular, and so is obviously not a good argument for the thesis that propositions are sets of possible worlds.

things as being a certain way, and that each proposition's constituents and structure yield just such an explanation (Ch. 4, §V). Obviously, this motivation is undermined if a structured proposition is supposed to primitively represent things as being a certain way.[6] So defenders of structured propositions should not claim that structured propositions primitively represent things as being a certain way.

Because of how propositions-as-sets-of-possible-worlds and structured propositions are motivated, neither of those accounts of the nature of propositions should be combined with the claim that a proposition primitively represents things as being a certain way. But none of this suggests that this claim should not be combined with—much less is not a result of—my own account of the nature of propositions.

There is a further reason that defenders of structured propositions should deny that a proposition primitively represents things as being a certain way. To begin to understand this further reason, consider that some defenders of structured propositions might say that the proposition *that A loves B* is the ordered set <A, *loving*, B> (Ch. 4, §VI). But—surely—they would not say that it is the ordered set <7, *being orange*>. And some defenders of structured propositions might say that the proposition *that dogs bark* is the state of affairs of *being a dog*'s standing in a certain relation R to *barking* (Ch. 4, §IX). But—surely—they would not say that that proposition is the state of affairs of my being seated. These two examples illustrate the following general point. If there are structured propositions, then (at least some of) the constituents of a structured proposition are intuitively correlated with how that proposition represents things as being (cf. Ch. 4, §V).

[6] Because I take this motivation to go hand in hand with a rejection of primitive powers relevant to representation, I say that this motivation is also undermined if a structured proposition's representing things as being a certain way relies on Zip or *Zipping* (see Ch. 4, §§VI, VII, and IX).

Suppose that propositions are structured. Then each proposition's constituents are intuitively correlated with how that proposition represents things as being. But suppose further that each structured proposition primitively represents things as being a certain way. Then—I shall argue—it is a mere coincidence that each proposition's constituents are intuitively correlated with how that proposition represents things as being.

Standard defenders of structured propositions deny that a proposition primitively represents things as being a certain way. Standard defenders add that a proposition's constituents are part of what explains how that proposition manages to represent things as being a certain way. So, for example, standard defenders of structured propositions say that having A, B, and *loving* as constituents (partly) explains how the proposition *that A loves B* manages to represent A as loving B.[7] Thus standard defenders can and should insist that it is no coincidence at all that that proposition's constituents are intuitively correlated with how that proposition represents things as being.

There are also nonstandard ways to keep this intuitive correlation from being a mere coincidence. For example, you might posit a single explanation of both *that A loves B*'s representing A as loving B and also its having A and B as constituents. But any such explanation is ruled out if there is no explanation of *that A loves B*'s representing A as loving B. So any such explanation is ruled out if the proposition *that A loves B* primitively represents A as loving B.

Or you might 'reverse' the standard explanation. That is, you might say that *that A loves B* primitively represents A as loving B, and then claim that this explains why that proposition has

[7] Standard defenders who are neo-Fregeans say that having the sense of 'A', the sense of 'B', and *loving* as constituents (partly) explains how the proposition *that A loves B* manages to represent A as loving B. My arguments to follow can easily be adapted to neo-Fregeanism.

A and B as constituents. But I shall now say why I think that this 'explanation' is no good.

Consider this question: Why does the ordered set <A, *loving*, B> have A and B among its members? This question might have no informative answer. Or this question might have an answer in terms of a set's being individuated by its members. Or it might have some other answer. But certainly the answer to this question is not that that set primitively represents things as being a certain way, not even if that set does primitively represent things as being that way.

Why does the state of affairs of R*'s relating A to *loving* to B have A and B as constituents? This question might have no informative answer. Or its answer might be in terms of how the identity of a state of affairs is partly determined by its constituents. Or its answer might be a causal explanation of how A came to be related by R* to *loving* to B. But certainly the answer to this question is not that that state of affairs primitively represents things as being a certain way, not even if that state of affairs does primitively represent things as being that way.

Why does an object composed of A, *loving*, and B have A and B among its parts? This question might have no informative answer. Or its answer might be in terms of what caused A, *loving*, and B to be appropriately interrelated so as to yield a composite object. Or its answer might be in terms of how a composite object is individuated by its parts. But certainly the answer to this question is not that that object primitively represents things as being a certain way, not even if that object does primitively represent things as being that way.

You might think that structured propositions are sets. Or states of affairs. Or composite objects. And you might think that something explains why a given structured proposition has the constituents that it does. But you should not say that that explanation is that that proposition primitively represents things as being a certain way—not even if you believe that it does primitively represent things as being that way.

Suppose, for the sake of argument, that the proposition *that A loves B* has A and B as constituents. Moreover, suppose, again for the sake of argument, that that proposition primitively represents A as loving B. Then—I have just argued—that proposition's primitively representing A as loving B does not explain why it has A and B as constituents. Then—as we saw above—that proposition's having A and B as constituents does not explain how it manages to represent A as loving B. Then—as we also saw above—there is no single explanation of both its having A and B as constituents and its representing A as loving B.

So I conclude that if the proposition *that A loves B* both has A and B as constituents and also primitively represents A as loving B, then the intuitive correlation between how that proposition represents things as being and its constituents is a mere coincidence. I have focused on the proposition *that A loves B*. But my argument focused on that proposition can easily be generalized to apply to all propositions. And that argument reveals that the view that each structured proposition primitively represents things as being a certain way has a sweeping result. This is the result that each proposition coincidentally has constituents that are intuitively correlated with how that proposition represents things as being. But I think that coincidence on such a staggering scale—recurring in each and every proposition—is absolutely unacceptable. So I conclude that defenders of structured propositions ought to reject the view—as in fact every single one of them does—that a proposition primitively represents things as being a certain way.

This objection to structured propositions that primitively represent things as being a certain way can easily be extended to propositions-as-sets-of-possible-worlds that primitively represent things as being a certain way. For defenders of propositions-as-sets-of-possible-worlds think that the members of the proposition *that A loves B* are exactly those possible worlds in which A loves B. Thus they think that that proposition's constituents (possible worlds in which A loves B) are intuitively correlated with how that proposition represents things as being (it represents A as loving B). This would be an unacceptable coincidence if that proposition primitively represented A as loving B. The point is general. So the thesis that propositions are sets of possible worlds that primitively represent things as being a certain way leads to unacceptable coincidence on a staggering scale.

My own account of the nature of propositions says that each proposition is a necessary existent that essentially represents things as being a certain way. My account does not imply that each proposition has constituents that are intuitively correlated with how that proposition represents things as being. So—given my own account—the claim that a proposition primitively represents things as being a certain way does not lead to unacceptable coincidence.[8]

IV. Simple Propositions

I have argued against propositions-as-sets-of-possible-worlds and against structured propositions (Ch. 3; Ch. 4; Ch. 5). So I have argued for the falsity of two views according to which propositions have constituents. But each of those views is committed to more than just the claim that propositions have constituents (see, e.g., Ch. 4, §§I–II). So the falsity of those views does not—not all by itself—imply that propositions do not have constituents. I shall now argue that propositions do not have constituents.

[8] I do endorse a correlation between what a proposition is about and how that proposition represents things as being. For example, *that Lincoln debated a senator* is about Lincoln, and represents Lincoln as having debated a senator. But this correlation is no coincidence. For I say that we should explain a proposition's being about an entity in terms of that proposition's representing that entity as being a certain way (Ch. 5, §VII).

As was emphasized in the previous section, both propositions-as-sets-of-possible-worlds and structured propositions imply that (at least some of) a proposition's constituents are intuitively correlated with how that proposition represents things as being. Moreover, those who think that complex propositions have propositions as constituents also endorse their own such intuitive correlation; for example, they think that the proposition that represents dogs as barking and A as loving B has *that dogs bark* and *that A loves B* as constituents, but not *that pigs fly*. With all of this in mind, it is hard to imagine a less controversial premise about the nature of propositions than the following:

(1) If propositions have constituents, then each proposition has constituents that are intuitively correlated with how that proposition represents things as being.

Here is a second premise:

(2) It is not the case that each proposition has constituents that are intuitively correlated with how that proposition represents things as being.

My defense of premise (2) builds on conclusions from earlier sections. Each proposition primitively represents things as being a certain way (§II). So if each proposition has constituents that are intuitively correlated with how that proposition represents things as being, then we face a staggering coincidence (§III). But we do not face that staggering coincidence. So it is not the case that each proposition has constituents that are intuitively correlated with how that proposition represents things as being. So (2) is true.

Premises (1) and (2) imply:

(3) It is not the case that propositions have constituents.

Propositions do not have constituents. In other words, propositions are simple. Note that this argument applies to all propositions. So it applies not only to propositions such as *that A loves B*, but also to propositions such as *that dogs bark and A loves B*. So (so-called) 'complex' propositions do not have constituents, not even constituents that are themselves propositions.

V. More on Primitive Representation

Michael Jubien says:

> In the end, it's implausible to think that *any* genuine Platonic entity could represent on its own . . . *Representation* is an 'intentional' or 'outer-directed' relation . . . Representation is ultimately the business of beings with intentional capacities, in short, thinkers . . . To hold . . . that propositions are *sui generis* doesn't relieve them of the burden of representation, and this is a burden they simply can't bear. (2001, 54)

So Jubien claims that no abstract object, not even a proposition, can represent things as being a certain way, at least not on its own. This claim leads Jubien (2001) to deny that there are propositions.

Jeffrey King (2007a, 135–6) and Scott Soames (2010, 32) believe that there are propositions. Even so, they agree with Jubien's claim that a proposition cannot, all on its own, represent things as being a certain way. They even agree with Jubien that representation is ultimately the business of thinkers.[9] For King and Soames think that a proposition represents things as being a certain way only because of our cognitive activity.

Here is my main response to Jubien and King and Soames: I have argued in this book that there really are propositions, and that they really have certain features. Among those features are being abstract, and also fundamentally and even primitively

[9] That representation is ultimately the business of thinkers is the standard view of those who deny that there are propositions. So—with the notable exception of the Stoics—this was the view of virtually everyone before the nineteenth century (see, e.g., Aquinas, *De Veritate*, Q.1, A.2, Reply [1994, 11]).

representing things as being a certain way. The arguments of this book for the existence and features of propositions are (so it seems to me) more compelling than the intuitions about representation that lead Jubien, King, and Soames to conclude that an abstract object cannot, on its own, represent things as being a certain way.

That is my main response. But I also realize that the intuitions had by Jubien, King, and Soames will be shared by others, others who will find the view of propositions that I defend to be mysterious, or spooky, or objectionably non-naturalistic, and so on. So it is worth exploring just how much mystery (spookiness, etc.) here really is due to my account of propositions in particular, and how much is inextricably bound up with representation itself. Along similar lines, it is worth exploring what must be done—beyond simply rejecting my account of the nature of propositions—to avoid all mystery (etc.) here.

The aspect of my view that is most likely to invite the charge of mystery (etc.) is its claim that each proposition primitively represents things as being a certain way; that is, each proposition represents things as being a certain way and there is no explanation of how any proposition manages to do this. And I shall focus on this claim in this section. But I want to start by discussing my claim that each proposition fundamentally represents things as being a certain way; that is, each proposition represents things as being a certain way, but not (even partly) in virtue of its being related to another entity that represents things as being that way.

You believe that the earth is round, and so have a true belief that represents the earth as being round. Someone else might believe that the earth is flat, and so have a false belief that represents the earth as being flat. Some sentences represent pigs as flying, and so are true if and only if pigs fly. And so on. There really are entities—and of course I think that propositions are among them—that represent things as being a certain way, and that, as a result, have truth conditions, and so a truth-value.

Now suppose, for reductio, that nothing ever *fundamentally* represents things as being a certain way. Then we have two options. The first option is that whenever *x* represents things as being a certain way, and so has a truth-value, it does so (at least in part) in virtue of being related to *y* ($\neq x$), which represents things as being that same way; and *y* represents things as being that way in virtue of being related to *z* ($\neq y$), which represents things as being that same way; and so on, ad infinitum. I do not think that anyone will endorse this first option.

The second option is a circle of representing entities such that *x* represents things as being a certain way, and so has a truth-value, (at least in part) in virtue of being related to *y* ($\neq x$), which represents things as being that same way; and *y* represents things as being a certain way in virtue of being related to *x*, which represents things as being that same way. Of course, the circle could be expanded to embrace more than two entities, *x* and *y*. But I do not think that anyone will endorse this second option, no matter how much the circle is expanded.

I think that the above reasoning shows that what we assumed for reductio is false. So we should all accept the result that some entities fundamentally represent things as being a certain way. That is, we should all accept the result that some entities represent things as being a certain way, but not in virtue of being related to another entity that represents things as being that way. (So it is not a mark against my account that it has this result, not even if fundamentally representing things as being a certain way turns out to be mysterious.)

We should all agree that some entities fundamentally represent things as being a certain way. This is the sort of representing that (so I say) is done by propositions. And it is the sort of representing that (so say we all) implies that the entity that does the representing has truth conditions, and so a truth-value. So an entity is a legitimate candidate for fundamentally representing things as being a certain way only if that entity has a truth-value.

Neither agents nor cognition nor minds have truth-values. So agents and cognition and minds clearly fail to fundamentally represent things as being a certain way in the relevant sense of 'fundamentally represent things as being a certain way'. The only contenders for thus representing directly in the realm of agents and their cognitive activity seem to be certain mental events, in particular those mental events that have truth-values.

With this in mind, consider that Soames tells us that the 'traditional' line has it that:

> ... propositions are both intrinsically representational, and that from which all other representational bearers of truth conditions—sentences, utterances, and mental states—inherit their representationality. (2010, 7)

But, departing from tradition, Soames himself believes that:

> Sentences, utterances, and mental states are not representational because of the relations they bear to inherently representational propositions. Rather, propositions are representational because of the relations they bear to inherently representational mental states and cognitive acts of agents.[10] (2010, 7)

So Soames seems to hold that certain mental events—'mental states' and 'cognitive acts'—are what fundamentally represent things as being a certain way (see also Soames, 2010, 103–7 and 2014, 91–124).

I shall focus on the mental events that are beliefs, that is, the events of one's believing that things are a certain way. Suppose, just for the sake of argument, that beliefs not only fundamentally represent things as being a certain way (and so have a truth-value), but also do so primitively. As far as mystery (etc.)

[10] I would never say that we must have paranormal power over platonic entities if our cognitive acts result, as Soames says they do, in there being propositions that represent things as being a certain way. I would never say this even though Soames calls the idea of 'grasping' a proposition a kind of 'platonic extrasensory perception' (2010, 7).

goes, this seems to be no improvement over the claim that propositions represent things as being a certain way, both fundamentally and primitively. And if you add that it is not objectionably mysterious (etc.) for events to primitively represent things as being a certain way just so long as they are *beliefs*, I do not see how you can object to my adding that it is not objectionably mysterious (etc.) for abstract objects to primitively represent things as being a certain way just so long as they are *propositions*.

Of course, those steadfastly opposed to the mysterious with regard to representation will say that if certain mental events fundamentally represent things as being a certain way, those events do not do so primitively. That is, they will say that there must be some explanation of how each such mental event manages to represent things as being a certain way.

Not just any explanation will do. For example, those steadfastly opposed to mystery may not say that a belief represents things as being a certain way because its object—a proposition—primitively represents things as being that way (cf. Ch. 1, §V). For that explanation reintroduces the allegedly objectionable mystery of primitively representing things as being a certain way. (That explanation also undermines the claim that beliefs fundamentally represent things as being a certain way.)

Or consider this idea: The explanation of a belief's representing (for example) dogs as barking involves an agent's predicating barking of dogs—but there is no explanation of how an agent manages to predicate properties of objects. This idea does not involve anything primitively representing things as being a certain way, not so as to have a truth-value. But this idea does involve an agent's primitively predicating properties of objects. So this idea does involve primitive powers relevant to representation. (This idea thus resembles accounts of structured propositions that invoke Zip and *Zipping*; see Ch. 4, §§VI, VII, and IX.) And primitive powers relevant to representation are no less mysterious than primitively representing things as being a certain way. So if an agent's having primitive powers relevant to representation is not objectionably mysterious, then neither is a proposition's primitively representing things as being a certain way.

Again, those steadfastly opposed to the mysterious with regard to representation will say that if certain mental events do fundamentally represent things as being a certain way, then there must be some explanation of how each such mental event manages to do so. And that explanation—they will add—cannot turn on any entity that primitively represents things as being a certain way, or on anything or anyone having primitive powers relevant to representation. Let us say that that explanation must be *naturalistic*. For although ardent non-naturalists could, for reasons of their own, resist anything that smacks of primitive representation, I suspect that most who object to my account of propositions on the grounds that it is unduly mysterious will do so because of sympathy with naturalism. Thus it is no surprise that King (2014, 48), immediately after objecting to primitive powers relevant to representation, says that he endorses 'an account of *naturalized propositions*'.

Unlike Soames, King does not think that mental events fundamentally represent things as being a certain way (see esp. King, 2014, 135–6). For rather than locating fundamental representation directly in the realm of agents and their cognitive activity, King seems to take sentences to be what fundamentally represent things as being a certain way. But King does insist that sentences represent things as being a certain way only because of the cognitive activity of agents. In particular, he takes sentences to represent things as being a certain way because of how agents interpret words or sentential relations or some similar entity. (See the sketch of King's view in Ch. 4, §IX.)

Suppose that, for each case of such interpretation, there is no explanation of how the agent manages to interpret the relevant entity in the relevant way. That is, suppose that, for each case of such interpretation, the agent primitively interprets the relevant entity in the relevant way. Then we have primitive powers relevant to representation. Then we have a view that is no less mysterious than the view that propositions primitively represent things as being a certain way. So, again, if an agent's having primitive powers relevant to representation is not objectionably mysterious, neither are propositions that primitively represent things as being a certain way.

But some defenders of King's view—including, for example, King—will be steadfastly opposed to the mysterious with regard to representation. So they will say that an agent's having primitive powers relevant to representation is objectionably mysterious. And some of them will add that there must be a naturalistic explanation of how an agent manages to interpret the relevant sorts of entities. And we have already seen that some defenders of Soames's view who are steadfastly opposed to the mysterious with regard to representation will say that there must be a naturalistic explanation of how a mental event manages to represent things as being a certain way.

I do not myself endorse naturalism (see, e.g., Merricks, 2006b). But perhaps you do. Then I can see why you would be, at least initially, inclined to deny that mental events primitively represent things as being a certain way and inclined to deny that agents have primitive powers relevant to representation and inclined to reject my account of propositions. For naturalism—however exactly it is defined—does seem to imply that there is a naturalistic explanation of every instance of representing things as being a certain way and of all cognitive activity.

But that is not all that naturalism seems to imply. Naturalism also seems to imply that there are no abstract objects. So naturalism also seems to imply that there are no abstract objects that represent things as being a certain way, primitively or otherwise. So to the extent that your theorizing here is driven only by what naturalism seems to imply, I think that you should deny that there are propositions—and so deny Soames's and King's views according to which there are propositions.

Moreover, I think that if naturalism drives your theorizing, you ought to be suspicious of metaphysical modality, and certainly of our ability to have knowledge of metaphysical modality (see Rea, 2002). As a result, for reasons defended in Chapter 2 (§§IV–VI), I think that you ought to be suspicious of logical validity, and certainly of our ability to have knowledge of logical validity.

Of course, naturalists do end up endorsing views that might have seemed, at first glance, to be ruled out by naturalism. For example, some philosophers who consider themselves naturalists endorse views about philosophy of mind that are not paradigmatically naturalistic. And some naturalists have endorsed the existence of sets because they believe that sets are required for mathematics, even though all abstract objects (sets included) seem to be, at least at first glance, non-naturalistic. Similarly, motivated by my arguments in Chapter 2 regarding logical validity, naturalists might shed their suspicions of metaphysical modality and even of modal knowledge.

And I suspect that King and Soames would say that their arguments for the existence of propositions are compelling enough to override naturalistic scruples against abstract objects, and even to override such scruples against abstract objects that represent things as being a certain way, albeit non-fundamentally and non-primitively. Similarly, I say that naturalists should go ahead and embrace abstract propositions that fundamentally and primitively represent things as being a certain way. And they should do this even if their naturalism made them, at least initially, suspicious of such propositions. So too should those who are not naturalists, even if they too were suspicious of such propositions. They should all do this because of the arguments in this book.

VI. Conclusion

I say that propositions are necessary existents that essentially represent things as being a certain way. This elegant account of the nature of propositions is partly supported by arguments earlier in this book for the conclusion that propositions really do exist necessarily and really do essentially represent things as being a certain way. This account is also supported by its explaining why propositions have the further features and play the roles that—as was shown earlier in this book—propositions really do have and really do play. This chapter developed all of these points while responding, along the way, to a few central objections to my account of the nature of propositions.

REFERENCES

ADAMS, ROBERT M. (1974) 'Theories of Actuality', *Noûs* 8: 211–31.

ADAMS, ROBERT M. (1981) 'Actualism and Thisness', *Synthese* 49: 3–41.

ADAMS, ROBERT M. (1986) 'Time and Thisness' in P. A. French, T. E. Uehling, Jr., and H. K. Wettstein (eds) *Midwest Studies in Philosophy, XI, Studies in Essentialism* (Minneapolis, MN: University of Minnesota Press).

ALGEO, JOHN (2001) *The Cambridge History of the English Language, vol. VI, English in North America* (Cambridge: Cambridge University Press).

ALMOG, JOSEPH (1986) 'Naming without Necessity', *Journal of Philosophy* 83: 210–42.

AQUINAS, THOMAS (1994) Robert W. Mulligan, SJ (trans.) *Truth*, vol. 1 (Indianapolis, IN: Hackett Publishing Company).

ARISTOTLE (1984) Jonathan Barnes (ed.) *The Complete Works of Aristotle: The Revised Oxford Translation* vols 1–2 (Princeton: Princeton University Press).

ARMSTRONG, D. M. (1986) 'In Defence of Structural Universals', *Australasian Journal of Philosophy* 64: 85–8.

ARMSTRONG, JOSHUA and STANLEY, JASON (2011) 'Singular Thought and Singular Propositions', *Philosophical Studies* 154: 205–22.

BEALER, GEORGE (1998) 'Propositions', *Mind* 107: 1–32.

BEALL, J. C. and RESTALL, GREG (2006) *Logical Pluralism* (Oxford: Oxford University Press).

BELL, JOHN and MACHOVER, MOSHE (1977) *A Course in Mathematical Logic* (Amsterdam: North-Holland).

BENACERRAF, PAUL (1965) 'What Numbers Could Not Be', *Philosophical Review* 74: 47–73.

BIGELOW, JOHN and PARGETTER, ROBERT (1989) 'A Theory of Structural Universals', *Australasian Journal of Philosophy* 67: 1–11.

BLANCHETTE, PATRICIA A. (1996) 'Frege and Hilbert on Consistency', *Journal of Philosophy* 93: 317–36.

BOBZIEN, SUSANNE (2003) 'Logic' in Brad Inwood (ed.) *The Cambridge Companion to the Stoics* (Cambridge: Cambridge University Press).

BOBZIEN, SUSANNE (2006) 'Ancient Logic' in Edward N. Zalta (ed.) *The Stanford Encyclopedia of Philosophy*, URL = <http://plato.stanford.edu/archives/spr2014/entries/logic-ancient/>.

BOGHOSSIAN, PAUL K. (1997) 'Analyticity' in Bob Hale and Crispin Wright (eds) *A Companion to the Philosophy of Language* (Oxford: Blackwell Publishing Ltd.).

BRAUN, DAVID (1993) 'Empty Names', *Noûs* 27: 449–69.

BRINGSJORD, SELMER (1985) 'Are There Set Theoretic Possible Worlds?', *Analysis* 45: 64.

BROGAARD, BERIT (2012) *Transient Truths: An Essay in the Metaphysics of Propositions* (Oxford: Oxford University Press).

BUCHANAN, RAY (2012) 'Is Belief a Propositional Attitude?' *Philosophers' Imprint* 12: 1–19.

BURGESS, JOHN P. (2009) *Philosophical Logic* (Princeton: Princeton University Press).

CARGILE, JAMES (1969) 'The Sorites Paradox', *British Journal for the Philosophy of Science* 20: 193–202.

CARGILE, JAMES (1979) *Paradoxes: A Study in Form and Predication* (Cambridge: Cambridge University Press).

CARTWRIGHT, RICHARD (1962) 'Propositions' in R. J. Butler (ed.) *Analytical Philosophy, First Series* (Oxford: Basil Blackwell).

CARTWRIGHT, RICHARD (1998) 'On Singular Propositions', *Canadian Journal of Philosophy, supplementary volume* 23: 67–83.

CHALMERS, DAVID J. (2011) 'Propositions and Attitude Ascriptions: A Fregean Account', *Noûs* 45: 595–639.

CHISHOLM, RODERICK M. (1976) *Person and Object* (LaSalle, IL: Open Court Publishing Co.).

CHURCH, ALONZO (1956) *Introduction to Mathematical Logic, vol. I* (Princeton: Princeton University Press).

COLLINS, JOHN (2007) 'Syntax, More or Less', *Mind* 116: 805–50.

COPI, IRVING (1972) *Introduction to Logic*, 4th edn (New York: Macmillan Publishing Co., Inc.).

COPI, IRVING (1978) *Introduction to Logic*, 5th edn (New York: Macmillan Publishing Co., Inc.).

CRESSWELL, M. J. (1985) *Structured Meanings* (Cambridge, MA: MIT Press).

CRIMMINS, MARK and PERRY, JOHN (1989) 'The Prince and the Phone Booth: Reporting Puzzling Beliefs', *Journal of Philosophy* 86: 685–711.

DAVIDSON, DONALD (2001) *Subjective, Intersubjective, Objective* (Oxford: Clarendon Press).

DIVERS, JOHN (1999) 'A Genuine Realist Theory of Advanced Modalizing', *Mind* 108: 217–40.

DUMMETT, MICHAEL (1978) *Truth and Other Enigmas* (Cambridge, MA: Harvard University Press).

ETCHEMENDY, JOHN (1990) *The Concept of Logical Consequence* (Cambridge, MA: Harvard University Press).

EVANS, GARETH (1982) *The Varieties of Reference* (Oxford: Oxford University Press).

FINE, KIT (1975) 'Vagueness, Truth, and Logic', *Synthese* 30: 265–300.

FINE, KIT (1985) 'Plantinga on the Reduction of Possibilist Discourse' in James Tomberlin and Peter van Inwagen (eds) *Alvin Plantinga* (Dordrecht: D. Reidel).

FINE, KIT (2007) *Semantic Relationism* (Oxford: Blackwell Publishers Ltd).

FITCH, GREG (1994) 'Singular Propositions in Time', *Philosophical Studies* 73: 181–7.

FITCH, GREG and NELSON, MICHAEL (2013) 'Singular Propositions' in Edward N. Zalta (ed.) *The Stanford Encyclopedia of Philosophy*, URL = <http://plato.stanford.edu/archives/win2013/entries/propositions-singular/>.

FORREST, PETER (1986a) 'Ways Worlds Could Be', *Australasian Journal of Philosophy* 64: 25–46.

FORREST, PETER (1986b) 'Neither Magic Nor Mereology: A Reply to Lewis', *Australasian Journal of Philosophy* 64: 89–91.

FREGE, GOTTLOB (1879) *Begriffsschrift* (Halle: L. Nelbert). Selections reprinted in Frege (1997).

FREGE, GOTTLOB (1892a) 'Über Sinn und Bedeutung', *Zeitschrift für Philosophie und philosophische Kritik* 100: 25–50. Reprinted in Frege (1997).

FREGE, GOTTLOB (1892b) 'Über Begriff und Gegenstand', *Vierteljahresschrift für wissenschaftliche Philosophie* 16: 192–205. Reprinted in Frege (1997).

FREGE, GOTTLOB (before 1895) 'Comments on *Sinn* and *Bedeutung*'. Published posthumously in Frege (1997).

FREGE, GOTTLOB (1914) 'Logic in Mathematics'. Published posthumously in Frege (1979).

FREGE, GOTTLOB (1918–19) 'Der Gedanke', *Beiträge zur Philosophie des deutschen Idealismus* 1: 58–77. Reprinted in Frege (1997).

FREGE, GOTTLOB (1923) 'Gedankengefüge', *Beiträge zur Philosophie des deutschen Idealismus* 3: 36–51. Reprinted in Frege (1977).

FREGE, GOTTLOB (1977) *Logical Investigations*, ed. P. T. Geach (Oxford: Basil Blackwell).

FREGE, GOTTLOB (1979) *Gottlob Frege: Posthumous Writings*, ed. Hans Hermes, Friedrich Kambartel, and Friedrich Kaulbach (Oxford: Basil Blackwell).

FREGE, GOTTLOB (1980) *Gottlob Frege: Philosophical and Mathematical Correspondence*, ed. Gottfried Gabriel, Hans Hermes, Friedrich Kambartel, Christian Thiel, and Albert Veraart (Chicago: University of Chicago Press).

FREGE, GOTTLOB (1997) *The Frege Reader*, ed. Michael Beaney (Oxford: Blackwell Publishers).

GENDLER, TAMAR SZABÓ and HAWTHORNE, JOHN (eds) (2002) *Conceivability and Possibility* (Oxford: Oxford University Press).

GILMORE, CODY (2014) 'Parts of Propositions' in Shieva Kleinschmidt (ed.) *Mereology and Location* (Oxford: Oxford University Press).

GRACIA, JORGE J. E. (1975) 'Propositions as Premises of Syllogisms in Medieval Logic', *Notre Dame Journal of Formal Logic* 16: 545–7.

GRIM, PATRICK (1984) 'There is No Set of All Truths', *Analysis* 44: 206–8.

GRIM, PATRICK (1988) 'Logic and Limits of Knowledge and Truth', *Noûs* 22: 341–67.

HANKS, PETER W. (2013) 'First-Person Propositions', *Philosophy and Phenomenological Research* 86: 155–82.

HANSON, WILLIAM H. (1997) 'The Concept of Logical Consequence', *Philosophical Review* 106: 365–409.

HAWTHORNE, JOHN and MANLEY, DAVID (2012) *The Reference Book* (Oxford: Oxford University Press).

HELLER, MARK (1998) 'Property Counterparts in Ersatz Worlds', *Journal of Philosophy* 95: 293–316.

JESHION, ROBIN (2002) 'Acquaintanceless *De Re* Belief' in Joseph Campbell, Michael O'Rourke, and David Shier (eds) *Meaning and Truth: Investigations in Philosophical Semantics* (New York: Seven Bridges Press).

JOHNSTON, MARK (2006) 'Hylomorphism', *Journal of Philosophy* 103: 652–98.

Jubien, Michael (1988) 'Problems with Possible Worlds' in David F. Austin (ed.) *Philosophical Analysis* (Dordrecht: Kluwer Academic Publishing).

Jubien, Michael (1991) 'Could This be Magic?' *Philosophical Review* 100: 249–67.

Jubien, Michael (2001) 'Propositions and the Objects of Thought', *Philosophical Studies* 104: 47–62.

Kaplan, David (1973) 'Bob and Carol and Ted and Alice' in Jaakko Hintikka (ed.) *Approaches to Natural Language* (Dordrecht: D. Reidel.)

Kaplan, David (1975) 'What is Russell's Theory of Descriptions' in Donald Davidson and Gilbert Harman (eds) *The Logic of Grammar* (Encino, CA: Dickenson).

Kaplan, David (1989) 'Demonstratives' in Joseph Almog, John Perry, and Howard Wettstein (eds) *Themes From Kaplan* (Oxford: Oxford University Press).

Katz, Jerrold (1996) 'Skepticism About Numbers and Indeterminacy Arguments' in Adam Morton and Stephen Stich (eds) *Benacerraf and his Critics* (Oxford: Blackwell Publishers Ltd).

Keller, Lorraine Juliano (2013) 'The Metaphysics of Propositional Constituency', *Canadian Journal of Philosophy* 43: 655–78.

Keller, Lorraine Juliano and Keller, John (2014) 'Compositionality and Structured Propositions', *Thought* 2: 313–23.

King, Jeffrey C. (2007a) *The Nature and Structure of Content* (Oxford: Oxford University Press).

King, Jeffrey C. (2007b) 'What in the World are the Way Things Might Have Been?' *Philosophical Studies* 133: 443–53.

King, Jeffrey C. (2009) 'Questions of Unity', *Proceedings of the Aristotelian Society* 109: 257–77.

King, Jeffrey C. (2011) 'Structured Propositions' in Edward N. Zalta (ed.) *Stanford Encyclopedia of Philosophy*, URL = <http://plato.stanford.edu/archives/spr2014/entries/propositions-structured/>.

King, Jeffrey C. (2014) 'Naturalized Propositions' and 'Criticisms of Soames and Speaks' in Jeffrey C. King, Scott Soames, and Jeff Speaks (eds) *New Thinking About Propositions* (Oxford: Oxford University Press).

Koslicki, Kathrin (2008) *The Structure of Objects* (Oxford: Oxford University Press).

Kretzmann, Norman (1970) 'Medieval Logicians on the Meaning of the Proposition', *Journal of Philosophy* 67: 767–87.

KRIPKE, SAUL (1979) 'A Puzzle About Belief' in Avishai Margalit (ed.) *Meaning and Use* (Dordrecht: D. Reidel).

KRIPKE, SAUL (1980) *Naming and Necessity* (Cambridge, MA: Harvard University Press).

KRIPKE, SAUL (2013) *Reference and Existence* (Oxford: Oxford University Press).

KURATOWSKI, KAZIMIERZ (1921) 'Sur la notion de l'ordre dans la théorie de ensembles', *Fundamenta Mathematicae* 2: 161–71.

LEONARD, HENRY S. and GOODMAN, NELSON (1940) 'The Calculus of Individuals and its Uses', *Journal of Symbolic Logic* 5: 45–55.

LEWIS, DAVID (1973) *Counterfactuals* (Oxford: Basil Blackwell, Ltd).

LEWIS, DAVID (1979) 'Attitudes *De Dicto* and *De Se*', *Philosophical Review* 88: 513–43.

LEWIS, DAVID (1983) 'Postscripts to "Counterpart Theory and Quantified Modal Logic"', *Philosophical Papers, Volume 1* (Oxford: Oxford University Press).

LEWIS, DAVID (1986a) *On the Plurality of Worlds* (Oxford: Basil Blackwell).

LEWIS, DAVID (1986b) 'A Comment on Armstrong and Forrest', *Australasian Journal of Philosophy* 64: 92–3.

LINSKY, BERNARD and ZALTA, EDWARD N. (1994) 'In Defense of the Simplest Quantified Modal Logic' in James Tomberlin (ed.) *Philosophical Perspectives, 8, Logic and Language* (Atascadero, CA: Ridgeview Publishing Co.).

MCDOWELL, JOHN (1994) *Mind and World* (Cambridge, MA: Harvard University Press).

MCGINN, MARIE (1984) 'Wright's Reply to Benacerraf', *Analysis* 44: 69–72.

MCGRATH, MATTHEW (2012) 'Propositions' in Edward N. Zalta (ed.) *The Stanford Encyclopedia of Philosophy*, URL = <http://plato.stanford.edu/archives/spr2014/entries/propositions/>.

MADDY, PENELOPE (1981) 'Sets and Numbers', *Noûs* 15: 495–511.

MARCUS, RUTH BARCAN (1946) 'A Functional Calculus of First Order Based on Strict Implication', *Journal of Symbolic Logic* 11: 1–16.

MARKOSIAN, NED (2004) 'A Defense of Presentism' in Dean W. Zimmerman (ed.) *Oxford Studies in Metaphysics*, vol. 1 (Oxford: Oxford University Press).

MATES, BENSON (1965) *Elementary Logic*, 1st edn (New York: Oxford University Press).

MATES, BENSON (1972) *Elementary Logic*, 2nd edn (New York: Oxford University Press).

MENZEL, CHRISTOPHER (1986) 'On Set Theoretic Possible Worlds', *Analysis* 46: 68–72.

MERRICKS, TRENTON (2001) *Objects and Persons* (Oxford: Clarendon Press).

MERRICKS, TRENTON (2003a) 'The End of Counterpart Theory', *Journal of Philosophy* 100: 521–49.

MERRICKS, TRENTON (2003b) 'Replies', *Philosophy and Phenomenological Research* 67: 727–44.

MERRICKS, TRENTON (2006a) 'Good-Bye Growing Block' in Dean W. Zimmerman (ed.) *Oxford Studies in Metaphysics*, vol. 2 (Oxford: Oxford University Press).

MERRICKS, TRENTON (2006b) 'Split Brains and the Godhead' in Thomas Crisp, Matthew Davidson, and David Vander Laan (eds) *Knowledge and Reality: Essays in Honor of Alvin Plantinga on his Seventieth Birthday* (Dordrecht: Kluwer Academic Publishers).

MERRICKS, TRENTON (2007) *Truth and Ontology* (Oxford: Clarendon Press).

MERRICKS, TRENTON (2008) 'Replies to Cameron, Schaffer, and Soames', *Philosophical Books* 49: 328–43.

MERRICKS, TRENTON (2009a) 'Propositional Attitudes?' *Proceedings of the Aristotelian Society* 109: 207–32.

MERRICKS, TRENTON (2009b) 'Review of Kathrin Koslicki, *The Structure of Objects*', *Journal of Philosophy* 106: 301–7.

MERRICKS, TRENTON (2012) 'Singular Propositions' in Kelly James Clark and Michael Rea (eds) *Reason, Metaphysics, and Mind: New Essays on the Philosophy of Alvin Plantinga* (Oxford: Oxford University Press).

MONTAGUE, RICHARD (1969) 'On the Nature of Certain Philosophical Entities', *The Monist* 53: 159–94.

MOORE, G. E. (1903) 'The Refutation of Idealism', *Mind* 12: 433–53.

MOORE, JOSEPH G. (1999) 'Propositions, Numbers, and the Problem of Arbitrary Identification', *Synthese* 120: 229–63.

PERRY, JOHN (1979) 'The Problem of the Essential Indexical', *Noûs* 13: 3–21.

PINILLOS, N. ÁNGEL (2011) 'Coreference and Meaning', *Philosophical Studies* 154: 301–24.

PLANTINGA, ALVIN (1974) *The Nature of Necessity* (Oxford: Clarendon Press).

Plantinga, Alvin (1979) 'De Essentia' in Ernest Sosa (ed.) *Essays on the Philosophy of Roderick M. Chisholm* (Amsterdam: Rodopi).

Plantinga, Alvin (1983) 'On Existentialism', *Philosophical Studies* 44: 1–20.

Plantinga, Alvin (1985) 'Reply to Critics' in James Tomberlin and Peter van Inwagen (eds) *Alvin Plantinga* (Dordrecht: D. Reidel).

Plantinga, Alvin (1987) 'Two Concepts of Modality: Modal Realism and Modal Reductionism' in James Tomberlin (ed.) *Philosophical Perspectives, 1, Metaphysics* (Atascadero, CA: Ridgeview Publishing Co.).

Plantinga, Alvin (1993) *Warrant and Proper Function* (Oxford: Oxford University Press).

Plantinga, Alvin and Grim, Patrick (1993) 'Truth, Omniscience, and Cantorian Arguments', *Philosophical Studies* 71: 267–306.

Pollock, John L. (1985) 'Plantinga on Possible Worlds' in James Tomberlin and Peter van Inwagen (eds) *Alvin Plantinga* (Dordrecht: D. Reidel).

Priest, Graham (1999) 'Validity' in Achille Varzi (ed.) *The Nature of Logic* (Stanford, CA: CSLI Publications).

Prior, A. N. (1960) 'The Runabout Inference-Ticket', *Analysis* 21: 38–9.

Proops, Ian (2011) 'Russell on Substitutivity and the Abandonment of Propositions', *Philosophical Review* 120: 151–205.

Pruss, Alexander and Rasmussen, Joshua (2015) 'Problems with Plurals' in Karen Bennett and Dean W. Zimmerman (eds) *Oxford Studies in Metaphysics*, vol. 9 (Oxford: Oxford University Press).

Quine, W. v. O. (1951) 'Two Dogmas of Empiricism', *Philosophical Review* 60: 20–43.

Quine, W. v. O. (1953) 'On What There Is' in *From a Logical Point of View* (Cambridge, MA: Harvard University Press).

Quine, W. v. O. (1969) 'Propositional Objects' in *Ontological Relativity and Other Essays* (New York: Columbia University Press).

Quine, W. v. O. (1982) *Methods of Logic*, 4th edn (Cambridge, MA: Harvard University Press).

Rea, Michael C. (2002) *World Without Design: The Ontological Consequences of Naturalism* (Oxford: Clarendon Press).

Restall, Greg (2005) 'Multiple Conclusions' in Petr Hajek, Luis Valdes-Villanueva, and Dag Westerstahl (eds) *Logic, Methodology and Philosophy of Science: Proceedings of the Twelfth International Congress* (London: King's College Publications).

RICHARD, MARK (1983) 'Direct Reference and Ascriptions of Belief', *Journal of Philosophical Logic* 12: 425–52.

RICHARD, MARK (1990) *Propositional Attitudes: An Essay on Thoughts and How We Ascribe Them* (Cambridge: Cambridge University Press).

RUSSELL, BERTRAND (1903) *Principles of Mathematics*, 2nd edn (New York: W. W. Norton and Co.).

RUSSELL, BERTRAND (1904a) 'Meinong's Theory of Complexes and Assumptions', *Mind* 13: 204–19, 336–54, and 509–24.

RUSSELL, BERTRAND (1904b) 'Dec. 12, 1904 Letter to Frege' in Gottfried Gabriel, Hans Hermes, Friedrich Kambartel, Christian Thiel, and Albert Veraart (eds) *Gottlob Frege: Philosophical and Mathematical Correspondence* (Chicago: University of Chicago Press).

RUSSELL, BERTRAND (1905) 'Necessity and Possibility' (manuscript). First published in Alasdair Urquhart and Albert C. Lewis (eds) *Foundations of Logic: 1903–05* (London: Routledge, 1994).

RUSSELL, BERTRAND (1907) 'On the Nature of Truth', *Proceedings of the Aristotelian Society* 2: 28–49.

RUSSELL, BERTRAND (1910–11) 'Knowledge by Acquaintance and Knowledge by Description', *Proceedings of the Aristotelian Society* 11: 108–28.

RUSSELL, BERTRAND (1912) *The Problems of Philosophy* (London: Williams and Norgate).

RUSSELL, BERTRAND (1913) *Theory of Knowledge* (manuscript). First published as *Theory of Knowledge: The 1913 Manuscript* (London: George Allen & Unwin, 1984).

RUSSELL, BERTRAND (1918–19) 'The Philosophy of Logical Atomism', *Monist* 28: 495-527; 29: 32–63, 190–222, and 345–80. Reprinted in *The Philosophy of Logical Atomism*, ed. David Pears (Chicago: Open Court Publishing, 1985).

SALMON, NATHAN (1986) *Frege's Puzzle* (Cambridge, MA: MIT Press).

SALMON, NATHAN (1987) 'Existence' in James Tomberlin (ed.) *Philosophical Perspectives, 1, Metaphysics* (Atascadero, CA: Ridgeview Publishing Co.).

SALMON, NATHAN (1989a) 'How to Become a Millian Heir', *Noûs* 23: 211–20.

SALMON, NATHAN (1989b) 'Tense and Singular Propositions' in Joseph Almog, John Perry, and Howard Wettstein (eds) *Themes From Kaplan* (Oxford: Oxford University Press).

SALMON, NATHAN (1998) 'Nonexistence', *Noûs* 32: 277–319.

SALMON, NATHAN (2007) 'About Aboutness', *European Journal of Analytic Philosophy* 3: 59–76.

SCHIFFER, STEPHEN (2003) *Things We Mean* (Oxford: Clarendon Press).

SEARLE, JOHN (1970) *Speech Acts: An Essay in the Philosophy of Language* (Cambridge: Cambridge University Press).

SIDER, THEODORE (2010) *Logic for Philosophers* (Oxford: Oxford University Press).

SIDER, THEODORE (2011) *Writing the Book of the World* (Oxford: Clarendon Press).

SOAMES, SCOTT (1987) 'Direct Reference, Propositional Attitudes, and Semantic Content', *Philosophical Topics*, 15: 47–87.

SOAMES, SCOTT (1989) 'Direct Reference and Propositional Attitudes' in Joseph Almog, John Perry, and Howard Wettstein (eds) *Themes From Kaplan* (Oxford: Oxford University Press).

SOAMES, SCOTT (1999) *Understanding Truth* (Oxford: Oxford University Press).

SOAMES, SCOTT (2008) 'Truthmakers?', *Philosophical Books* 49: 317–27.

SOAMES, SCOTT (2010) *What is Meaning?* (Princeton: Princeton University Press).

SOAMES, SCOTT (2014) 'Why the Traditional Conceptions of Propositions Can't Be Correct' and 'Cognitive Propositions' in Jeffrey C. King, Scott Soames, and Jeff Speaks (eds) *New Thinking About Propositions* (Oxford: Oxford University Press).

SORENSEN, ROY (2001) *Vagueness and Contradiction* (Oxford: Oxford University Press).

SPEAKS, JEFF (2014) 'Propositions are Properties of Everything or Nothing' in Jeffrey C. King, Scott Soames, and Jeff Speaks (eds) *New Thinking About Propositions* (Oxford: Oxford University Press).

STALNAKER, ROBERT (1976) 'Propositions' in Alfred F. MacKay and Daniel D. Merrill (eds) *Issues in the Philosophy of Language* (New Haven, CN: Yale University Press).

STALNAKER, ROBERT (1987) *Inquiry* (Cambridge, MA: MIT Press).

STALNAKER, ROBERT (2003) *Ways a World Might Be: Metaphysical and Anti-Metaphysical Essays* (Oxford: Clarendon Press).

STALNAKER, ROBERT (2011) 'The Metaphysical Conception of Analyticity', *Philosophy and Phenomenological Research* 82: 507–14.

STALNAKER, ROBERT (2012) *Mere Possibilities* (Princeton: Princeton University Press).

Stanley, Jason (2011) *Know How* (Oxford: Oxford University Press).
Sutton, Catherine S. (2012) 'Co-located Objects Tally-Ho! A Solution to the Grounding Problem', *Mind* 121: 703–30.
Szabó, Zoltán Gendler (2000) 'Compositionality as Supervenience', *Linguistics and Philosophy* 23: 475–505.
Tarski, Alfred (1936) 'Über den Begriff der logischen Folgerung', *Actes du Congrés International de Philosophie Scientifique* 7: 1–11. Reprinted in Tarski (1956).
Tarski, Alfred (1938) 'Der Aussagenkalkül und die Topologie', *Fundamenta Mathematicae* 31, 103–34. Reprinted in Tarski (1956).
Tarski, Alfred (1956) *Logic, Semantics, Metamathematics: Papers from 1923 to 1938*, ed. John Corcoran, 2nd edn (Oxford: Clarendon Press).
Thomson, Judith Jarvis (1998) 'The Statue and the Clay', *Noûs* 32: 149–73.
Turner, Jason (2005) 'Strong and Weak Possibility', *Philosophical Studies* 125: 191–217.
van Inwagen, Peter (1986) 'Two Concepts of Possible Worlds', *Midwest Studies in Philosophy* 11: 185–213.
van Inwagen, Peter (2004) 'A Theory of Properties' in Dean W. Zimmerman (ed.) *Oxford Studies in Metaphysics*, vol. 1 (Oxford: Oxford University Press).
van Inwagen, Peter (2006) 'Names for Relations' in John Hawthorne (ed.) *Philosophical Perspectives*, 20, *Metaphysics* (Oxford: Blackwell Publishers Ltd).
Williamson, Timothy (1994) *Vagueness* (London: Routledge).
Williamson, Timothy (1998) 'Bare Possibilia', *Erkenntnis* 48: 257–73.
Williamson, Timothy (2002) 'Necessary Existents' in Anthony O'Hear (ed.) *Logic, Thought and Language* (Cambridge: Cambridge University Press).
Williamson, Timothy (2006) 'Conceptual Truth', *Proceedings of the Aristotelian Society, supp. vol.*, 80: 1–41.
Williamson, Timothy (2007) *The Philosophy of Philosophy* (Oxford: Blackwell Publishers Ltd).
Williamson, Timothy (2013) *Modal Logic as Metaphysics* (Oxford: Oxford University Press).
Wright, Crispin (1983) *Frege's Conception of Numbers as Objects* (Aberdeen: Aberdeen University Press).

INDEX

The manufacturer's authorised representative in the EU for product safety is Oxford University Press España S.A. of El Parque Empresarial San Fernando de Henares, Avenida de Castilla, 2 - 28830 Madrid (www.oup.es/en or product.safety@oup.com). OUP España S.A. also acts as importer into Spain of products made by the manufacturer.
Printed and bound by CPI Group (UK) Ltd, Croydon, CR0 4YY
10/02/2026
02051498-0003